South Korea's
Minjung Movement

Studies from
the Center for Korean Studies

Studies on Korea: A Scholar's Guide, edited by Han-Kyo Kim. 1980

Korean Communism, 1945–1980: A Reference Guide to the Political System, by Dae-Sook Suh. 1981

Korea and the United States: A Century of Cooperation, edited by Youngnok Koo and Dae-Sook Suh. 1984

The Reluctant Crusade: American Foreign Policy in Korea, 1941–1950, by James I. Matray. 1985

The Korean Frontier in America: Immigration to Hawaii, 1896–1910, by Wayne Patterson. 1988

Korean-American Relations: Documents Pertaining to the Far Eastern Diplomacy of the United States. Volume III. *The Period of Diminishing Influence, 1896–1905,* edited and with an introduction by Scott S. Burnett. 1989

Diplomacy of Asymmetry: Korean-American Relations to 1910, by Jongsuk Chay. 1990.

South Korea's Minjung Movement: The Culture and Politics of Dissidence, edited by Kenneth M. Wells. 1995.

SOUTH KOREA'S MINJUNG MOVEMENT

The Culture and Politics of Dissidence

Edited by Kenneth M. Wells

UNIVERSITY OF HAWAI'I PRESS, HONOLULU

95 96 97 98 99 00   5 4 3 2 1

A Study from the Center for Korean Studies, University of Hawai'i
The Center for Korean Studies was established in 1972 to coordinate and
develop the resources for the study of Korea at the University of Hawai'i. Its
goals are to enhance faculty quality and performance in Korean studies;
to develop comprehensive, balanced academic programs; to stimulate research
and publications; and to coordinate the resources of the University of Hawai'i
with those of other institutions, organizations, and individual scholars engaged
in the study of Korea. Reflecting the diversity of the academic disciplines
represented by affiliated members of the University faculty, the Center seeks
especially to promote interdisciplinary and intercultural studies.

Library of Congress Cataloging-in-Publication Data
South Korea's minjung movement : the culture and politics of
dissidence / edited by Kenneth M. Wells.
p.   cm.
Revisions of selected papers presented at the International
Conference on the Korean Minjung Movement held at Indiana Univ. at
Bloomington in Nov. 1989.
Includes bibliographical references and index.
ISBN 0–8248–1700–1 (alk. paper)
1. Populism—Korea (South)—History—20th century.
2. Nationalism—Korea (South)—History—20th century.   3. Korea
(South)—History—1960–1988.   I. Wells, Kenneth M., 1953–
II. International Conference on the Korean Minjung Movement (1989 :
Indiana University)
DS922.25.S68   1995
951.9504'3—dc20   95–17225
CIP

Designed by Kenneth Miyamoto

Contents

Preface

THIS VOLUME has its origins in an international conference on the Korean *minjung* movement held at Indiana University at Bloomington in November 1989. With participation by nearly thirty scholars from both hemispheres, east and west, the conference was the first outside South Korea to attempt to come to terms with a phenomenon that has had, and may continue to have, a considerable impact on the social, political, and cultural character of modern South Korea. In an attempt to capture as composite a picture of the minjung movement as possible, the conference was interdisciplinary by design, drawing on the methods and findings of anthropology, history, literary criticism, religious studies, and sociology.

The chapters in this volume are for the most part revisions of selected papers presented at the conference. The chapter by Paik Nak-chung, who was invited to the conference but was prevented by the Korean government from participating in it, is a translation of an article he published in *Ch'angjakkwa Pip'yŏng* (Creation and criticism) in spring 1989. In faithfulness to the conference deliberations and the subject matter itself, no attempt has been made to select contributions that form any consensus on the issue. Even so, readers will find a great deal of commonality among the writers on the roots of the minjung movement, its importance for contemporary Korea, and the intricacy of the issues such an inquiry entails. Further, the combination of perspectives of those who, like Kang Man'gil, Choi Chungmoo, and Paik Nak-chung, speak from within the movement, with those of us who necessarily must adopt a more distant position, makes this a truly valuable collection.

Chapters are arranged according to disciplinary focus, moving from general analyses to more specific case studies. The chapters by Kang Man'gil, Kim Hyung-A, and myself deal with historiographical issues; those by Chung

Chai-sik and Donald Clark, with philosophical/religious themes; those by Choi Chungmoo, Nancy Abelmann, and Kim Seong Nae, with anthropological aspects; and those by Paik Nak-chung, Marshall Pihl, and Choi Hyun-moo, with literary movements. Although one volume cannot be as comprehensive as the subject warrants, I feel constrained to offer on behalf of the contributors our regret at one particular omission: the important feminist critique of the terms and procedures of the minjung movement which was presented at the conference by Cho Hae-joang of Yonsei University, a revision of which she has been unable to contribute, for personal reasons, to this volume.

Finally, I wish to acknowledge my indebtedness to institutions and individuals who have made this volume possible. The conception of the conference owes a great deal to ideas contributed by Choi Chungmoo and Choi Kyeong-Hee, who also aided me in finding the most appropriate scholars to participate in the conference. George Wilson and Jurgis Elisonas have supported the venture through its entirety, while Sue Tuohy concerted the Indiana University East Asian Studies Center and Conference Bureau with great efficiency, besides assisting in the procurement of conference and editorial grants. Within Indiana University, the conference was sponsored by the Department of East Asian Languages and Cultures, the East Asian Studies Center, and the offices of International Programs, Research, and the University Graduate School, and of the vice president and chancellor. Outside grants were received from the Korea Research Foundation and the Korean Committee of the Social Science Research Council, which latter organization also provided funds for editorial expenses relating to preparation of this volume.

Finally, the rather complex business of fashioning the individual chapters, typed on a truly daunting variety of word-processing programs from different hardware systems, into one uniform document was rendered inestimably less burdensome by the patient and skillful work of Benita Banning of Indiana University's East Asian Studies Center and Julie Gordon and Dorothy McIntosh of the Division of Pacific and Asian History at the Australian National University. Any editorial weaknesses, needless to say, are solely my responsibility.

Introduction

Kenneth M. Wells

THE FIVE YEARS since the conference on the minjung movement at Indiana University has been a period of considerable historical "density." The import of the concatenated events following the June 1987 uprising—the long-awaited "triumph" of the minjung—and troubling questions over the precise direction upon which the subsequent South Korean government and, indeed, the majority of the populace have embarked, have necessitated considerable revision of the chapters dealing with the contemporary manifestations of the movement. This introduction sets out the issues addressed in this volume in light of recent developments.

Much of the conference discussion itself centered on the question "Who have been and who now are the minjung?" The conference began with a very makeshift definition of the minjung movement as a form of populist nationalism. Because the movement has historically been concerned with nationalistic projects—redefining social relations during the 1860–1895 Tonghak movement, liberating the nation from the Japanese in the period from 1905 through 1945, eliminating military rule in South Korea, and reunifying the country—the nationalist element in this rough definition evoked little unease. "Populism," however, proved contentious and catalyzed the earnest and highly spirited debates that characterized the conference throughout, for it was here that the question of the identity of the "people," and those who could be called the minjung, arose. It proved far easier to use the term "minjung" as an adjective—minjung theology, literature, historiography, and so on—than as a noun referring to any specific group of Koreans. As an adjective, the term could refer to the qualities and objectives of various endeavors. But insofar as delineation of these qualities and objectives presupposed an identifiable element among the Korean people that embodies them and indeed has initiated, sustained, and will

1

continue to support the movement, discussion had constantly to return to the question "Who were/are the minjung?"

One conference participant queried whether it really mattered who the minjung are, whether indeed it mattered if they existed concretely at all. In the main, it was thought that it did matter, first because the term ought not to become an academic interest with no real accountability, and second because large numbers of real people have been involved in a movement which has had indisputably significant effects.

One of the most recent of these effects, however, the June 10 uprising of 1987, has covered the issue with confusion. Through this uprising, in which a large spectrum of Korean society was represented, the then president, General Chŏn Tuhwan (Chun Doo-Hwan), was forced to abandon thoughts of a second term and concede to the people the right to elect their president directly. A promising opportunity was given the opposition to field a winning presidential candidate the following December. But the opposition split and defaulted the elections to the ruling party, and subsequent events have doused the euphoria and muddied the picture. It is difficult, for example, to see how the 1988 Seoul Olympic torch burned for the minjung or precisely how their interests have been served by Kim Yŏngsam's (Kim Young Sam) merger with the governing party and subsequent election as president, erstwhile dissident though he is.

Thus, events since the June uprising have raised the question of minjung character and identity in an urgent way. The conference, which in any case preceded such developments as Kim Yŏngsam's election, did not of course resolve the issue. A very general understanding emerged that the minjung are Koreans, predominantly workers in agriculture and urban industries, who retained the values and sentiments of the Korean masses in the face of militaristic rule and cultural and economic systems imposed directly or otherwise by foreign governments or interests, along with those among intellectuals, writers, politicians, and professionals who have supported their aspirations. Beyond this, it was recognized that the movement has deeply penetrated large numbers of Koreans' consciousness of themselves and their nation and has permeated almost every area of life and mode of expression on the southern half of the peninsula.

A nation or class or individual has not just one but many histories, and one should assume the existence of as many histories as possible. "How many historical paths are there?" is a salutary question to ask oneself when looking at "national" experience, especially where there is a tendency to restrict significance to select types of phenomena. This book cannot, of course, explore all paths, but it does strive to present a multifaceted cultural analysis and critique of an entity that does not lend itself to easy classification in terms of hardheaded structural analysis.

Like many other nations, Korea has suffered a turbulent, often violent, century. Three wars have been fought on its soil since 1894. The last of these, the Korean War of 1950–1953, was a bitter internecine conflict in which the stakes were raised devastatingly high by the military involvement of Cold War forces. The century has been dominated in economic and political fields by imperialist encroachments, most concretely by the Japanese colonial occupation of Korea from 1905 to 1945, but continuing thereafter under the baleful influence of the hostile interests of the United States and former USSR and, in the south, under alleged neocolonial economic predations by Western capitalist powers. From the Yŏsun rebellions in 1948 to the 1960 student uprising and 1980 Kwangju rebellion, South Korea's history has been marked by bloody clashes between military regimes and a disaffected populace.

It is therefore understandable that, for many, "minjung consciousness" owes its rise to these violent episodes of the last one hundred years. This book, however, assumes rather than delves into the conflagrations: its master narrative is the struggle for cultural definition, for the sense of what it means to be and act as "the Korean people" amid the far-reaching global and domestic changes that have affected them personally—issues that in some ways lie behind and are even deeper than the conflagrations themselves. Suffering, intrinsic to all definitions of the minjung, relates to that violence, but not only to that violence; and it is one of the strengths of this interdisciplinary collection that it explores dimensions of the minjung phenomenon which relate to more subtle forms of violence, cultural in particular.

To take one example, the Cheju Island rebellion in 1948 (part of the much larger left-wing Yŏsun uprisings) is one of the most often cited episodes of violence during the formative years of the Republic of Korea under Syngman Rhee. It might seem perplexing, therefore, that Kim Seong Nae's chapter on a Cheju shaman's dreams tucks this uprising into a corner and exalts above it the remembrances of a single individual. Her chapter violates the normal rule of considering who was fighting for whom—indeed, the question of "sides" itself. We are left in doubt about the actual role of her husband and how he really died, and nowhere does the shaman tender an opinion on the ideology of it all. Of course, the shaman is not supposed to represent herself only, and we await further anthropological investigations to corroborate or fill in the canvas, but as it is the chapter serves some important functions.

First, it throws light on the personal history and experience of a survivor of the Cheju uprising, who had to tend to the business of living in impoverished circumstances. It reveals what is often occluded in accounts of the violent struggles and shows that individual suffering is not necessarily the same as, and is certainly not as simple as, the stark ideological conflict usually depicted in studies of the Cheju uprising. No attempt is made to force an analogous relation between the suffering during the violence and the suffering of the shaman: to do so would mean subordinating the latter to the former. In this way, the study challenges ideas of what the "real" history of an event is and implies that the shamanic narrative should be given equal weight, where human life and values are concerned, to the commonly received perspectives. Second, by presenting an *actual* case of a shaman in connection with an experience considered as part of the soil from which minjung culture has sprung, this chapter cautions us against a naive acceptance of the *projected* image of the shamanism/minjung connection of many writers and activists. Finally, the whole ethnographic study calls into question the unitary nature of minjung culture.

The theme of cultural unity crops up repeatedly throughout the volume. Kang Man'gil proposes a definition of the minjung as a confederation of classes that hold certain crucial values and objectives in common; Choi Chungmoo writes of the ideal of a "cultural commonality" held by minjung cultural activists; and Nancy Abelmann describes the same presumption of minjung solidarity among students participating in a farmers' movement in the 1980s. One can with justice claim that to a considerable degree the minjung movement *is* a struggle to achieve a unified vision of Korean culture: the struggle against oppressions is cast in cultural terms. As Marshall Pihl points out, with a nod toward Georg Lukács, the minjung literary product moves from its political-historical context to an imagined future of harmony under a unified view of human existence. The cultural relevance of minjung literature, he believes, "is demonstrated by the fact that it has been welcomed at many levels of Korean society," and its power lies in its attention to the need to find value in individual life rather than only in idealized rhetoric concerning nationhood. Choi Hyun-moo, pursuing a different emphasis, claims that it is actually the minjung linkage with nationalism—the search for all-inclusive culture—that distinguishes it from Western proletarian literature, which defines itself as a class culture. This link with the "national" question she deems to be the decisive condition of the minjung movement, and from it stems its ambivalence regarding culture.

As Pihl observes, Paik Nak-chung explains this ambivalence as a dialectic between two impulses: one that refuses to allow national issues to overarch and relativize the immediate tasks of the oppressed people; and one that recognizes the commonality of origin, interest, and context that makes it meaningful to talk of a nation. And in his chapter, Paik gives a detailed and concrete account of the literary products of this dialectic. But if in literature the ambivalence is a dialectic, in social science it appears to be more a confusion of cultural with economic categories. A large part of my own discussion addresses this dilemma; and Kim Hyung-A, examining the socioeconomic theories of two leading minjung exponents, Pak Hyŏnch'ae and Han Wansang, concludes that there is a fundamental contradiction between such approaches that attempt to link minjung-ness to a social or economic class and the commonly espoused cultural pretensions of the movement to represent the nation in essence and totality.

Naturally enough, minjung culturalists define themselves in contradistinction to other competing versions of cultural content and method. Both Choi Chungmoo and I mention their hostile critique of the culturalists of the 1920s and 1930s. Chung Chai-sik's masterly discussion of the impact of the Korean Confucian tradition on the people and society indicates how uncomfortable adherents of that long-lived, official version of culture were with any suggestion of popular determination of social and cultural forms. Rhetorically opposed to any hierarchical conception of society and imposed cultural values, minjung culturalists fault the 1920s culturalists for having made a halfhearted break from elite culture and methods, replacing a Chinese tradition with subservience to Western or even Japanese culture.

A question here is whether the difference is so marked as claimed. My own position is that there has been more of a transition and refocusing than a rupture. Choi Chungmoo inclines to the view that the change in terminology masks the fact that the culturalism of the minjung has also failed to throw off sufficiently the old cultural idealism: "advocates of the culture movement argue that cultural unity should precede national unity and that, indeed, the spiritual realm of national unity cannot be achieved without it."

There is certainly the same *idea* here of culture as in the colonial period; and there was, after all, a *vnarod* movement in the 1930s, as there has been in the 1980s. One may suspect that the fact that the colonial movement was coopted by the Japanese authorities, who held all the advantages, not least in linguistic practice, has encouraged the unexamined claim that the culturalists then were dupes or collaborators of the Japanese. Choi Chungmoo draws attention to the employment—indeed the initiation—by South Korean regimes of folk-cultural symbols and the partial failure of minjung activists to anticipate the double-edged nature of their cultural sword precisely because of their idealist notion of popular culture.

But the dilemma goes deeper than this. If the leadership of the contemporary "new culture movement" differs from the semi-Confucian movement of the 1920s and1930s mainly in the terminology it employs and little at all in its idealist conception of culture, it is unclear how the relationship between the leaders and the "people" differs. The didacticism of the contemporary "enlightenment" literature and histories, for example, which aim to facilitate the "awakening" of the minjung to their qualities and mission, leaves an ambiguous impression of the kind of authority that is tacitly assumed. In a hard-hitting analysis that cares more about actions, and deconstructs avowed intentions in the light of these actions, might not the minjung culturalists appear as cultural hegemonists?

Rather than tackling this issue head on, discussion in this book elucidates the central motif of the cultural movement: autonomy. The sense of ambiguity is in part attributable, one imagines, to the sense that Korean identity is under threat, that autonomy is the condition of national reunification, and that autonomy rests on attainment of a united, genuinely Korean culture. All three chapters on minjung literature suggest that the sense of threat impels the movement to adopt what at times appears to be a decidedly nationalistic focus. What, in this case, is the engine of minjung cultural development: an internal dynamic, outside pressures, or some dialectic of the Native versus the Other?

Here we impinge on the relation of the minjung movement to global developments. The oft-claimed uniqueness of the movement cannot be taken at face value. Chung Chai-sik expresses the Korean neo-Confucian subscription to universalism, and evidently it is not simply democracy's threat to hierarchical power and privilege that served to make the Confucian hangover a foil for minjung self-definition, but its distaste for nonuniversal culture: "local" was always "vulgar" for Korea's Confucian establishment, despite its parochial politics. The turn by minjung culturalists to shamanism as the unique locus of Korean culture must be understood in this light.

In minjung Christian theology the issue is more complex. Donald Clark's highly informative and careful chapter describes the use of suffering, or *han*, in minjung theology to express the unique quality of Korean spirituality. This han arises from the historical experience of Koreans, whose geopolitical position has brought unusual collective and individual suffering upon them. Among non-Christian minjung exponents, han occurs as a result of the injustice of others who harbor insidious designs, or of adverse structural arrangements set up by dominant powers. In Christianity, however, the suffering of Christ and of humans ultimately derives from the evil present in all humans. Thus, as Clark indicates, care is generally taken by minjung theologians to prevent self-righteousness that may issue from the concept of han, and this does create some distance from other versions of the minjung's sufferings. Even so, the uniqueness of the Korean minjung is upheld in minjung theology, and its relation to liberational theologies elsewhere remains largely unexplored.

Of course, to treat South Korea's minjung movement as a purely Korean phenomenon would be to say that it bears no relation to global conditions. And it is essential to the drive for autonomy in culture, economics, and politics that the Korean people be viewed in an adversarial relation to global forces, particularly to the cultural and economic pressures which comprise the major effects of "neocolonialism" or the momentum of "international capitalism." Among the contributors to this volume there is a general consensus that if the minjung movement is to be historicized, it must be regarded not as a purely Korean phenomenon, nor as a by-product of neocolonial forces, but as the authentic *Korean* response to global movements as they impinge on domestic life: a conjunction of historical developments at least partially lend the minjung its character. But one would like to push further here, to see Korea as more positively part of the contemporary world, and ask, "How far is the minjung critique of global capitalism and internationalization of culture universalizable?"

Minjung activists and theorists have hardly had the leisure to consider the possibility of extending their critique to other nations' situations. Yet the reverse does seem to apply. Kim Hyung-A indicates the adoption of Marxist and Weberian analyses by minjung theorists, Lukács' literary theory is explicit in Pihl's discussion and implicit in Paik's, while Choi Chungmoo judges that the minjung culture movement "is implicitly utopian socialism." This suggests that non-Korean categories are deemed universal enough to apply to Korea. There is understandably some prickliness among minjung theorists on this issue, but it is questionable whether there is cause to fear an ironing out of cultural specificity under the application of "classical" social and historical interpretations, which talk of general conditions within which cultural variation can enjoy considerable scope. Marxism, for example, does not posit an identical beginning for civilizations and so leaves room for "universal" tendencies to develop from any number of beginnings and to include the logic of those beginnings at each point.

The issue of universality in minjung thought has not, admittedly, been resolved. In concrete movements, as in the case of the student involvement in the 1980s Koch'ang farmers' movement presented in Nancy Abelmann's chapter, the need for more rigorous attention to the question becomes clearer. The dilemma for activists desirous of uniting theory with practice is that the *rural* minjung is where the most indigenous of the "nonofficial" (nonsinicized, nonwesternized, nonelite) Korean sources lie, whereas it is in relation to the *urban* minjung that issues of dramatic social change, modernity, and the impact of global capitalism arise most sharply. Without unduly exaggerating the situation, Abelmann does draw attention to the gap in understanding between the students and farmers, where the latter complained of students' ideological obsessions and desired to pursue their interests practically rather than "heroically." Significantly, and for the students frustratingly, martyrdom was not high among the farmers' values; rather, it was human concern for the parents of slain students and to avoid further such incidents—and the need to follow agricultural seasons.

A parallel may be drawn with the Tonghak movement of the latter decades of the nineteenth century, a movement commonly appealed to as an example of minjung solidarity and power in action. From one point of view, the breakthrough of that peasant and dissident literati-based movement came when the farmers began to conceive of their grievances not simply as local injustices but as a *national* issue, an aspect of the contradictions within the nation's social and economic structures and an effect of imperialist rivalry over Korea by its neighbors. Nevertheless, the farmers' army, when poised to take Seoul, was persuaded by promises of redress of specific grievances and consciousness of the agricultural calendar to return to their farms. In the 1980s also, tensions surfaced between the farmers' sense of their own goals and the root-and-branch approach of the students, who were ideologically committed to transformation of the whole national system. In the end, in June 1987, it was largely the urban laborers who carried the movement forward. Their subsequent lapse into a kind of middle class as their lot has improved has further frustrated activists and may represent a setback to the project of universalizing an autonomous minjung culture, at least in Korea.

The minjung quest for autonomy and its ambiguous connection with global developments has to be understood against the overwhelming desire to formulate a method of achieving national reunification. Again, the national question comes urgently to the fore. Choi Hyun-moo devotes a substantial part of her discussion to the way in which minjung literature by the 1980s situated the national question within the global context. And yet if, as Choi Chungmoo observes, national reunification is, for minjung activists, "coterminous with decolonization," the notion of Korean and global developments conjoining in a positive sense is hardly to be admitted. Where overcoming the national division is predicated on decapitalization, understood as complete self-determination of Korean society, the idea of even a dialectical relation to international forces is not gladly entertained. Possibly for strategic reasons, minjung theorists have not shown concern for the dangers inherent in adopting an overtly nationalistic rhetoric and approach to the "national" question, where all problems are attributed to the division, and the division to the actions of non-Korean forces or their domestic servants. What for Paik Nak-chung is a rather delicate dialectic, for many activists is more a confrontation between Koreanness and inimicable outside forces with which negotiation is not to be countenanced. Strategy aside, in light of the chilling manifestations of a nationalistic solution to national problems in contemporary Europe, questions *should* be raised about the direction of minjung nationalism. The more firmly the motif of autonomy is wedded to a drive for cultural hegemony, the more likely it is that an impatient leadership will turn to statist solutions. There is considerable relevance for Korea in Simone Weil's observations on the French experience (*The Need for Roots* [London: Routledge & Kegan Paul, 1952], 106):

> when the illusion of national sovereignty showed itself to be manifestly an illusion . . . [p]atriotism had to change its meaning and turn itself towards the State. But thereby it straightway ceased to be popular. . . . Thus it happened that, by an historical paradox which at first sight seems surprising, patriotism changed to a different social class and political camp. It had been on the Left; it went over to the Right.

The pressing issue for the present, however, is the identity of the minjung. As some key expectations or predictions of the direction in which the minjung will lead Korean society when they come into their own founder on post-1987 developments, the crisis of identity strikes at the root of the minjung theorists' reading of history and contemporary culture. If the contributors to Hagen Koo, ed., *State and Society in Contemporary Korea* (Ithaca: Cornell University Press, 1994), are correct, it would appear that the middle class (of which a large number were formally putative minjung) is gaining the upper hand in the struggle for cultural hegemony. Put differently, the minjung overthrow of the military culture may have paved the way for the flowering of a "civil" society that does not subscribe to the supposed values of the minjung.

This is not altogether surprising and certainly does not necessarily imply minjung failure or a misreading of history on its own. Events often take their course with unnerving disregard for what goes on inside our heads, and this waywardness that events exhibit in regard to our ideas need only precipitate a crisis where ideas are held inflexibly or where a literal congruity is demanded between ideas and events. Paradoxically, the anxiety to discover a "law" of Korean autonomous historical and cultural development—something universal for Koreans—has become so embedded in the particularization of the circumstances which inspired it, that the minjung movement may have become a political device of the moment, borne away by time rather than remaining active within it. But it is too early to judge: to say that the minjung conception has been superseded or annulled is to claim to know where Korea is headed now. However much we desire to speak *to* the present, speaking *of* the present demands much greater humility.

1

The Cultural Construction of Korean History

Kenneth M. Wells

IN WHAT SENSE does a cultural idea exist in history? If an idea has a history, then we may say it exists as a subject of historical inquiry, that is, it exists in terms of historical method. But the question of how a notion such as minjung exists in history—or, who the minjung are—presents the historian with a peculiar species of problem, as the idea of minjung is not simply a subject of history but a theory of history. It is, further, a judgment on the present and a prescription for the future. In this sense it belongs to that class of historical approaches exemplified by class analysis, where the subject—class—is also the interpretation.

But minjung presents an even more complex problem. As we shall see, minjung historians in South Korea claim that their notion of the nature and role of the minjung arises out of empirical investigation of minjung activity in Korean history. The problem here is that the minjung are not normally defined as a class or any specific social group, which means one needs to establish an idea of what constitutes the minjung in the first place. Admittedly, one requires an idea of class also when one identifies classes in society, but this is not quite the same problem. One may take a group—say, those who do manual labor in cities—whose existence affords little argument and give them a term like "urban proletariat" by which to make other claims which may or may not be useful. "Minjung," however, refers less to such a group than to a *quality* which, it is claimed, can be found in the past, is active in the present, and will determine Korea's future. In the final analysis, minjung is applied, not to people who form a group within a structure of social relations by virtue of their *doing* something, but to "the people" who form the dynamic of history by virtue of their *being* something—the bearers of certain values and qualities. The term belongs to populist idealism, culturally defined.

What we are dealing with here, evidently, is the impact on the course of history of shared cultural ideas, as distinct from (but not as opposed to) social, economic, and political structures. Examination of culture as a historical agency involves two main levels of analysis. On one level, it involves examination of how people form and relate to understandings of the world and themselves, to values, to ideas of the "good," and so on. On another, it concerns investigation of the relation between these understandings and ideas, and the things that "happen" in history. Although South Korean minjung historians pursue both these levels in order to support their claim that the minjung are the dynamic force of Korean history, it is their activity in the latter area which is the primary concern of this chapter.

It must be stated at the outset that there is no single minjung theory of Korean history. Who qualify for the term "minjung" and why are extremely vexed questions that are almost irremediably confounded by the intense nationalist feelings and political stakes entangled in them. A conclusion drawn from one source of minjung history may be refuted by another, and many an observation will be weakened by numerous qualifications. This problem is compounded by the fact that many minjung theorists have hardly clarified their positions, which often appear to involve confusing inconsistencies. However, it is not my purpose to mount a critique of the minjung movement, still less to satisfy or side with any of its competing versions, but rather to try to understand it in terms of a cultural construction of Korean history. In this respect, I believe it is possible to preface the discussion with some generally valid observations.

First, South Korean minjung historiography is interventionist. It challenges histories that assume the Korean story can be told adequately by raising questions only about institutions of power—who mismanaged Korea in the nineteenth century, how Japan seized Korea, what policies and what organs directed economic development, and so on—by asking other questions, such as who have ensured the continuity of the majority Korean culture and how they have developed it in face of attempts to thwart or distort it. It questions why historical inquiry has been limited to certain subjects and restricted to certain sources. Minjung historians have broadened the sources of Korean history to include oral traditions, popular theater and dances, shamanist and other religious rituals and beliefs, and literary journalism. In these, as well as in other more traditional sources, they claim to find the script of a cultural drama according to which Korea's history must be interpreted and in which the minjung play the leading roles.

Second, in this drama the minjung are *sufferers*. They suffer from all the forces that have appeared to be in control of the nation at various times: the Yangban aristocracy up to the end of the nineteenth century, the Japanese empire from 1905 to 1945, the superpower division of the nation thereafter, the "neocolonial" pressures of the United States and Japan, and their own despots and military dictatorships. How, then, do they play the leading roles? Rather than rendering them passive and mute, this suffering, according to the interpretation, gives the minjung an acute sense of the stark *difference* between their values and those of their oppressors. Every victory of the non-minjung forces is therefore pyrrhic, for it only furthers the development of minjung culture and strengthens the resolve of the minjung not to be assimilated by "values" whose alienating cruelty has been exposed. Herein lies the brittleness of non-minjung forces, which, in the struggle over national culture, including political culture, cannot possibly win on such terms. At least, such is the logic. How far "reality" respects this logic is a question which is now prompting some reformulation of the theory and which will be addressed toward the end of this chapter.

Third, since its logic of historical development leads to minjung ascendancy, minjung history is predictive. This can be understood in a strong sense, where society is understood to proceed according to scientific laws; in a weak sense, where the prediction goes no further than that the minjung will (or does) take charge of Korea's history; or in a conditional sense, where it is claimed that, *provided* the minjung are given charge, Korea's history will follow a certain desirable course. But whichever sense applies, history that does not have this predictive bent, based on a minjung-centered interpretation of history, is not minjung history. For this reason Yi Kibaek's innovative and important "new theory" of Korean history (in which, in any case, Korean cultural history revolves around changes in the leadership elite) can hardly be regarded as minjung history.[1] This impulse to predict derives from the oppositional, often dissident, nature of the wider minjung movement in South Korea and reflects its predilection for Marxist analysis.

This is especially clear in the case of social scientists such as Pak Hyonch'ae, who adheres to a strong view of prediction and whose "minjung economics" consists in treating the minjung as a classical Marxian "class."[2] For Pak, the behavior of groups is determined by their relation to production, and so in principle the course of society can be predicted according to this relation. In this case the minjung have to be defined in terms of a relation to production, that is, as a structural agency. Their suffering, then, is the result of this relation, and the self-awareness induced by this suffering is understood as a rise in class consciousness.

It is here that confusion arises over what constitutes the minjung. The confusion comes from trying to explain the role of cultural movements in history in terms of the way socioeconomic classes relate to each other. But there appears to be no clear statement among minjung historians that minjung culture can be reduced to class consciousness or is created by position in the overall social structure. And unless minjung culture is regarded as a derivative of a structural pattern replicated throughout much of the world, this is hardly possible. Further, not only the working people suffer, and the suffering does not ensue only from economic conditions. Students, teachers, writers, artists, and journalists also suffer, and although their socioeconomic

positions differ significantly from those of the "workers," they see their relationship with the workers not as a transitory alliance based on a temporary
common cause but as a coalition based on a vital cultural unity. In Chapter 2
of this volume and elsewhere, Kang Man'gil describes this as a class confederation.[3] This solidarity is based on the idea that they all suffer, albeit in
different measure, under the implementation of values that they all find
alienating. If the desirable Korean cultural values repose most purely among
the workers, this is because their greater suffering has had a more refining
effect, which is a very different thing from claiming that these values themselves derive from class composition.

Fourth, minjung historians are deeply concerned with the division of the
Korean nation into two states and maintain that reunification must or will be
achieved through the strength and according to the values of the minjung.
There is a strong tendency here to interpret the minjung in the context of
international power structures, particularly because the division of Korea
into two states is a most tangible common cause of suffering. In this case
those who suffer because of the division and other effects of "neocolonialism" or international capitalism exist as a class by virtue of their relation to
world forces, while any Koreans who benefit from this arrangement can be
considered agents of these forces. This view is common (though by no
means unchallenged) among minjung theorists, and there is nothing contradictory in approaching Korean historical experiences from this angle. But if
it is supposed to account for the nature of minjung culture, the question
again becomes confused. For it is surely not the intention of minjung theorists to suggest that the Koreanness of minjung values is a *product* of international power configurations or that once the international causes of
suffering are removed minjung culture will lose its raison d'être and be
replaced by some other structurally dependent system.

Finally, minjung historiography cannot properly be understood from the
standpoint of developments in Western theory and practice. It is particularly
important not to approach Korean "cultural" history as though it were in the
grip of the disputations over postmodernism and deconstructionism that
preoccupy Western academics or took its cue from developments in the
French Annalist tradition or the "new cultural history" movement in the
English-speaking world. It is undeniable that some minjung theorists do
draw ideas from such sources, and it is one of the ironies of the movement
that some of its strongest proponents advance it by applying frameworks
developed in the West. Nevertheless, the notion of the minjung is not an
outgrowth of such frameworks, and as a cultural phenomenon it arises out of
a Korean sense of the basis of national society and of how history works.

The Role of the Historian in Korea

The earliest written record we have by a Korean historian is Kim Pusik's
twelfth-century official history of the Three Kingdoms, the *Samguk Sagi*. A

Confucian scholar in a predominantly Buddhist state, Kim Pusik was concerned to present a correct view of the past, that is, to show how the course of government and society was determined by the moral example of the rulers. Kim's victory over the rebellion led by the Buddhist monk Myo Ch'ŏng was more than a political triumph: it was a victory of the rational Confucian view of how history worked over a "superstitious" view that related the fortunes of the state to geomantic principles. By the onset of the Chosŏn dynasty at the end of the fourteenth century, the office of historian was a real institution, and the court historian could advise the king that he had two things to fear: the mandate of heaven and the historian's brush.

Under the neo-Confucian Chosŏn dynasty, which continued up to the Japanese occupation in 1910, the state was believed to rest on the ideal of civilization laid down in the Confucian classics. In the accumulating accounts of the *Kukcho Pogam* (twenty-eight volumes by the end of the dynasty), the Chosŏn historians drew lessons for present rulers from the behavior and its consequences of past rulers, and conformity to the *tao,* or way of *t'ien* (heaven; *ch'ŏn* in Korean), was to be the basis of Korean civilization. History was not studied in terms of structures but of approximation to this cultural ideal, and it was not change that was anticipated so much as a stable harmony. Predictions about the future consisted in very general moral observations about whether the rulers' conduct would benefit or harm the kingdom. Even in the writings of Yulgok (Yi I, 1536–1584), the most practical and prescient of the Chosŏn scholar-officials, one finds an almost mystical view of the source of harmony: a good person, through moral self-transformation, can transform the entire social and natural order of the universe.[4]

This view of history was official, elitist, and initially drawn from China, and its propagation was accompanied by suppression of other viewpoints. There is, in fact, considerable dissonance between the claims made in the *Kukcho Pogam* and the more descriptive records of the *Chosŏn Wangjo Sillok* (the veritable records of the Chosŏn dynasty). The historians said that employment by Chosŏn monarchs of shamans to perform rain-dances in times of drought was unthinkable, as such matters as drought and flood depended on the virtue or otherwise of the ruler. But the dynastic records stated that shamans were called upon for such services during the reigns of T'aejong (1400–1418), Sŏngjong (1469–1494), Chungjong (1506–1544), and Injo (1623–1649), and for other purposes throughout the dynasty.[5]

There was, therefore, a cultural struggle involved in the Confucian scholars' writing of history, a struggle to reform the nation according to the (Chinese) Confucian values in place of the native shamanist and indigenized Buddhist values. Shin Hŭm, a renowned seventeenth-century Confucian scholar, stated that the Chosŏn dynasty's guiding principle was to emulate Chinese civilization. Although Korea had come a long way, the fact that shamanism and Buddhism still held sway over some, he lamented, signified that Korea was still a land of "barbarians."[6] In the eighteenth century, this view was challenged by the rising *silhak* scholars, who urged that Korea's history be examined and judged as the history of the Korean people rather than in terms of conformity to a Chinese ideal. Although it did not repudiate Confucianism as such, the silhak movement was regarded as a threat to the founding principles of the dynasty and was soon crushed.

It is important to note that the struggle was not over whether a nation was founded on a cultural ideal but over what that ideal ought to be in the case of Korea. It would not be inappropriate to describe traditional Korean history writing as a type of cultural idealism. When the role of the people in Korea's history is the issue, the struggle was over elitist versus populist idealism. Thus Chŏng Tojŏn (?–1398), the leading ideologue of the Chosŏn dynasty in its foundation years, stated that the "mind of the king is the foundation of the government," and that local magistrates are "the parents of the people," as their welfare depends on the magistrates' virtue.[7] In reply, the silhak scholar Tasan (Chŏng Yag'yong, 1762–1836) called for a people-centered history, culture, and administration.[8]

Thus, when we turn to Korean minjung historians, we should be wary of understanding their thought or method according to recent Western developments. They have their own tradition of cultural historiography, and it should be no surprise to discover elements of this tradition in minjung writings. The role of the historian still is to instruct or warn the rulers of the consequences of ignoring the proper cultural basis of the nation, as was the case with traditional court historians. But now, what the (recalcitrant) rulers must fear is not heaven's mandate but the mandate of the people—and the historian's word processor. Now, any right to rebel is not founded on a Mencian ideal of the Way of Heaven, but on a notion closer to the silhak position: the Korean laboring masses, in whom repose the sources and values of Koreanness and the dynamic of Korean history. The people, the masses, are not the object of Confucian paternalism but are the nation's backbone, its shape, and, most important, its compass bearing.

The idea of a mandate of the people is notoriously subject to manipulation, whether naively or by design. What "the people" means when their mandate is invoked depends very often on which interest group is invoking it. In October 1989, the then president of South Korea, No T'aeu (Roh Taewoo), in a speech he delivered at George Washington University, appealed to the classical precept "The wish of the people is the will of heaven." This he claimed to be the basis of his determination to listen to the people and act on their wishes.[9] Yet there were significant numbers of people and important representatives of groups of people in Korea to whom Mr. Roh was determined not to listen: he chose which voices represented the "people." The government in the south has also been adept at managing the idea of indigenous culture. It has been quick to assume the role of arbiter of national culture by sponsoring cultural festivals, exhibitions, and centers and designating human beings as "Living Cultural Treasures" of Korea.

Naturally, those regarded as dissidents in the south make their own choices about who the people are and express their own views on culture through art, drama, literature, and the movements they create or support. But the term "dissident" assumes a legitimate and nonlegitimate or official and nonofficial polarity. And it is quite true that minjung ideology has arisen in great part out of a sense of this polarity. At least the minjung have had a definite counterpoint in the government, which has been determined to interpret and dispose of the will of the people in accord with its own power interests. Consequently, the minjung issue is a struggle over legitimacy, and the articulators of minjung ideology—or ideologies—consciously and often vehemently represent to the Korean people two stark choices: leadership of and by the minjung into a new era of reunification as a genuine Korean nation; or perpetuation of an alien system of politics that makes the continuing tragic division of the nation the cornerstone of power.

But despite the impression created by the media, especially in the West, the view that the issue is limited to an argument between dissidents and successive South Korean governments is misleading. The idea, again abetted by the media, that this seeming sudden rise of "populism" in South Korea is a new development of the 1980s is also a misconception. Debate over the nature and role of the "people" in Korea extends back for centuries, and in terms of modern history, at least to the 1880s. It is hardly surprising, therefore, that much of the debate today focuses on the late nineteenth century in both historical and literary fields.

The Role of the People

Between the decline of the Chosŏn dynasty around the turn of the century and the appearance of the present minjung theory of the people's role in history, there arose a strong culturalist movement among Korean nationalist intellectuals, whose views on the people retained some vestiges of the traditional outlook and at the same time contained some elements of the current (unofficial) position. Yet although this suggests a continuity in terms of issues debated, a fundamental transition has taken place in twentieth-century Korean nationalism regarding the role of the people in effecting change. This is essentially a transition from culturalism to populism. I am using these terms, not generally, but specifically in the context of modern Korean nationalism. Culturalism refers to movements from the late nineteenth century which placed hopes of a new, strong Korean nation in the enlightened reformation of ideas and ideals concerning human social and political relations. These movements carried over the neo-Confucian faith in the civilizing function of education and moral self-improvement. They believed in the force of ideas, including imported ideas, to change national character and therefore the national state. Essentially, political change had to be preceded by cultural change, a change which could be planned and deliberately implemented by intellectuals.[10] The people, called the *minjok,* were to be *made* into a nation.

In the populist view, the people make and inform the nation. The minjung have to be Korean, and can only be Korean, not a social grouping generalizable over all nations. Hence minjung theology, which is more popular in Protestant than Catholic circles, is not the same as liberation theology, even though obvious comparisons can be drawn in some areas. Nor among leftist historians is a class struggle involved pure and simple, even though there is clear Marxist inspiration in many aspects of their writings. When the minjung are considered in relation to the problem of reunifying Korea, a Leninist theory of imperialism may serve as a framework, but there is always an irreducible remainder in the concept of minjung which its champions consciously uphold. This remainder appears at times to be the unique spirit of the Korean people, which no general theory can contain: it is a historical law of development peculiar to Korea. Minjung is even more basic than the traditional nationalist term for the people, "minjok," because the minjok as a whole are not yet properly imbued with the original minjung qualities, and consequently are not yet fully propelled in the proper direction by the minjung historical dynamic.[11]

Two groups in particular have been active in promoting this role: the Korean History Research Association *(Han'guk yŏksa yŏn'guhoe)* and the Historical Issues Research Center *(Yŏksa munje yŏn'guso)*. The former publishes the journal *Yŏksawa hyŏnsil* (History and Reality; first issue 1989), while the latter publishes the journal *Yŏksa pip'yŏng* (Historical Criticism; first issue 1987). In order to relate the minjung to concrete historical effects, the term is frequently identified with a specific group or movement among the Korean people. This is given added urgency where a historical lineage is required to give legitimacy to contentions that this or that movement in the present is the true focus of the minjung. And here, the objectives and methods of the two associations do show similarities to cultural history writing in the West, in particular with the approach of the Center for Contemporary Cultural Studies at Birmingham. They are, to use the terminology of the Birmingham group, anxious "to recover past struggles in order to create a politics for the present," to "link the politics of history-writing to the sense of history active within contemporary cultural and political movements," and so to argue that "historiography is concerned not with the past but the relation between the past and the future."[12]

This relation is, of course, recognized by most theorists on history writing, and quite specifically in the works of Herbert Butterfield, R. G. Collingwood, and E. H. Carr. But there are important differences. In drawing attention to the link between the way we construe the past with the political fashion of the moment, Butterfield was sounding a warning and making a plea to treat the past with a little more respect. For Collingwood, the task was to find out how the present came to be what it is—part of the human response to the summons to self-understanding. Carr maintains that because we are trying to find out how things work in history, we always have an eye on the future.[13]

For members of the Korean History Research Association, however, the concern is so much with the future—particularly with a Korea united in the future[14]—that the object is not to minimize but to maximize the intrusion of the future into the past; not to find out how the present came to be but to exclude from it its aberrant features. The dominant tone, therefore, is unabashedly exhortatory, and any such notion as academic distance from one's subject is not simply given short shrift, but is opposed as a fundamental misunderstanding about the unavoidable relation between history writing and the construction of the future.[15]

There are, of course, historiographical issues here which have to do with the relationship between concepts and their supposed historical referents. Although the focus of this chapter is on the concept of the minjung rather than the historical movements as such, my purpose is to examine how minjung historians propose that this concept interacts with the historical group or movement to which it refers. But the nature of this interaction is also an idea, of which there are many varieties. And it seems to me that, here, much of the Korean minjung historiography requires explanation. In their concern to offer solutions to the discontents and divisions on the Korean peninsula, many academics in South Korea over the last two decades have produced versions not of what the minjung has been so much as what it ought to be. One might consider this to be of no consequence if the objective is to promote a political idea and movement. But insofar as this aspect of the campaign is directed at a highly educated audience, any weakening of the term's link with history is bound sooner or later to threaten its inspirational effectiveness. The question is whether the referent of the term "minjung" is more a set of ideas than something identifiable in the past.

One of the major continuities of the debate over the nature and role of the minjung, a term that also appears in the *Tongnip Sinmun* (Independence News) in the 1890s, is precisely this problem which surrounds the attempt to link such a term to historical events, movements, structures, and persons. It may be argued that the attempt to make the link is based on a mistaken idea that an analytical term can have an actual, literal counterpart in history. Wittgenstein, for instance, held that the attempt to link a term with a referent is based on a fundamental confusion over the nature of language, and the same objection may be raised against trying to link "minjung" too directly or literally to something in the past. But the methodological dilemma facing historians who deny the past any reality independent from their terminology has been demonstrated recently in connection with history influenced by the New Historicism in literary criticism: shock at finding denials of or justifications for the Nazi holocaust based on exactly the same principles as those espoused in the New Historicism has exposed its methodological weakness. Historians, and cultural historians among them, should not be in any hurry to abandon an empirical approach to evidence.

But a more fruitful approach, and one that is heedful of Korean historiographical traditions, would seem to be to find a *cultural* referent for the term. Once this is done, movements and groups can be analyzed in relation to a cultural struggle, with all its attendant social and political power conflicts. The nature of the term "minjung" may require us to adopt this approach—to regard, in short, culture as history.[16] It is in this sense that I propose now to examine the history of the notion of the people in modern Korea.

Culturalism and the New Citizen

Although I find it justifiable to speak of a transition from culturalism to populism in view of a fundamental shift in perception of the role the people play in Korean history, there were antecedents of the latter in the culturalist movements. Indeed, insofar as the minjung historians, literary critics, and others argue that national reunification will be achieved through expansion of minjung *culture,* they share the basic premise of the culturalists concerning the modus operandi of Korean history.

In some studies of modern Chinese nationalism, culturalism is defined as the conviction that, as a nation has a cultural and intellectual foundation, any changes that nationalists might advocate require modification of that cultural-intellectual base.[17] Korean culturalism, which also grew out of a neo-Confucian tradition, easily fits this definition in the sense already indicated above. But there are two essential differences.

First, for a large proportion of Korean culturalists, thought and civilization themselves were founded on a religious outlook. Culturalism's most prominent advocates were Protestants and members of the indigenous Ch'ŏndogyo (Religion of the Heavenly Way; formerly *Tonghak*), who quickly swamped the moderate Confucian reformers. Their predominance possibly precluded, until the mid-twentieth century at least, the appearance of areligious or antireligious nationalist intellectuals similar to Liang Ch'i-ch'ao in China. Ch'ŏndogyo adherents desired national restoration through egalitarian but conservative values, which they claimed resided in the people. The Korean Protestants were more iconoclastic. From the 1890s they organized nationalist clubs, published journals and newspapers in the vernacular script, and mounted a campaign for the adoption of new social, political, economic, and legal values and institutions, which reflected the liberal-democratic views of England and the United States of America at the time. But both religious groups saw a necessary connection between religion and civilization. They tended to regard the "people" religiously: they were amenable to spiritual transformation, whence would issue a national transformation.

Second, from 1910 to 1945 Korea was under a Japanese colonial occupation that made it difficult if not impossible for the culturalists to implement their ideals politically. This external restraint on their activities, including speech and publication, threw culturalist politics into some confusion and exposed it to charges of compromise, even collaboration. Consequently, culturalism and its ideas began to lose favor steadily from the mid-1920s, and the focus of nationalist debate shifted more to the socialists. This, in combination with the fact that socialist ideas were introduced to Korea by waves of Koreans returning from abroad, seems to be responsible for the common assumption that there was a complete break between the culturalist and the later "populist" positions on the people. But what occurred was less of a break than a transition.

The most significant departure by the culturalists from the traditional view of the people was the idea that they were no longer subjects but citizens. This was a far-reaching departure, calling into question the strict hierarchical cosmology that had been reflected in detail in the traditional state and society of the Chosŏn dynasty. A principal theme of the 1896–1899 Independence Club and of enlightenment campaigns up to 1910 was that citizens were horizontally linked in a sort of collective responsibility for the nation. Nation building was the work of the people—their right and responsibility. For the Protestants, this was guaranteed by the doctrines of stewardship and the priesthood of all believers.[18]

In an August 1896 editorial of *The Independent,* a newspaper published by the Methodist Sŏ Chaep'il, the government was called upon to rule in the interests of the people. Who were the people? "This word 'people' is a new word in Korea but the readers of this paper know what a mighty word it is and how irresistible its claims are in the long run. Today may be dark for Korean people but they may rest assured that their cause will inevitably triumph."[19] From the context of this statement, it may be concluded that the people were those upon whom the administration, particularly its legal offices, weighed heavily—namely, almost all who were not of noble blood or official rank. But since the paper was published wholly in English, its "readers" could hardly be numbered among such as these. There were a number of reasons why the paper was published in English (and the first ever Korean vernacular newspaper, the *Tongnip Sinmun,* was published alongside it), but the inexorable "cause" of the people was clearly considered to be new not only to the government but to the people themselves. The culturalists' attitude toward the people was paternalistic, and their enlightenment campaigns assumed dire ignorance on their part.

The traditional view of human nature, that it is distinguished by a capacity for moral understanding and therefore morally educable, was applied more democratically than before to include the lowest classes. The people remained a moral category. But now, they were not simply beings whose moral quality depended on the example of their superiors; they were independently responsible. The decline of the nation was partly their responsibility, in that, by entrusting their property, their families' fates, their very lives to officials, they had allowed the latter to usurp the position of "master" *(chuin)*, which belongs to the people.[20] In particular, the ignorance of the people was a moral failing on the part both of the ruling class that kept education to itself and of the commoners whose shortsightedness prevented them from seeking practical knowledge.[21]

To become "masters" of their nation therefore required a change of heart and mental attitude. But the real change that was urged at the end of the nineteenth century was, rather, a change of masters; what was demanded of the people was a shift of loyalty—from the monarchy to the nation-state. The people were to be mobilized to serve the ends of a strong, proud member of the world of nations. This was presented to the people as a radical shift from toadyism to independent statehood, from corrupt self-seeking to public altruism. The watchword was *chaju tongnip,* self-reliant, self-directed independence from personal to national levels.[22]

Above all, the people had to *work* for the new nation, to strengthen it so that it could catch up and keep up with other nations.[23] The new citizen was to be a patriot, which meant putting the reputation, glory, and profit of the nation before even one's own life.[24] While it was implied that by working for the nation the people were working for their own as well as others' good, at least in the long run, it was clear in practice that for some time to come the people would be expected to shoulder a rather heavy burden of labor. "Your labor is the foundation of the country," taught the radical reformer, Yu Kiljun, implying that the better their labor the better the nation.[25] Prosperity, it was argued, would result from intensive development and improvement of agriculture.[26]

Doubtless—they at least said so—the early culturalists envisaged the people turning into able citizens in time, when such close supervision would become unnecessary. And a tremendous amount of work was devoted to gaining legal rights and protection for the people. But the people nevertheless did not naturally possess the requisites of citizenship: they were not the repository of national values. In 1898 Yun Ch'iho wrote of the "abominable indifference of the general public" to the political life of their country,[27] and even by 1910 a prominent nationalist, Kim Ku, complained that the people "did not even know what a nation was."[28] There was little hesitation in proclaiming that the initiative and leadership lay with the newly Western-educated elite.[29] The masses had no national values, no national consciousness—that was the problem, the reason for their becoming the object of the culturalists' intense campaigning.

From 1910 to 1918, the period Koreans remember as the Dark Ages, it was again religion which provided the most potent symbols. In particular, the Korean people as a whole were conceived of in the Protestant church as a suffering people, a type of Israel, exiled within their own land. Sermons on Nehemiah's rebuilding of Jerusalem and Moses leading the Children of Israel out of bondage, and school dramas enacting Queen Esther saving her people made the Japanese nervous and gave the Koreans identity and hope.[30]

This idea of the people as a suffering people and a remnant of the people which holds within itself the true form of Korea is a theme carried over by the minjung movement. And of course the culturalist views did not vanish with the introduction of populist ideologies, for the former contained elements which neither the populist Right nor Left wished to repudiate. Nevertheless, it would be simply wrong to claim that populism grew directly out of the culturalist principles or even out of a rethinking of the culturalist position. Historically, the transition to populism was sparked by the return to Korea of waves of students who, while studying in the enemy's universities in Tokyo and Kyoto, had become inspired by the Marxist theory of society and Lenin's theory of imperialism.

The Shift to Populism

The shift away from the culturalist view of the people as citizens serving a modernized nation-state and toward the position that the people are the makers of Korean history commenced in earnest in the early 1920s. The failure of the very costly March First movement of 1919 and the dismal response of the League of Nations to overtures by the Korean Provisional Government in Shanghai provoked impatient repudiations of the culturalist position. The mood was set by the brilliant scholar-activist Sin Ch'aeho, whose pre-1920 writings, while reflecting Western ideals of patriotism and enlightenment, had already introduced the idea of the "broad masses" as the dynamic force of history. After 1920, Sin moved more and more away from concepts of nation and patriotism in favor of the people as a key category with their own culture and social values.[31]

But it was chiefly socialism that redefined the people. Not only did converts to Marxism returning from Japan argue a different relation of the people to national life and the colonial power, but numbers of key leaders of the culturalist stream also defected to socialism. Many of these were Protestants. By and large they remained Protestants, but they still regarded their action as a defection. They no longer believed that the people had lost independence through moral negligence and spiritual poverty and therefore no longer had any faith in the culturalist cure. However, the Protestants, Ch'ŏndogyo adherents, and many Buddhists also, continued to hold an ethical view, if now in relation to the imperialist Japanese. Consequently, some adopted ethical socialism, supposedly on the basis of Kant's maxim that no human being should be treated simply as a commodity or an object of any sort. But they held in common with the Marxists and Marxist-Leninists the conviction that the human beings who make history are the workers.

Because of the continuing nationalistic nature of Korean movements, however, the workers were called upon to struggle less against an oppressing class than against an oppressing nation, the Japanese. On instructions from the Comintern, the Marxist-Leninists agreed to form a united front with other socialist groups and the nonsocialist nationalists in 1927. The leaders of all streams remained the highly educated, and even where farmers' cooperatives were established and labor action organized, the socialists' approach to the people was only a little less didactic and top-down than the continuing enlightenment campaigns of the culturalists. But the rhetoric certainly was different, and Korea awaited only the removal of the Japanese imperialists for the workers to establish a proletarian paradise. In the 1930s, however, the Japanese tightened their grip over all aspects of Korean life, incarcerated socialist and nationalist leaders alike, and began to invade China. The debate over the people awaited a liberation in 1945 that was quickly followed by national division into two states. Minjung historiography being a phenomenon of the south, I shall limit my discussion to the debate there.

Under President Syngman Rhee (1948–1960), both culturalists and socialists were suppressed in favor of a policy of promoting a simple nationalism of unity. Independence movements of the Korean race against the Japanese race were extolled as the genuine nationalist past, and the institution of liberal democracy (supposedly) in continuation of Rhee's diplomatic struggles in the West during the colonial era was promoted as the only legitimate activity in the present. This official nationalism was explicitly anticommunist and in general looked with disfavor on theories concerning the masses, particulary in the wake of considerable prosocialist uprisings and their bloody suppression in Cheju Island and Yŏsu between 1947 and 1949. The Korean War of 1950–1953 deepened this bitter legacy, and Park Chunghee's military rule from 1961 to 1979 was, if anything, even more actively suppressive of debate on national issues of any kind other than the threat from the north.

This long period of suppression of thought and restrictions on any non-official organization among the South Korean people appears to have influenced to a considerable extent the current notion of the role of the minjung in Korean history. As there is nothing in the present or the recent past to serve as an example of a minjung organization of Korean society, it is necessary to seek minjung culture in predivision history. And since the relaxation of publication laws early in 1987 (when President Chŏn Tuhwan [Chun Doo-Hwan] resigned), a phenomenal number of journals, academic and otherwise, have appeared, as well as monographs and novels on minjung themes. Old novels banned by the former regimes have been published; North Korean works of history and literature have become available on the shelves of Seoul bookstores. The most intensive development of the minjung theme is taking place in the fields of literature and history. Because the chapters by Paik Nak-chung, Choi Hyun-moo, and Marshall Pihl in this volume treat the subject of minjung literature in detail, I shall focus my own discussion on minjung histories.

The Minjung in History

A considerable rewriting of Korean history is taking place, which echoes the themes of minjung literature. The writers do not, of course, always see eye to eye, yet all share the aim of rediscovering the minjung in the present by finding their imprint in the past. The most notable events in this program of rewriting were the formation in Seoul of the aforementioned Historical Issues Research Center *(Yŏksa munje yŏn'guso)* and the Korean History Research Association *(Han'guk yŏksa yŏn'guhoe)* in February 1986 and September 1988, respectively. These societies consist mainly of a new generation of historians who desire to throw off the restraints of conservative, especially ruling-class, views of Korean history and pursue in its place a history of the people based on a scientific methodology.

What is meant by "scientific"? According to the Korean History Research Association's *Manifesto,* "only that study of history which has its roots in the social forces which generate historical progress is scientific, and its scientific integrity can be verified only through social practice."[32] Concerning these social forces it states: "We are conscious that the agents of social transformation and progress are the minjung, and our quest is for a history which accords with the will and the worldview of the minjung." The type of interaction assumed here between history and history writing, between the past and the future, is clear enough: how yesterday is understood determines what is done today to shape tomorrow. Presumably the results, the "social practice," will justify the view that is forwarded concerning the past.

Despite their privileged position as agents of Korean history, the minjung are not yet sufficiently aware of this. While reflecting that "Now that we are in a new historical phase leading towards the democratization of society and the unification of the nation, research on modern and contemporary Korean history can no longer stop within an ivory tower nor be simply transmitted didactically to the masses," the Historical Issues Research Center goes on to state that the "time has come when the minjung, the subjects *(chuch'e)* of Korean society and Korean history, must recover the knowledge of their own history."[33] Accordingly, the Korean History Research Society has busied itself with a program of publication and mass education designed to popularize the fruit of its research in order to guide the people's historical consciousness in the correct direction.[34] It might be objected that the "will and the worldview" of the minjung was already leading not only themselves but also the researchers in the right direction, as they are the only source of the historians' apprehension of the correct direction in the first place. But I do not think mention of formal logical difficulties here has much point: the general confusion surrounding the undefined use of "scientific" and the circular logic in the apologetics of the intellectuals' link with the masses is long familiar to us all. What is important for historiographical purposes is to find out what kind of history is being done.

If we concentrate on the younger minjung historians, those who succeed Kang Man'gil, whose contribution to minjung historiography is considerable and merits a study in its own right,[35] it is evident that they do believe they have a vantage point from which to view the recent history of the minjung. This vantage point is the history of mass movements in the nineteenth century (and perhaps earlier)—that is, before the "Great Interruption" (my term). This Great Interruption is the dislocation of Korean history by the Japanese occupation from 1905 to 1945, during which the minjung will and worldview was stifled, the course of Korean history was wrested from them, and with it the means of their self-knowledge. The regimes of the post-1945 era in the south have continued this dislocation by maintaining a bureaucratic-military state.[36] Only now are the people recovering their consciousness as the masters of Korean history, and the historians can assist in this recovery.

Thus a position has been found which justifies the new historians' claim to enlighten the people concerning their own mission without falling back on a position that transcends minjung history. On the contrary, they base their claim on their immersion *in* minjung history. To be more precise, their role is a maiuetic one: by writing their history and elucidating their culture they bring the minjung to self-awareness, even if sometimes the tone is didactic and assertive. Thus also the intellectual is saved, its leadership in the people's revolution is affirmed, albeit by the intellectuals themselves, as it was in Europe in May 1968. And, very importantly, this account of their interaction with the minjung has given them a platform from which to attack the legitimacy of the rulers, at least up to 1992. By writing a *people's* history of the 1860–1895 Tonghak movement and the later independence struggles against the Japanese colonial regime, pointed questions are raised about the position of South Korea's recent rulers. The post-1945 regimes and their intellectual supporters are tarred with the same brush as the previous oppressors, and the implication is clear that they, too, are "foreign" to the Korean Volk [folk], indeed, are representatives of foreign powers and systems.

A recent study of the Tonghak movement opens with the observation that, to date, writings on this movement have paid scant attention to what shape of society and economy was envisaged by the peasants who participated in the rebellion. Knowing this would be to know the mind and will of the minjung.[37] In his *Declaration*, Chŏn Pongjun, the "Mungbean" General, described the minjung socially as commoners, "untouchables" (butchers, tanners, and so on), and slaves, and economically as peasants, small merchants, and the unemployed. Generally, they comprised the mass of people who suffered under the "feudal" system of Yangban, plutocrat and bureaucrat.[38] Their economic vision was to replace feudal control of land and produce with peasant ownership of land, economic autonomy for small farmers, and the lifting of restrictions on small merchants (to break official monopolies).[39] Their social and political vision was emancipation of the untouchables and slaves, equal access to employment at all levels regardless of lineage, and local self-rule based on the *chipkangsŏ* (peasant councils) that were formed during the rebellion.[40] The guiding principle of their vision was the religious notion of the Oneness of Heaven and Humanity *(in nae ch'ŏn)*.

Although there is nothing remarkable or innovative in the methodology employed here, or in fact any real contribution to our knowledge of the subject, the author clearly believes that the Tonghak movement is the proper place to look for the minjung spirit and dynamic of Korean history. Not only were the "feudal" rulers caught up in contradictions which the peasant movement would have solved or avoided, but all the other alternative visions for national reorganization of salvation at the time were either also doomed by internal contradictions or based on alien systems that had little part in minjung culture. The selection of the Tonghak movement implies a rejection of the 1895 Kabo reforms, the 1896–1899 Independence Club, the enlightenment campaigns up to 1910, and the whole culturalist movement during the colonial period.[41]

Although many articles use Marxist analytical terms,[42] a comparison with North Korean writings in the thirty-three-volume *Chosŏn Chŏnsa* (1980)[43] shows important differences. Concerning the Tonghak movement, the North Korean historians praise it for its principle of the Oneness of Heaven and Humanity, interpreting this as a repudiation of transcendental ideas of God, heaven, and so on, and as an affirmation of the material processes of history. But it is faulted for being insufficiently revolutionary in its objectives. It is not linked with any minjung property or lineage, but is lumped with a bourgeois phase in Korean history that includes the Independence Club and everything else up to the March First movement in 1919. This latter movement is the terminal point of the bourgeois phase; thereafter socialism ascends through development of labor and farmers' movements to the attainment of the Democratic People's Republic of Korea (DPRK) in 1948.

Kang Man'gil offers the suggestion that, by including all movements as integral parts of Korean history, the North Korean treatment may be superior to those South Korean studies which exclude "non-minjung" elements.[44] Even so, the North Korean application of the classical Marxist phases to Korea is overly mechanical and ignores the importance of the deep cultural differences found by the South Korean scholars. But the difference is influenced by their different agendas. North Korean scholars aim to present an official version of Korean history that legitimizes the DPRK. South Korean minjung historians aim to present the *nonofficial* past as the legitimate Korean history, with a view to bypassing the present (South Korean) rulers and reunifying under minjung leadership.

Conclusion

The culturalist view of the people as new citizens who, upon receiving the requisite training, would build a new, strong nation-state as responsible political and economic beings began in the late nineteenth century with considerable force but declined in the 1920s in the face of the Japanese occupation and the rise of socialist thought. It nevertheless undermined to some degree the former hierarchical concept and ordering of the Korean state by inculcating the doctrine of the horizontal relationship of all citizens and by energetically expanding modern education down through the ranks of Korean society. The idea that every Korean was responsible for the fate of the nation and must therefore participate in its political life was vigorously propounded by the culturalists from the late 1890s.

Underlying their activities was the conviction that politics, and indeed the formation of a nation-state, grew logically and chronologically out of the development of a healthy national culture. Under the influence of Protestant doctrines and their assumption that the Western political form also derived from its cultural base, many Korean culturalists purposed to create a healthy national culture through the spiritual, moral, and mental transformation of the people. In this sense, the people were not regarded as the locus of Koreanness or the source of national values; in fact, on such they stood in dire need of enlightenment.

Populism did not so much develop the theme of the people's political responsibilities and rights, which was more or less retained, as introduce a new notion of the nature and role of the people, a new definition of the minjung. Socialists in the 1920s had already emphasized that the people were the engine of historical development. In recent years, however, the minjung have been further defined as a cultural group; as not only the motive power of history but the guardians of national values who will determine the future (united) shape of the nation. Minjung historians reject the idea that culture can be imported or even imposed from above by Koreans themselves. As dissidents in search of a position from which to assail the ruling ideology and by which to formulate the means of national reunification, some have nevertheless turned to "scientific" approaches to social analysis which did not grow up on Korean soil. This attempt to combine structural analysis with a virtual cultural idealism regarding the sources of nationhood seems to be responsible for confusion and disagreement among minjung historians about the nature of the minjung. In some ways, the apparently successful June 1987 movement has brought issues to a head.

The June 1987 movement, in which a large, concerted uprising of Koreans representing diverse social groups forced the government of Chŏn Tuhwan to accede to demands for democratic reforms and elections, was initially hailed as a triumph of a minjung coalition of students, activists, and laborers, and a vindication of minjung theory. But subsequent developments have been ambiguous enough to raise serious doubts over whether this victory marked a turn toward or away from minjung direction of Korean history. Reunification seems no closer under the present regime, Kim Yŏng-sam's merger with the ruling party does not reflect minjung aspirations (although in 1993, Han Wansang, author in 1981 of *Minjung Sociology*,[45] was appointed Deputy Prime Minister for Reunification Affairs, he had to resign due to conservative pressures), and the rudder of Korean society appears to be in the hands of the economic middle class. The 1987 experience can be viewed as a large question mark over the accuracy of minjung history: does it in fact falsify the whole hypothesis?

It is difficult to grasp the seriousness of the question without appreciating the fact that the desire to predict the course of minjung history is spurred by a more deep-seated desire for the reunification of the implacably divided nation. The possibility that events following the June 1987 uprising expose a serious misreading of Korean society before 1987 has thrown the minjung movement into a state of crisis.[46] Recent debate rages over the import and validity of "internationalization"—not only of the economy but of Koreans' conceptions of their own culture and their chosen path to reunification.[47] Is this new "middle class" which is not altogether heedful of "minjung" values and directives an unwelcome feature of global capitalism triumphing in socialism's dark hour?—or is it perhaps a development that is integral to Koreans' own identity and desiderata concerning the peninsula and its place in the world?

For anyone wrestling with the nature of minjung historiography, this conundrum raises anew an old difficulty: how far can one cast the "people" in the image of our mental frameworks and our desires for the future without doing violence to their historicity? What happens to the study of the past when it is decided in advance what the end of all the past is to be?

But it would also be historically misleading to conclude that the usage of the term "minjung" and the way in which it is applied to Korea's past, present, and future is simply an idealistic manipulation on behalf of its users' ideologies. For the whole phenomenon, including minjung historiography itself, is a stage in a palpable, sustained conflict that has been taking place in Korea since the demise of the "old order" over the proper source and form of social and political organization for the peninsula. It may have been a crucial mistake to try to identify the minjung with a class or any other grouping based on social origin, but the idea of the minjung has had concrete effects on recent Korean history, has galvanized large numbers of Koreans into consequential action, and deeply affected intellectual, literary, and political culture. To conclude in the spirit of Korean historiographical tradition, the lesson of June 1987 is a renewed appreciation of the powerful agency of cultural notions in history. But there is also a warning: the more the term "minjung" comes to refer simply to itself, the more one may have to conclude that, on account of the minjung, the people do not exist.

2

Contemporary Nationalist Movements and the Minjung

Kang Man'gil

Translated by Roger Duncan

As one who has been intimately involved in the evolution of a minjung view of Korean history and deeply concerned with finding an approach to the imperative of national reunification that is both faithful to positive indigenous traditions and workable in the contemporary world, my aim in this chapter is to present a *practitioner's* perspective on the identity of the minjung. In our historical research we have naturally sought to link the term to those who comprise the leading force of the national movement throughout modern Korean history. To many Western scholars, however, the minjung that emerges from this linkage appears to be a rather vague entity: an oppressed social stratum which transcends historical periods. Although I do offer a sharper definition, my principal objective here is accordingly to determine whether the minjung can be usefully understood in terms of a European-style social class.

The contemporary history of Korea can be divided roughly into three periods: capitalistic aggression at the close of the nineteenth century; colonial rule in the first half of the twentieth century; and national division in the latter half of the twentieth century. The national movement has struggled throughout each of these periods: first to maintain sovereignty in the face of the aggression of capitalistic powers, then to gain liberation from colonial rule, and finally to overcome division and reunify the nation. Korean historians have, since liberation in 1945, actively pursued an investigation of the developmental process of the national movement and have now achieved a somewhat systematic understanding of at least the modern national movement. Nonetheless, we have still not gained a clear answer about which social class has been the leading group of the national movement throughout these three periods.

The national struggle against the predations of foreign capitalism in the

31

latter half of the nineteenth century is often defined as a movement of the bourgeoisie (following the European model), but we do not yet have sufficient empirical studies to demonstrate that the Korean bourgeoisie was mature enough at that time to lead a national movement. It is now sometimes argued that it was the largely peasant minjung, rather than the bourgeoisie, who led the national resistance of the late nineteenth century. The argument that the bourgeoisie formed the leading social class of the national mobilization for liberation from the colonial rule of Japan in the first half of the twentieth century is rarely heard now. That does not, however, mean that scholars agree that a European-style proletariat played the leading role in the national movement as a whole during that period. Some scholars argue that the bourgeoisie led the struggle for national liberation up until the March First uprising, after which the proletariat took charge, but increasing numbers of scholars are now arguing that the group which steered the struggle throughout the entire colonial period is something we call the minjung. Virtually nobody argues that a European-style bourgeoisie or proletariat is leading the national movement of the second half of the twentieth century. Most scholars consider the minjung to be the leading force of the post-1945 national project of overcoming national division and achieving reunification by peaceful means rather than by war or revolution.

Despite the importance assigned to the minjung as the leading force of the modern and contemporary national movements, very little historical research has been done regarding what political forces and social strata comprise the minjung. Only recently have some studies begun to examine what historians have meant by the term "minjung."[1] Looking at the way in which historians' perceptions of the minjung have evolved may be one way to clarify its nature, but it seems to me that we must first deal with the concrete issue of which social strata have constituted the minjung during the modern periods of Korean history.

The Colonial Period Minjung

We can find use of the term "minjung" in magazines and newspapers, such as the *Tongnip Sinmun* (Independence News), in the latter half of the nineteenth century. But it was used at that time, along with such other terms as *paeksŏng, sŏmin,* and *inmin,* simply to indicate the general populace and not to designate an entity responsible for a historical task like the national movement.

It seems likely that the first treatise to employ the term "minjung" to designate the leading group of the national movement was "The Declaration of the Korean Revolution" (Chosŏn hyŏngmyŏng sŏnŏn sŏ) written by Shin Ch'aeho in 1923. Prior to writing this declaration, Shin had used the term to refer to the people in general or to masses lacking any historical consciousness rather than to the group responsible for the development of history, as when he lamented, "How can we preserve the nation with the minjung great only in number?"[2] At one time, he thought that historical progress came about only through the efforts of a few heroes, and somewhat later he began to think that modern-style citizens (kungmin) played the main role in creating history.[3] But from around 1920, he began to consider the minjung to be the leading group of the national liberation movement.

At the time of writing the declaration as the manifesto of the Righteous Brotherhood (ŭiryŏldan), a violent revolutionary independence movement organized in China after the March First movement of 1919, Shin considered the independence movement to be revolutionary, declaring, "To preserve the existence of the Korean people, the Japanese robbers must be expelled; the only way to expel the Japanese is through revolution."[4] Regarding the stratum to carry out the revolution, he said, "Because the revolution of today is a revolution by the minjung and for the minjung, it is called the 'Minjung Revolution' and the 'Direct Revolution.'"

It is necessary to consider why Shin Ch'aeho, who in the precolonial years of the Taehan Empire (1897–1910) had regarded heroes and citizens as the entities responsible for the development of history, came in the 1920s to look upon the minjung as the leading force of the national liberation movement and of historical development. It is, of course, possible that once the Korean peninsula became a Japanese colony he was no longer able to consider the citizens as fulfilling this role because the Korean people no longer had a state of their own. Shin himself tells us, however, that it was the March First movement that led him to discover the minjung:

> The 1884 coup d'état was nothing more than a dramatic struggle between special forces in the palace, and the Righteous Armies that were inspired to action through the ideas of scholars who were fulfilling the traditional duties of loyalty to king and love of country before and after the colonization of 1910 occurred. Such patriots as An Chunggŭn [assassin of Prince Itō Hirobumi in 1909] and Yi Chaemyŏng, who attempted to assassinate Yi Wanyong, the pro-Japanese minister of the Taehan Empire, displayed zeal in their violent acts, but they were not backed up by any fundamental minjung capacity. The hurrahs of the March First Movement showed a consensus of the minjung spirit but lacked any violent nucleus.[5]

This shows that, to Shin, the modern Korean national movement was first infused with a minjung spirit during the March First movement. Needless to say, here Shin uses the term "minjung" to refer neither to individuals, such as An Chunggŭn or Yi Chaemyŏng, nor to the scholars who were the commanders of the Righteous Armies. Unfortunately, he never clearly or directly explains in "The Declaration of Korean Revolution" to which social class the minjung belonged as the leading group of the revolution. He does, however, make some statements that explain the minjung indirectly, which we can use to draw the following inferences.

The minjung are those who suffered directly from Japan's colonial rule.

In Shin's words, the "minjung are those who can neither live nor die according to their own will, since they are poverty-stricken under heavy taxation,
harassed with debts, and restricted in their liberty of action."[6] Similarly, the
minjung are those who are opposed to Japanese rule and struggle for the
nation's liberation. Shin says that the minjung are those "who continuously
progress in order to fulfill their goal with the intention of not living if they
cannot achieve independence and of not yielding if they cannot expel the
Japanese from Korea."[7]

Shin's minjung are not collaborationists like those who sought to obtain
limited autonomy while accepting Japanese rule, not culturalists like the
advocates for the so-called cultural movement that aimed to preserve
Korea's culture under Japanese rule, nor gradualists who asserted that Korea
was not yet ready and needed to prepare for future independence.[8] It seems
that Shin's definition of minjung may particularly indicate the proletariat of
the oppressed colonial nations in Asia. "The beastly people of the capitalist,
imperialist countries are full to bursting with the blood, flesh, and bones of
the proletarian minjung of all the colonies in the Orient," he observed.
"They torment the proletarian minjung, especially those of all the colonies
in Asia where our minjung live under circumstances more miserable than
death."[9]

To summarize, Shin Ch'aeho considered the minjung to be the general
public of the oppressed nations, especially colonies in Asia, who not only
suffered under colonial rule but actively struggled against it and aspired to
national independence. As for the societies of the oppressed colonial nations
of Asia, and especially Korean society, a European-style bourgeoisie had not
emerged before colonization. Consequently the bourgeoisie neither seized
power by revolution nor became the leading group in resistance to imperialist aggression. Even after their country was reduced to a colony, they were
unable to take the lead in the national liberation movement on their own.

A European-style proletariat did begin to grow in those colonial societies
where the bourgeoisie was unable to develop as the leading historical force
and the leading force for national liberation; in Korea, the colonizing power,
Japan, structured active industrial investment in such a way that indigenous
industrial capitalism was not able to develop. Thus the most important
matrix of the proletarian classes, industrial labor, was not a major component of Korean colonial society. In 1930, twenty years after colonization,
the total number of factory workers in Korea, male and female, was only
83,900.[10] That represented only 0.4 percent of the 1930 total (Korean and
foreign) population in the peninsula of 20,256,563. Nearly 80 percent of the
population were peasants, and although there were some laborers who were
not factory workers, they were for the most part day laborers on civil engineering projects, who were difficult to organize and train.

After the 1930s, as Japanese imperialism launched full-scale aggression
against China, Korea became a supply base and was penetrated by Japan's

monopolistic capital, so that industrial capitalism based on war industries developed to some degree, leading to an increase in the number of factory workers. Nevertheless, the potential of the proletariat as the leading force of history was so weak that the Korean Communist Party declared, upon liberation on 15 August 1945, that Korea had not reached the level of a socialist revolution but rather stood at the level of a bourgeois democratic revolution (although the party did say that the proletariat should exercise hegemony).

Because of the conditions of colonialism in Korea in the first half of the twentieth century, a European-style bourgeois class was not able to lead the national liberation movement on its own, nor was a European-style proletariat able to develop enough to take the bourgeoisie's place; thus the minjung were perceived as the leading force of the national movement.

The minjung that arose under these conditions to take charge as the dynamic force of history did not comprise a single class comparable to the European-style bourgeoisie or proletariat, but rather constituted a class confederation that arose in Korea and the other colonial societies of Asia. It is therefore difficult to render the term "minjung" into English. The minjung of the first half of the twentieth century were, as Shin Ch'aeho explained in part, a confederation of classes that included intellectuals, peasants, workers, and even petite bourgeoisie who suffered from and struggled actively against colonial rule. Thus the minjung movement was oriented toward a national front rather than a single-class front.

During the colonial period, the minjung as a class confederation was considered the leading group of the national liberation struggle, as neither the bourgeoisie nor the proletariat could lead the movement single-handedly. As a consequence, within the movement there was a split between rightists (nationalists) and leftists (communists and socialists); we can also confirm, however, that incessant efforts were made to bring the two forces together in a united front in order to strengthen the power of resistance. In this case, the leading force of the national liberation movement was described as the nation as a whole, minus the pro-Japanese elements. This is how most Koreans conceive of the minjung today.

For instance, "The National Revolution," the organ of the Korean National Revolutionary Party, an entity which favored violence and was organized in 1935 in China as a joint front of left- and right-wing national forces, set forth the following political program that argued for the arming of the masses for the purpose of armed resistance:

> The national unification front cannot be controlled by the "isms" or political program of any particular class. If, under circumstances such as the present when the "isms" and political programs are opposing each other, we try to control everyone with the "ism" or political program of a particular class, we shall end up with one particular class exercising dictatorship over the nation or with all the members of the nation except for that particular class excluded from the united front of the national movement.[11]

The minjung, as a confederation of all the militant anti-Japanese classes who led the way in the movement for national liberation, endeavored to become the matrix for a united front that brought together the independence movement forces of both Left and Right. This is the historical significance of the minjung in the first half of the twentieth century.

The Minjung in the Period of National Division

In spite of these efforts to create a united front of Left and Right during the colonial period, the Korean peninsula was divided into South and North upon the liberation of 15 August 1945, and the Left–Right ideological confrontation intensified. The two states established in the north and south referred to the people they governed as the *inmin* (people) and the *kungmin* (citizens), respectively. Consequently, the minjung referred to here—the minjung that was already the leading force of the national liberation movement during the colonial period and that formed the united front of leftist and rightist forces—was broken down into inmin and kungmin, so that the term "minjung" was for some time rarely used.

Throughout the 1950s, the two Korean states each clung to their respective methods of forced reunification, either by revolution (North Korea) or by advancing north (South Korea). The outbreak of the 19 April 1960 revolution, however, led to the renewal in South Korea of the minjung as the leading force in historical progress. Scholars then actively tried to define the concept of minjung academically and theoretically. Despite differences in time and circumstances, scholars in the 1960s and Shin Ch'aeho in the colonial period alike viewed the minjung as a class confederation rather than a single class. In forwarding this view, they espouse several common notions. The minjung came into being through class contradictions and, more importantly, national contradictions. The minjung is centered around workers and farmers but includes minor landowners, national capitalists, and the urban middle class.[12] Changes must be made in the national view of history so that the minjung can become the standard by which to see history, and furthermore there must be established a broad historical value system which embraces all classes of the nation.[13] The minjung is transcendent, encompassing categories like class, nation, and citizen *(simin)*;[14] in fact, it is only by class confederation that the minjung can be objectively categorized.[15]

What is the most important task the class-confederation minjung must confront in the second half of the twentieth century as they create Korean history? National reunification is quite naturally perceived as the primary task, and the minjung seen as the leading force in the movement for peaceful national reunification that has emerged since the 19 April 1960 revolution.

The minjung of the colonial period was a class confederation composed of intellectuals, workers, peasants, and petite bourgeoisie opposed to and resisting colonial rule, and the minjung of the period of national division is, as far as the south is concerned, composed of the same groups opposed to and resisting the national division system. But whereas the minjung of the colonial period consisted mostly of peasants in combination with a small number of workers and a very small number of petite bourgeoisie and intellectuals, the composition of the minjung of the post-1945 period has changed greatly, with a radical increase in the proportion of workers and petite bourgeoisie, a small increase in the proportion of intellectuals, and a decrease in the proportion of peasants.

The present-day minjung differs from the colonial minjung not only quantitatively, in the increased proportion of workers, particularly factory workers, but also qualitatively, in the greater degree of organization and training. At the same time, there is also an important difference between the intellectuals who played an important role in developing the national liberation movement and the intellectuals who have fulfilled a similar role for the national reunification movement. The anticolonial intellectuals who may be numbered among the minjung were extremely limited in number, and most of them went into exile and devoted themselves to the cause of national liberation while living in foreign countries, such as China. This made it difficult for them to link their movement directly with the constituent elements of the minjung, the workers and peasants who remained inside the country. By contrast, the antidivisionist intellectuals of the post-1945 period have been able to connect directly with the main elements of the minjung to lead the national reunification movement—the minjung movement of this period. During the period of national division, and especially during the 1970s and 1980s, antidivisionist intellectuals, comprised mostly of students, have gone directly to the villages and factories—at times becoming peasants and workers themselves—to organize and lead the peasants' and workers' movements.[16]

Conclusion

Although I have examined in some detail various aspects of the question of the identity of the minjung, my investigation has, as mentioned at the beginning, focused on identity in relation to the question of whether or not the minjung bears similarities to a European-style social class. By way of conclusion, I would like to reiterate briefly the kind of definition of the nature of the minjung that arises when we base our approach to the problem on the results of current research in Korea.

The minjung is not a single class like the bourgeoisie or proletariat of Europe, but rather a class confederation composed of anti-Japanese and anticolonialist intellectuals, peasants, factory workers, and petite bourgeoisie and was the leading force of the national liberation movements of oppressed colonial societies, particularly in Asia. Although the minjung, as the leading group of both the national liberation and national unification struggles, has been composed of the various classes mentioned above, its class composition has shifted decidedly toward a worker-centered constituency during the period of national division.

We can confirm that, among the constituent elements of the minjung in the period of national division, workers have not only increased in quantity, but are also much more organized and better trained, whereas intellectuals have greatly reduced the gap in historical understanding, worldview, and actual livelihood existing between themselves and workers and peasants. The national reunification movement, led by a minjung that has advanced in many aspects beyond the colonial minjung, has developed in tandem with these changes in the class makeup of the minjung: it is expected to rise to the multilayered task of class, national, and human liberation.

Although we have looked only at the Korean case here, neither Right nor Left was capable of leading the national liberation movement on its own; and when the formation of a joint front of Left and Right was aspired to or actually achieved for a time, the minjung—neither bourgeoisie nor proletariat—was seen as the leading force of the national liberation movement. This fact stands in contrast to the conventional view that, in the colonial period, the leading force of the right-wing national liberation movement was a European-style bourgeoisie and that of the left-wing national liberation movement was a European-style proletariat.

In Korean history, during the period of national division after 1945, when the national reunification movement focused on such forceful and violent means as advancing northward or armed uprising, emphasis was placed on the kungmin (bourgeoisie) and the inmin (proletariat) as the leading forces; however, once the argument for reunification by peaceful means gained broad support, the minjung began to lead.

Thus, just as the purpose of the colonial national liberation movement was not simply to liberate the nation from its colonial bonds but also to raise Korea's historical development to a higher stage, so must the goal of the national reunification movement of today be, not simply national reunification, but the enhancement of the historical development of the Korean nation. It is here that the historical significance of the minjung as the leading force of the Korean national movement lies.

3

Minjung Socioeconomic Responses to State-led Industrialization

Kim Hyung-A

ONE OF THE MOST controversial and yet influential issues for the minjung movement during the 1980s was that of self-identification: providing a definition of the key concepts of minjung. Who are the minjung and under what conditions (social, political, economic, religious, and cultural) is an individual person or group categorized as minjung? Generally, the notion of minjung was premised on a putative historical unity of the suffering people of Korea. In this ongoing debate, two prominent academics, Pak Hyŏnch'ae and Han Wansang, have been regarded as the most eminent expositors of the "two types of concepts in regard to the minjung."[1] The former regards the minjung as the social classes of laborers, farmers, and urban poor who are the end products of the capitalist system (though in his initial proposal, Pak also includes certain progressive intellectuals as a minjung component); and the latter regards the minjung as the various social groups who are largely excluded from the political, economic, and cultural means of power in society.

Irrespective of their current relevance or coherence in rationale, the two theories examined here both had a significant impact on conceptualizing minjung thinking, particularly in regard to defining the constituency of the minjung, their status, and their role. Although in my view neither theory satisfactorily characterizes the minjung or explains their specific motivation and their background, both have been prevalent in shaping general perceptions of the minjung in ideal terms. They have therefore had both an academic and a practical political impact. This chapter will examine each of these approaches in more detail and, in particular, will consider how they relate to minjung ideals as a whole and their applicability to the minjung movement in practice.

Korean Minjung Theory: A Social-Class Approach

In his essay "Examination of the Characteristics of Minjung in Terms of Social Class" (Minjunguĭ kyegupchŏk sŏnggyŏk kyumyŏng), Pak Hyŏn-ch'ae, economic analyst, generally defines the components of minjung in terms of four classes: laborers (as the basic component); farmers (as small-scale producers); small-scale commercial operators and the urban poor; and certain progressive intellectuals.[2] Of these, Pak identifies three groups—namely laborers, farmers, and urban poor, who make up the largest proportion of the minjung—as the end product of the production process in the capitalist economic system. Pak argues that "the minjung are composed as a single entity within which each component group transmutes into the various categories which correlate to one another in a circulatory system."[3]

He refers to this process as involving the disintegration and specialization of farmers (which occurred with the rise of capitalism); their alienation from their subsistence life-style as a result of new production and distribution mechanisms; and their subsequent transformation from owners of capital (albeit poor) into either urban poor or laborers for wages. Through this circulatory process, farmers, laborers, and the urban poor emerge together as the victims of capitalism. According to Pak, therefore, the notion of minjung is essentially dependent on economic variables, and the analysis of this notion in terms of its reality requires an examination of that social class which, in the process of the development of capitalism, is the poorest. Upon the basis of this premise, Pak not only restricts his concept of minjung to three groups, namely the laboring farmers, laborers, and the urban poor, but also limits his theoretical explanation to these three groups.

Pak first defines farmers as a "general farming stratum" (*nongmin-ch'ŭng*) who have historically been slaves, known as the "agricultural producers" (*nongŏp saengsanja*) in both Ancient and Middle Age societies. In contemporary capitalist society, Pak argues, farmers became an "entity in a transitional stage" (*kwadogijŏk chonjae*) because of the nature of their production. In other words, they must either specialize or disintegrate as farmers if they are to survive in a capitalist society. Pak differentiates farmers into two types within the farming stratum. One type can be identified in a capitalist environment in which farming is connected to economic progress, and comprises six categories: (1) agricultural proletariat and wage-laborers; (2) semiproletariat or petty farmers; (3) tenant farmers; (4) medium-scale farmers; (5) large-scale farmers; (6) large-scale landowners. The other type can be identified in a noncapitalist system in which farming may be said to comprise four categories: (1) poor farmers; (2) medium-scale farmers; (3) wealthy farmers; and (4) landowners.

Of these components of the farming stratum, Pak stresses that only the poorest categories of laboring farmer (*kŭllo nongminjŏk pŏmju*) represent a component of the minjung. In the capitalist system these exclude large-scale farmers and large-scale landowners. In a noncapitalist system they exclude wealthy farmers and landowners. The theoretical basis for Pak's concept relies on two factors: first, farmers who manage their own means of production are initially encouraged and inspired by capitalist principles; and second, as small producers whose means of production depends entirely on the strength of their capital, they are bound to react and respond to the demands of market conditions. Hence, farmers are forced either to specialize (and become petty capitalists) or to disintegrate into wage-laborers. Pak's theory is clearly identical with the Marxian notion of the position of peasants and handicraftsmen in capitalist society. Karl Marx stated:

> For it is also a law that economic development distributes functions among different persons; and the handicraftsman or peasant who produces with his own means of production will either gradually be transformed into a small capitalist who also exploits the labor of others, or he will suffer the loss of his means of production . . . and be transformed into a wage-laborer. This is the tendency in the form of society in which the capitalist mode of production predominates. . . .[4]

Pak argues that market conditions and the strength of capital affect not only the basic production mode but also the scale of production and the nature of products. These changes, resulting from the capitalist transformation of agriculture and the restructuring of productivity, however, gradually transform farmers into a different stratum or social class. Such a transformation is inevitable because farmers are forced either to abandon their calling or to specialize due to the comprehensive penetration of commercial agricultural development, mechanized farming, and the monetary economy. This emerging production process is significant to the composition of minjung because, through this process, farmers, who suffer the loss of their means of production and thus abandon their livelihood, will be transformed either into the class of urban poor or into laborers.

In brief, Pak's attempts to illustrate the conditions of petty farmers and their gradual disintegration in the process of capitalism also clearly reflects the Marxist view that states:

> The lower strata of the middle class—the small trades people, shop-keepers, and retired tradesmen generally, the handicraftsmen and peasants—all these sink gradually into the proletariat, partly because their diminutive capital does not suffice for the scale on which Modern Industry is carried on, and is swamped in competition with the large capitalists, partly because their specialized skill is rendered worthless by new methods of production. Thus the proletariat is recruited from all classes of the population.[5]

Second, Pak defines the "laborer" class as the "basic component of minjung" *(kibonjŏgin minjung kusŏng)*. He also sees it as the basic class of capitalist society, which possesses the capacity of self-reproduction, for it provides the key to the relationship between capital and wage labor. Pak argues that "laborers are the propertyless [thus the proletariat] because . . . they don't own the means of income unless they sell their labor as a commodity."[6] He sees laborers as an oppressed and exploited group, noting that laborers are mostly the ruined craftsmen and farmers who, in the relationship between wages and capital, are reduced to the class of wage-laborers either in capitalist farming or manufacturing industries.

Furthermore, wage-laborers will gradually fall into the class of urban poor as they lose their labor power because of ill health or old age. This gradual degradation, however, does not merely depend on ill health and old age, but rather on the structural contradictions of modern capitalist society. In regard to these structural contradictions, Pak points to two dominating social factors: (1) that modern capitalist society circulates around the production of commodities, and the relationship between capital and wage labor in this context is entirely aimed at profit making based on free labor; and (2) that the control of reproduction (of labor power) in capitalist society is determined by the changing phases of the industrial cycle. It will therefore not only sustain the industrial "reserve army" during periods of average prosperity but will also result in masses of unemployment during periods of stagnation.[7]

Under this social structure, laborers become exploited and victimized both physically and psychologically: they are obliged to compromise their working hours or conditions, which inevitably leads to various barriers to employment (consequent upon accidents, illness, early retirement, and so on); and they live in permanent uncertainty because of the precarious nature of their means of subsistence. Furthermore, "their wage is valorized politically so that it does not exceed that of the reproduction cost of social labor power. Furthermore, this wage is determined extremely flexibly in order to satisfy the demand which arises from the circulatory process of capitalist reproduction. Laborers are, overall, left in the condition of a casual work force or in a state of unemployment rather than in a usual state of employment."[8] Nevertheless, laborers constitute the basis of capitalism and of the minjung as the "alienated class" (*sowedoen kŭrŭp*) in capitalist society, comprising the majority of its population. Moreover, in Pak's view, laborers are the most progressive social stratum of today's society, because they are the propertyless class that leads the struggle against the fundamental contradiction of modern capitalism.[9]

Third, Pak defines the urban poor as the lowest stratum (*ch'imjonch'ŭng*) in capitalist society, comprising a variety of classes under three categories: (1) urban handicraftsmen (independent petty producers) and petty tradesmen; (2) industrial wage-workers (laborers) and temporary casual workers with low wages and precarious positions in small and medium businesses; and (3) the unemployed. Of the three categories, the unemployed make up the main component of the urban class and comprise two groups, one able and willing to work and the other neither able nor willing to work. The oppressed conditions of the urban poor, therefore, are destined to continue and recur unjustly; a relative surplus population of unemployed, an army of "informal" labor, is an inevitable outcome. In relating the capitalist production mode to the economic degradation of the components of the minjung, especially laborers, Pak writes:

> In a capitalist society, where the motive of production does not depend on the satisfaction of demand as determined by the requirements of society but on profit, capitalism of its very nature . . . seeks unpaid labor without any justification. Laborers are, therefore, expected to be paid a low wage, to endure hard labor and to work extended hours; farmers are forced to apply low labor costs and to charge low prices for agricultural products so as to satisfy the requirement of cheap raw materials for industry; and the urban poor face the imposition of a huge burden, especially when the demand for (virtually) unpaid labor becomes excessive, even though their situation may be cyclical. This major separate antagonistic relationship between each minjung component and capitalism is the principal foundation which leads the minjung components to have uniformity of economic interest. And this common basis for economic interest also supports the historical fact that minjung components have represented different elements of the social system of circulation, which correlate to each other in the process of existence.[10]

Of course, Pak's socioeconomic perspective is heavily affected by Korean-style industrialization led entirely by a bureaucratic authoritarian state, which in part accounts for his rather rough-and-ready form of Marxism.

Relevance of the Class Approach

Much of Pak's thought is based on his analysis of proletarianization defined as an increase in the number of people who lack control over the means of production and survive by selling their labor power.[11] Although much sociological understanding of industrialization is based on the European experience, in recent times this has been countered by dependency, world-systems, and bureaucratic authoritarianism theories. Pak's analysis attempts to focus on the causes and effects of proletarianization expressed in industrialization theory in the Korean context.[12]

While proletarianization is regarded as "the single most far-reaching social change that has occurred in the Western world over the past few hundred years,"[13] possibly nowhere has this occurred more dramatically than in Korea, where comprehensive proletarianization commenced only in the early 1960s and changed the country from a predominantly peasant agricultural society into a dynamic industrial nation in less than thirty years.[14] The rapid economic pace in Korea has, in fact, not only brought the "curtailment of history" in terms of national productivity and industrialization, but also the reshuffling of social structures regarding social stratification and the dynamics of the ruling elite.

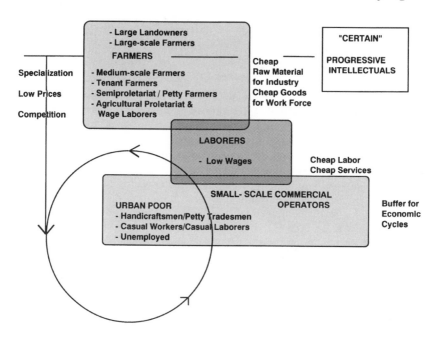

Proletarianization — The Circulatory System

In Europe there had been a strong, articulate artisan culture, and through industrialization which, according to Tilly and others,[15] had taken over five centuries to develop in a slow and continuous process, artisans and their culture had fallen victim to capitalists, creating major resentment. The main cause of resentment in workers in newly industrialized countries, however, has been the inability of the economy to absorb the rapidly growing labor force into full-time employment at adequate wage levels over much shorter time frames, leaving many workers in casual employment without contracts or government labor protection. In world-systems theory, it is argued that this informal sector of the economy subsidizes formal capitalist enterprises by generating low-cost materials and services for their workers to enable them to subsist on low wages. Pak and others refer to "semiproletarianization," which posits that the expansion of world capitalism was essentially a search for a low-cost labor force, and that, therefore, a capitalist would "prefer to have his wage-workers located in semi-proletarian rather than proletarian households."[16] The Korean experience, however, contradicts the semiproletarianization thesis put forward by world-system theorists and is also very different from the European experience of proletarianization, in terms of its rapid development, its politico-economic form, and its sociocultural dynamics.

Although Korea experienced quite significant proletarianization during Japanese colonization, the end of World War II abruptly ended that process, with South Korean industry virtually coming to a complete halt from 1945 to 1953. Import-substitution policies, reliant on U.S. aid, achieved little in the way of industrialization during the next eight or nine years (until 1961). Park Chung Hee's decision to pursue export-oriented industrialization after 1962, and especially through his Yusin program of heavy industrialization after 1972, however, led to a phenomenal increase in production for both domestic and overseas markets. Production that initially focused on light-manufacturing goods shifted gradually to higher value-added items, and the labor force changed its structure accordingly. By the late 1980s the majority of industrial workers were employed in heavy and chemical industries such as automobile, steel, shipbuilding, machinery, and petrochemicals.[17] In one generation a sophisticated, dynamic industrial society was created; but, ironically, that society also fell into a "crisis of unbalanced development,"[18] which forced alterations not only in the scale of Korean proletarianization but also in the characteristics of social conditions.

Korean proletarianization, for example, generated massive migration from the rural sector and, despite the largely unsophisticated background of these immigrants, rapidly created a workforce of manual production workers and white-collar salaried workers, with a substantial increase in female participation, especially in clerical fields. "Because of this compressed industrial transformation," observes Hagan Koo, "the Korean population has greater heterogeneity and internal status differentiation than its European counterparts—a numerically significant white-collar stratum exists alongside a large industrial proletariat."[19] As elsewhere, Korean capitalists have pursued a strategy for ensuring a cheap and flexible work force, but due to the absence of protective labor laws and government support for the maintenance of both low wages and cheap raw materials have not had any disincentive to operate within a formal wage system. In this environment labor unions have not been able (at least until 1987) to exert any real influence on wage fixing. Wages in Korea are thus largely a product of supply and demand in a labor market where the repression of labor action has not only given the capitalist the upper hand but "has facilitated the uninhibited absorption of labor into formal, capitalist enterprises."[20]

It should be noted that Pak's comments on the circulatory nature of the economic role of the three key components of the proletariat—laborers, small-scale producers (including farmers), and the urban poor—incorporate the capitalists' need for both cheap raw material and cheap labor. Government pricing policies, to illustrate this point, have not only forced millions of Koreans to migrate to urban centers in search of more secure incomes, but have also stabilized urban consumer prices, allowing urban workers to survive on low wages and thus reducing the pressure on capitalists for wage increases. The low economic capacity of the rural sector and the full (not casual) commitment to urban industrial work greatly facilitated the massive proletarianization that is evident. This phenomenon has been further reinforced by the establishment of industrial towns such Ulsan, Ch'angwŏn, Okpo, Kuro, and Kumi, which now have sophisticated working-class communities and minjung solidarity.

How is it that Korean workers have so readily adapted to industrialization? Hagan Koo (Ku Haegŭn) identifies a number of key factors: a high level of urbanization and formal education; a large volume of geographic and social mobility since the colonial period; and compulsory military service for men, which taught them time orientation and subjugation to formal authority.[21] Perhaps an even greater factor was the absence of any cultural inhibitions to proletarianization. The absence of any significant artisan culture and the ready acceptance of the low ranking afforded by the Korean Confucian system to artisans and merchants, meant that workers experienced proletarianization "without any proud working-class cultural heritage."[22]

Historically, the position of the labor movement had been weakened by the fact that, after liberation from Japan, it had been embroiled in extreme political conflict between the Left and the Right, and that subsequently the mobilization of labor had been equated with communism.[23] This factor was all too easily exploited by both the government and capitalist enterprises. Workers, therefore, responded and adapted to their new role on an individual basis, putting up with long hours, hazardous conditions, low wages, and authoritarian management. The extreme interventionist authoritarianism of Korean governments suppressed the formation of any effective labor movement, kept labor unorganized, and prevented it from linking up with other sectors from the time of the Syngman Rhee government (except for the brief interregnum of the Chang Myŏn administration of 1960–1961). During the 1980s, however, Korean workers attracted substantial support from religious and intellectual communities, which struggled for human rights and democratization.

In summary, industrialization in Korea is characterized by proletarianization, not semiproletarianization, and has placed the prototypical industrial proletariat and modern white-collar workers side by side. The government's role has probably been the single most important determinant in this process, and its agricultural pricing policies have ensured that it developed as an urban phenomenon which, by drawing on rural workers of the lowest class, facilitated a smooth adaptation to the industrial work pattern and authority structure. The lack of an effective counterideology in the early phases of proletarianization led to extremely low levels of industrial conflict; but during the 1980s, along with a reduced capacity to supply additional labor commensurate with continued industrial growth, a strong union movement developed. This development reflects in part "the density of proletarian experiences among Korean workers,"[24] which in the late 1980s combined with other minjung elements to force democratic reforms and has progressively obtained improved salaries and conditions for workers.

Korean Minjung Theory: An Alienation Approach

Han Wansang, former professor of sociology at Seoul National University, conceived the notion of minjung in terms of the relationship between "rulers" and "subordinates," or the "ruling" and the "ruled," in modern Korean society.[25] His analysis reiterates an argument from "The Politics of Mass Society" by William Kornhauser suggesting that Korea is a "naked society" where two social groups, the "ruling elite" and the masses, stand against one another. This is so because "there isn't any particular [intermediate] pressure group which struggles for the development of democratic institutions while at the same time representing the masses [minjung] who are subject to the ruling elite."[26] The existence of the minjung, in Han's view, is based on the premise that possession of power which determines social stratification or groupings not only characterizes social order but also creates inequality in that order. Furthermore, the people with no power within this order become excluded from the three essential means of power—namely, political, economic, and social.

On this basis, Han defines the notion of minjung as "the people who are in the 'ruled' position even though they make up the majority. They co-exist as a united group who are never from one single stratum, but from many groups and strata. Minjung are the resistance force who boldly struggle against the unjust political power."[27] Han nevertheless categorizes minjung into three types. First, he identifies the "politically ruled people" (*chŏngch'ijŏk minjung*), who are excluded from the means of rule consisting of the power to command, mobilize, and also to suppress. Hence, those who possess that power are designated as the "political ruling group" in contrast to those without power, who are identified either as the "politically ruled group" or the "political minjung." Han regards the "political minjung" as the central dynamic of the minjung component of modern society. His view is very similar to the Weberian notion that, "bureaucratic organization is technically the most highly developed means of power in the hands of the man who controls it."[28] He argues that this has been particularly so under the authoritarian ruling structure of Korea.

Second, Han refers to the "economically ruled people" (*kyŏngjejŏk minjung*), who are excluded from the means of production which control the entire array of activities and functions related to production, consumption, and distribution. These people become the minjung of the economic dimension and are identified as "economic minjung." They are exploited and controlled by the ruling groups (in this case, capitalists), and are by necessity taken more seriously in modern society because their proportion in the population is growing rapidly.

Third, Han identifies the "culturally ruled people" (*munhwajŏk minjung*), who are excluded from access to public recognition in the form of honor and prestige. Honor and prestige, which enable certain individual persons or groups to enjoy public recognition and the privileges of status in society while influencing social values, are monopolized by these "culturally ruling groups." In general, they are recipients of an advanced education that provides them with the necessary requirements for a privileged life-style, including opportunities to obtain knowledge, social contacts, skills, qualifications, and so on. They are also the engineers of "high culture," which reveals certain typical features of cultural sophistication. They thus become not only the trendsetters of the privileged life-style but also a separate group which, in the words of Max Weber, "rests upon distance and exclusiveness"[29] from what Han terms "popular culture" *(taejung munhwa).*[30] This perception is particularly important to understanding Han's concept of minjung, which rests basically on its antithetical relation to the "status stratum" or "status groups" defined by Weber:

> In contrast to classes, status groups are normally communities. They are, however, often of an amorphous kind. In contrast to the purely economically determined "class situation" we wish to designate as "status situation" every typical component of the life fate of men that is determined by a specific, positive or negative, social estimation of honor. This honor may be connected with any quality shared by a plurality, and, of course, it can knit to a class situation: class distinctions are linked in the most varied ways with status distinctions.[31]

In his discussion of the concept of the minjung and the classes, Han himself refers to the Weberian theory on social stratification based on the multidimensional "status situation" of society.[32] In Han's view, the cultural minjung, in contrast to the culturally ruling groups and thus the high-status groups, are the victims of lack of opportunities for honor and prestige. Conflict between ruling and ruled groups within the society is therefore particularly severe when the opportunities for a higher education are concentrated predominantly in the ruling groups (as a status stratum). What Han focuses on here is the bureaucracy as a social phenomenon which, according to Weber, created a new channel of power and rose as a social stratum based predominantly on the educational certificate:

> Differences of education, in contrast to the class-forming elements of property and economic function, are nowadays undoubtedly the most important factor in the creation of status difference. It is essentially the social prestige of education . . . that the modern official owes his position to in society. Whether one likes it or not, education is one of the strongest social barriers. . . .[33]

Access to education was not only available exclusively to the ruling class *(yangban kyegŭp)* throughout the Chosŏn dynasty, but also "the civil examination system (restricted in any case to candidates of yangban status) gave the authorities the machinery with which to control entry to the ruling class."[34] Therefore, polarization of the high-status groups and the ordinary people (minjung) based on educational qualification created a fundamental barrier in Korean society.

In examining the history of societies, argues Han, one finds that the structural inequality emerging from power structures is a universal phenomenon regardless of system, time, or place. The specific characteristics of ruled and ruling groups are therefore determined according to each social order (feudal, capitalist, or communist), or the "three means" of power (political, social, and economic) and other factors such as religion or ethnicity. The question is, which of these orders or means will dominate society as the most powerful? The nature of society thus changes automatically once the characteristics of the two juxtaposed social groups are changed. In this regard, Han emphasizes the Weberian view of the "structure of power" that consists of various strata arising from "all those having vested interests in the political structure. . . ."[35]

With reference to the consciousness of the minjung, particularly their self-awareness and acceptance of their fate in life, Han separates the minjung into two types: the sleeping minjung (chŭkchajŏk minjung) and the awakened minjung (taejajŏk minjung). Here he applies to Korean society the Marxist distinction between a class "for itself" and a class "in itself;" the latter being a social and economic unity which lacks self-consciousness and the former a unit the members of which share a common viewpoint and act together. According to this view, the sleeping minjung are a single identity in terms of their role in the economy and society, but do not recognize their unitary identity. The awakened minjung, however, understand themselves as such, and undertake political and social action to further their common interests.[36] The sleeping minjung are those who are not aware precisely of their social stratum as the excluded "ruled people," despite the fact that they are politically excluded, economically alienated, and culturally ignored by both intellectuals and ruling elite.

In general, the sleeping minjung are "not capable of observing themselves and their social conditions critically from an objective perspective."[37] They are a people with a passive character who are "uneducated" and "do not attempt to resist [the dictates of the ruling groups] but rather obey them like a herd of sheep."[38] In this way, the sleeping minjung are "most obedient and convenient servants" of the ruling groups, "helplessly manipulated" by the latter's pretensions, "just as morphine addicts are intoxicated by morphine."[39] The sleeping minjung tend to be "deceived by the ruling elite's false propaganda and are deceived into thinking they might accomplish something," argues Han, "because the ruling elite exercise a special leverage decorated with appealing rhetoric designed especially for their effective control."[40] Nevertheless, Han concludes that blame should not be laid on the sleeping minjung for their passivity and lack of self-awareness, because "they are not voluntarily sleeping, but are conditioned to be so indefinitely."[41]

The awakened minjung, on the other hand, understand their existence in the context of prevailing social structures, particularly power structures, as the "ruled people." They are the intelligentsia who are fully aware of the social imposition under which they suffer not only social and political injustice and economic disadvantage but also alienation from the means of political power. Nevertheless, intellectuals have the social and moral responsibility to educate the sleeping minjung to develop their self-consciousness, so that they also "can be independent variables who determine history and the structure [of society]."[42] Conscientization, says Han, is a "thought process of the minjung whereby they transform themselves from the historical object to the historical subject."[43]

In regard to these people's self-awareness of their life fate as the minjung, however, Han distinguishes three phases. In the first, the awakened minjung possess a "structural thought" *(kujojŏk sago)*, which Han refers to as the concept of "sociological political imagination," quoting A. Fasola-Bologna, who in turn refers to C. Wright Mills.[44] Han argues that this notion differentiates "personal trouble" and "public issues" and provides evidence for his theory that structural thought by the awakened minjung is possible through "sociological imagination." Furthermore, through this structural thought, the minjung in the first phase build their self-consciousness in response to social injustice. In the second phase, the awakened minjung become critical of their ruling structure: they are the "critical people" who understand fully the falsehood of the ruling groups and willingly indict them. Their criticism, however, does not seek a kind of "touch-up" of the existing system but stands for a "fundamental exposure of the ulterior motives of the ruling dynamics and ideology of the ruling groups."[45]

In the third phase, the awakened minjung transform themselves into a people of action, into (antigovernment) activists. They do not merely think structurally and expose the falsehood of the ruling groups, but take more direct action which aims to promote fundamental change of the existing social order, especially of structural inequality. Therefore, the action employed by these minjung represents a concrete development of an "antigovernment movement." The most ideal and radical type of minjung engage in this movement because they genuinely believe in their cause as a struggle for justice and humanity. Therefore, they are prepared to sacrifice themselves in a spirit of martyrdom based on religious belief and hope, and to challenge the ruling order for their cause.[46]

Relevance of the Alienation Approach

To understand Han's theory of minjung, it is important to note his views on the makeup of the ruling groups during the industrialization of the early 1960s to the mid-1980s. One should also note changes in the political, social, and cultural environment in Korean society, particularly since the promulgation of the Yusin constitution in 1972, because through this constitution the regime transformed two main structures of the ruling order: first, it consolidated the industrialization strategy from one of import substitution in the 1950s to an export-oriented one commencing in the 1960s; and second, it

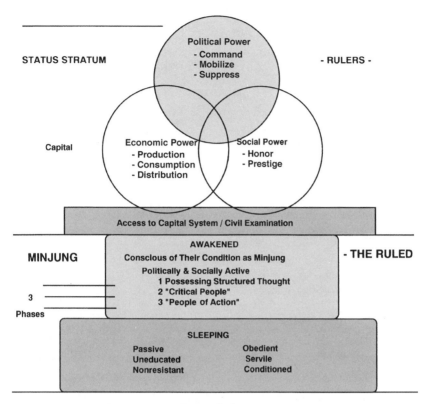

Han's Alienation Analysis of The Minjung Components

established the dictatorial bureaucratic authoritarian state. James Cotton, in his study of the state in South Korea, writes:

> Throughout this period [from the early 1960s to the mid-1980s], bureaucratic direction was one of the most significant features of state policy and capability. Though the character and membership of those who commanded the upper reaches of the state varied from a military clique to a bureaucratic–security–business coalition, the mechanisms of the state remained insulated from wider popular forces for more than two decades. Business remained subordinated, labor was corporatized, and political forms were manipulated (on occasions, forcibly) to prevent effective institutional challenges to the prevailing order."[47]

The creation of this bureaucratic authoritarian state brought about two major social changes, first in social stratification and second in social and cultural values. There arose a newly created "status stratum" known as the "newly rising ruling group" *(sinhŭng yangban)*. This consisted of three subgroups, namely, technocrats, a coalition group from the military and bureaucracy, and newly established conglomerates. In addition, the prevailing social trend in values reflected the overall beliefs and values of the *sinhŭng yangban,* which focused on educational qualifications, efficiency, and quick-thinking salesmanship.

Such a tendency, according to Han Wansang, is an outcome of the "over-heated competition"[48] experienced in everyday life, which not only drives society to seek a "short-cut method" (based on expediency and effective-ness) but also confuses society's moral standpoint. Han argues: "[The people's] sense of value, developed after the birth of the Third Republic of Korea in May 1961, mainly focussed on 'short-cut method policy' [*p'yŏn-ppŏpchuŭi*]. This method is also the system which underlies all kinds of criminal activities and thus fundamentally destroys human quality, human-ity, as well as the roots of social order."[49]

As already mentioned, Han's approach was based on the Weberian theory of social stratification, with particular focus on the social collision of the high-status stratum and the rest of the social strata. However, in the Korean context, due to the historical role of the state in a rigid Confucianist culture (with its tradition of bureaucratic order) and the extreme authoritarianism since liberation, the political dimension has had a greater impact on one's status situation than in the European context to which Weber refers. Han is eager to point this out, for otherwise the tendency might be to associate class with status without reference to the dominant influence of political power on both, when such power has traditionally been a stepping-stone to the acquisition of wealth (class) and social honor and prestige (status).

In contrast to Pak, Han does not focus on class only but broadens his analysis to "bases for communal action" (rather than to physical "communi-ties"), and is thus able to identify a broader range of factors affecting social conflict in Korea. Economic class and status stratum are separate determi-nants of the extent to which a people will seek radical ideals as a strategy to combat the ruling structure for access to power and thus to status, so long as the strategy is perceived to serve a specific purpose such as socialism, Marx-ism, or the *chuch'e* ideology of Kim Il Sung. Exponents of the minjung movement in the 1980s, in fact, made significant headway through such rad-ical ideals up to the collapse of the military dictatorship of Chŏn Tuhwan in 1987. They had proved that such an ideological strategy, applied strictly to an illegitimate and undemocratic political system, not only generated a powerful energy for mobilizing the masses (minjung), but also created an opportunity for a major shake-up of the sociopolitical perspectives of the ruling elite, whether in power or in opposition. In this regard, the theories of Han, as well as Pak, were fundamental to the formation of minjung thought in the 1980s.

Participatory Democracy: Response of the Opposition

Although making no claims to be an intellectual in his own right, Kim Taejung (Kim Dae Jung) has been preeminent among politicians prepared to use minjung rhetoric in appealing for support. It is therefore useful to consider Kim's employment of the term "minjung" as an example of attempts to link minjung theory with political practice before discussing the likely fate of the minjung political movement.

In "Kim Dae Jung: Conscience in Action," Kim's spokesman, Ch'oe Wŏn-sang, and coauthor Han Hwagap focus on the extent to which minjung energy had been generated and the national potential this power represented. They outline the basic standpoint of Kim and his party, the Democratic Party (DP), in regard to the masses as follows:

> the power of the masses (minjung) will be a great factor in Korean society as well . . . the masses will become, with their firmly established values, the engine of national progress in politics, economy, society, and culture; no national leader will be able to ignore their role and expect to preserve internal political and social stability. In the process of building up and further developing their power, it may seem that the masses have followed the existing national leadership. However, as their power consolidates, they might even brush aside the leadership that is now in place. Therefore, the present leaders must humbly accept the advice that they faithfully serve the minjung as they would serve "Heaven."[50]

Kim Taejung, who is recognized as the "leader of the democratic opposition to a whole sequence of authoritarian regimes"[51] since the early 1960s, and who narrowly avoided the death sentence during the regimes of both Park and Chŏn, writes:

> the masses have consistently been the motivating force in History. We have survived because of their vision, their yearning for what is right and just which, though flickering, is not yet extinguished. When we consider the rise and fall of the Silla, Koryŏ, and Chosŏn dynasties, no matter who played the clown, only those who had the support of the masses, who were squirming in the gutters of society and seemingly powerless and ignorant, were the ones to prosper. Those who did not have the support of the masses fell. From a long-range perspective, the mind of the masses was the mind of heaven.[52]

Therefore, it is no surprise that Kim advanced very much the same concept of minjung as the other minjung proponents. What is more notable about his political stance is that he not only criticized the conduct of the United States "in most Third World nations"[53] including Korea, but also alerted the United States to the need to improve its understanding and attitudes toward these countries' political, social, and economic conditions. In the case of Korea, Kim argued, an alternative economic program was the only way to rectify the evils of the social system and achieve an industrial democracy, the substance of which had been systematically subverted by the government in the process of industrialization. The alternative he offered was a "Mass-Participatory Economy":

The goal of my program [Mass-Participatory Economy] was, and still remains, a proper balance across three major objectives: growth (efficiency), equitable distribution of income, and price stability. These three objectives often conflict with one another. Because a unilateral imposition of one leader's preference can only result in public discontent, the three objectives must be balanced by full participation of the masses. That is the goal of my program for a Mass-Participatory Economy.[54]

The operation of pluralism in all aspects of political, social, and economic decision making is what Kim proposed to his constituents, the nation, and to neighboring countries, including the United States. He passionately sought people power through industrial democracy:

Today, in advanced countries, where there is industrial democracy, the masses have freed themselves by their own power from their traditional exploited status and have acquired a solid position of equality with capitalists in such fields as politics, the economy, and culture. A clear example of this popular phenomenon is seen in the fact that labor parties and social democratic parties in many countries are now in power.[55]

Here it is important to consider the relevance of this so-called industrial democracy, or Mass-Participatory Economy, that emphasized public consensus as the top priority in Korean democracy. Kim's visionary program, in this regard, was an overall representation of not only the Korean people's aspirations but also the voice of the Korean minjung against antidemocratic governments, particularly during the 1980s, as articulated in the theories of both Pak Hyŏnch'ae and Han Wansang.

The importance of the two theories (of Pak and Han), therefore, lies in their attempt to rationalize and articulate the essence and concept of minjung which, according to minjung exponents, were built primarily on the historical suffering, termed *han* (insoluble resentment or sorrow), of ordinary Korean workers, the "subjects of history."[56] Although each theory had its flaws in premise and logic, they nevertheless identified essential characteristics and socioeconomic and political dynamics in Korean society that raised the common people's consciousness of the han built up over many centuries of oppression. Thus the two theories, in effect, rationalized, legitimized, and even radicalized the opposition movement of the minjung (known widely as the minjung movement in the 1980s) in their struggle for democracy.

The Changing Socioeconomic Environment

On 29 June 1987, however, No T'aeu (Roh Tae-Woo), then president of the ruling Democratic Justice Party, announced his eight-point declaration, which led not only to his becoming president of the Sixth Republic of Korea through the election of December 12, but also and more importantly brought about dramatic change in public opinion toward government. Subsequently, the majority of the populace, including Korean workers, no longer pursued the minjung movement, or at least its more radical form, when responding to conflicts arising from political, economic, and cultural alienation and exclusion.

The populace was relatively content with the newly elected government, which, in principle, adhered to democratic process. This public contentment, especially after the appointment of the civilian government led by Kim Yŏngsam (inaugurated on 25 February 1993) seems ironically to have blurred the identity of minjung into obscurity. This is so because President Kim has not only promoted the creation of a "New Korea" built on "change and reform," but has also projected a government image with totally new faces by appointing either academics or former leading thinkers of the minjung movement to key cabinet and other important positions.[57] The appointment of Han Wansang himself in the dual position of deputy prime minister and National Unification Board minister (1993–1994) is one example.

Two changes reveal workers distancing themselves from the radical elements of the minjung movement after the June 1987 revolution. First, they began to take action without reference to solidarity with other minjung constituencies such as students and other oppositional activists, and kept "away from these 'outside agitators.' "[58] Their primary concern, as opposed to students or intellectuals, was the "practical solution of labor rights and immediate rice-and-soy-sauce economic issues [rather] than political reforms. . . ."[59]

Second, the vast improvement in the economic circumstances of Korean workers resulted in a widespread upgrading of their status. This was accompanied by a change in the market situation of many workers, the adoption of a nonproletarian life-style, and the development of relationships with the established middle class, leading to what Weber called "anticipatory socialization" and the emergence of a self-conscious middle group with bourgeois status. The existing concept of the minjung—that is, the image of people who are economically excluded and socially and politically alienated—no longer fits the self-identity and aspirations of these newly upwardly mobile Korean workers.

This turnabout in the masses' attitude to the minjung movement, whether of "minjung" workers or the general populace, however, came about despite whatever various levels of minjung consciousness prevailed after 1987. Han's distinction between the "sleeping" and the "awakened" minjung has proved quite irrelevant; for the overwhelming majority of the masses have come to share the same position on the fundamental principles of democracy in recent years, regardless of their intellectual and educational differences.

The factors identified by Han and other minjung activists that led to social alienation included not only the work situation but also the location of one's domicile, one's rise in the hierarchy of the community or enterprise, marriage, education, and socioeconomic aspirations. I would suggest that, given the role of each of these factors in contemporary Korea, the continued rise of workers, through the acquisition of wealth, to the status of the middle class will ensure that the more radical socialist ideals of earlier decades, especially of the mid-1980s, will become more and more remote. Furthermore, it would seem that those who led the minjung movement as leading activists and thinkers in the 1980s—namely, students and intellectuals— have come to realize that their radical ideology of the late 1980s cannot generate either energy or purpose for the mobilization of the masses as long as the state observes the democratic process. The reflections caused among Koreans by the collapse of the socialist bloc in Eastern Europe in 1989 and of the former Soviet Union in 1990 have only hastened and vindicated this change of perspective.

Conclusion

Despite each having distinct premises and logic, the two theories of Pak and Han bear similarities in their conclusions—namely, that the components of the minjung are the end products of exclusion from society. The minjung, according to Pak, are the economically alienated proletariat class. Han, on the other hand, identifies the minjung as those people "excluded" from that ruling power which controls various opportunities in society. Hence the minjung, whether the alienated people or the excluded people, are the victims of social and economic structures. Similarly, the thinking of both Pak and Han is based on the polarization of Korean society into the ruling group and the minjung. This polarization is seen as the cause of two major types of conflict: political and economic.

Economic conflict, as analyzed by Pak, is exacerbated by the ruling group's tendency to depend on foreign capital, a tendency that has continued allegedly since liberation. This dependence, according to Pak, is strongly opposed by the nationalistic consciousness of the minjung. He argues that internal class conflict is the outcome of social conditions which, in a broader context, are linked to national conflict, partition, and dependence. Each of these forms of national disintegration he deems the result of dependent politics, a dependent economy, and a dependent culture. Therefore, the laborers, farmers, and urban poor of the minjung, who actively struggle against these conflicts, in effect not only lead the people's movement toward social reform, but also lead the nationalist movement and the movement for national reunification. These movements, in his view, all have an interdependence based essentially on class conflict resulting from differences in socioeconomic status. However, as Han Sangjin argues,[60] the cause and effect relations of class conflict do not necessarily correspond to the national and international determinants of partition and political power.

I would argue that Pak's theory of minjung is also flawed in other respects. First, it contradicts the Korean national ideal of fraternity; for by defining the minjung as the proletariat he leaves no room for reconciliation with capitalist elements and intrinsically rejects the possibility of national unity, creating merely an exclusionary proletarianism. Moreover, the notion of minjung is much more complex than that outlined in Pak's theory and has had a much longer history than the process of proletarianization in Korea on which Pak's thinking is focused. The development of minjung as a conscious and active force was based theoretically as much on social and political conflict throughout history as on relatively recent economic conflict.

I would suggest that, in view of Pak's conceptually and historically narrow perspective, his theory is neither an adequate exposition of the complexities of the concept of minjung nor a basis for a viable ideology. It would seem that his motivation for applying "minjung" to the Korean proletariat was to take advantage of the nationalistic sentiment associated with the term in the 1970s and 1980s in order to confront the blatant exploitation of workers under Yusin policies, but without looking beyond Marxian ideology.

Han, on the other hand, attempts to accommodate a wider range of social strata and groups in an equally broad range of social, political, economic, and cultural issues, but fails to recognize that minjung cannot be grasped as a static entity or stratum. Furthermore, his identification of minjung as the group alienated from power in society, but with the goal of overcoming their alienation, encouraged a utopian dream which captivated their imagination and inspired hope. It is, however, contradictory to maintain that the minjung can retain their status as minjung if they do extricate themselves from the clutches of power in the manner Han suggests. For in the process of so extricating themselves, they inevitably destroy the very causes that create their status as minjung (in Han's definition). Still, it is not contradictory for the people both to achieve this goal and to remain the subjects of history.

The people as the subjects of history (my preferred description of minjung) have existed throughout history, including today. However, today they have gained access to economic power through high income and the acquisition of wealth, social power through education, and political power through democratic institutions, and a wider consciousness and understanding of their condition and aspirations. Therefore they no longer fit Han's definition of minjung in terms of alienation from power. His definition, based on the long history of the people's suffering, was effectively applied to a particular period in Korean history in which the minjung again suffered alienation from power under Yusin policies. To the extent that Han's focus gave impetus to the process of empowerment, his theory bore real significance, but as a comprehensive minjung thesis it lacks relevance to today's subjects of history, who have new perceptions and agenda.

Although Pak and Han's expositions did not provide the basis for a viable comprehensive analysis of minjung (especially as "subjects of history") they did contribute significantly to the debate on the plight of the underprivi-

leged in Korea in the 1970s and 1980s. In pinpointing economic power as a
key factor in the determination of one's share in the nation's wealth and production, Pak's arguments motivated workers to mobilize and seek fair wages
and better conditions of employment. He focused the minjung movement
on a particular issue which had not been of significant concern prior to
industrialization and, again, is now becoming of less concern as workers
move beyond the proletariat and acquire their own economic power.

Han highlighted the alienation of commoners from social, economic, and
political power and prestige and identified access to education as a key to
acquiring social and political prestige. He inspired ordinary people to
engage in education, especially in what Han termed "conscientization," that
is, "a thought process of the minjung whereby they transform themselves
from the historical object to the historical subject."[61] He convinced the
minjung of the need to conscientize and encouraged them to struggle for a
society that would adopt a path of "holistic development" *(ch'ongch'ejŏk
palchŏn)*. "Holistic development" means that "economic growth and distribution of income rise concurrently and material wealth and extension of
human rights go hand in hand."[62]

To what extent do these theories regarding minjung remain relevant to
the masses in the Korea of today? Today's minjung (mainly the "proletariat"
class) might say that Pak's theory provided a valuable insight into the dynamics of proletarianization in Korea during industrialization under Yusin
policies and continues to remind them (especially the workers) that the
masses' solidarity is their strongest and most effective weapon.

Korea in 1994 contrasts markedly with the working conditions and
income levels of Korean workers/laborers in the 1970s and 1980s. Moreover,
the overall level of education of Korean workers has risen significantly since
the early 1970s. However, the image of minjung as workers who fight against
capitalists/employers in principle remains, even though Korea exhibits a different work mentality, characterized by the so-called short-cut method and
3-D phenomenon (avoidance of Dirty, Dangerous, and Difficult work),[63]
and exhibits a materialistic value system.

In regard to the future of the minjung, almost no one expects a sudden
resurgence of minjung influence. Today the image of minjung as a term representing the majority, according to minjung commentators, is in crisis.[64]
The lack of capacity of the remnant minjung movement to attract the
masses on any issues reflects its own demise. Minjung organizations and
their campaigns have been replaced by community action *(simin undong)*
on a range of issues such as antipollution campaigns *(pan konghae undong)*
and consumer campaigns against price rises and inferior-quality products.

The notion of minjung as put forward by minjung exponents was, in
reality, putative. It attempted to define what was essentially a nondefinable
entity and struggled to encapsulate notions of a suppressed people, striving
to rise above their condition characterized by economic hardship and a lack

of personal freedom. The minjung concept heavily relied on emotional responses under such banners as nationalism, anti-imperialism, and anticapitalism, and dressed itself up in ideological concepts drawn from Western thinkers such as Marx and Weber. Any attempt to come to terms with the concept failed to realize that the characteristics of minjung and their response to their condition were in constant flux and could not be fixed within any specific group, set of circumstances, ideology, or socioeconomic theory. Such attempts gave rise to simplistic analytical frameworks which imposed on the concept a character that ignored the dynamics of their changing condition, status, and chosen responses in a rapidly changing world. Perhaps that is why the strong expositions of Pak and Han, which did not accommodate change, are the putative concepts rejected by today's subjects of history.

4

Confucian Tradition and Nationalist Ideology in Korea

Chung Chai-sik

THE SPREAD of nationalism on a global scale is a result of the westernization and modernization of non-Western societies.[1] In Korea, too, the awakening and spread of nationalism has been a result of the increasing encroachment of Western military, economic, and cultural power from the beginning of the nineteenth century and the colonization of the country by imperial Japan. Nationalism has emerged as the primary ideological force and stimulant to awaken all Korean people to national awareness and political action during times of momentous sociopolitical transition.

In Korea, nationalism has undergone several transformations. Starting out as a xenophobic reaction to outsiders, it was transformed into traditional reform movements as well as a bourgeois, progressive enlightenment movement. Later it developed into an anticolonial mass movement which accommodated an ever-widening participation of the people at large in the political, social, and cultural life of the nation. During the waning days of the Chosŏn dynasty and the colonial period—the formative years of nationalist ideology in Korea—how did Confucianism, which had most broadly defined the nature of man, culture, and society in traditional Korea, assume the responsibility for maintaining the collective identity in the modern world in terms of inherited symbols, shared cultural values and sentiments? What were the limits of Confucian nationalist ideology in redefining a collective identity and in articulating political and social programs for modern Korea to move effectively on toward the goal of creating a modern nation-state?

Uses of the Past: Confucian-Style Reactions to External Incursions

To discuss the intellectual origins and development of Korean nationalism, it is necessary to trace the political and intellectual history of nineteenth- or even eighteenth-century Korea. But for now we shall begin with the development of nationalism as an ideological movement since the latter half of the nineteenth century. The Korean response to Japanese and Western incursions during the latter half of the nineteenth century showed patterns similar to the responses to Western incursions in China after 1840 and in Japan with the Meiji Restoration of 1868. Unlike China, Korea did not show a wide-ranging ethnic, linguistic, and regional variation; all Koreans shared a more or less homogeneous culture and a tightly knit patrimonial social order during the long rule of the Chosŏn dynasty.

The values and norms of neo-Confucian orthodoxy at the center, maintained by the *yangban* elite, had far-reaching effects as they filtered down to large numbers of ordinary people, inducing them to follow neo-Confucian principles in regard to family structure, rituals, and social relations. Nevertheless, the ecumenical, high culture of the elites derived from China—such as the Confucian classics, literary Chinese, the civil service examination, and the Sinocentric worldview—remained separate from the popular culture of the masses based on the shamanistic tradition, which was deeply rooted in the native soil. The ruling yangban elites expected the lower masses of the people to fall voluntarily into line, but by failing to take into account the ordinary folk and the needs of their everyday lives, the rational moral discourse of the yangban remained largely irrelevant. Despite the elaborate means of moral education and social control enforced upon the people, a wide gulf separated the world of neo-Confucian moral principle (*i*) from the actual experience of the common people. This kind of dualism in Korean culture would later have considerable implications for the development of Korean nationalism. This study will trace the unfolding of nationalistic ideology in Korea by focusing upon the thought of Confucian intellectuals in recent times.

Neo-Confucianism, or *Ch'eng-Chu* philosophy, started as the vital ideology of the Chosŏn dynasty at its inception, providing a spiritual direction for the new dynasty and guidelines for the construction of a new state and society. Reaching its zenith around the sixteenth century, however, the Ch'eng-Chu orthodoxy began to lose its original vitality, increasingly becoming merely a handed-down, stagnant tradition. The fact that the orthodox tradition no longer commanded the unquestioning loyalty of the people at large became evident as more people, disillusioned with the reigning orthodoxy, began to seek fulfillment of their frustrated wishes through such neo-Confucianism alternatives as the *Silhak* (practical or real learning) and *Wang Yang-ming* schools, and even through such unusual heterodoxies as the belief in the Buddha to come (*Mirŭk* or Maitreya), the geomantic prognostication of the *Chŏnggamnok*, which promised a millennial salvation from deprivations in this world, and especially Catholic Christianity, then known as *Sŏhak* (Western learning).

By the eighteenth century, Catholicism, with its dangerous messages of Christian individualism, universalism, and the eschatological hope for otherworldly salvation, appeared to the Confucian ruling elites in Korea to be a subversive religion that devalued the world, destroying the fabric of Confucian family life and the society as a whole. After the nineteenth century, however, with American and French vessels intruding on the coasts of Korea, the threat of Western incursion had become more real. Christianity, which was suspected as a front for Western encroachment, was condemned by the Yi Korean Confucian government as the most dangerous "heterodoxy" *(idan, sahak)* that posed a direct threat to the existing state and society.

If "nationalism is essentially an anti-feeling" and "feeds and fattens on hatred and anger against other national groups," as Jawaharlal Nehru pointed out, we can already find tangible expression of such a negative character of national awareness in the attitude of the Korean yangban elites toward the alien religion of Westerners.[2] In the series of persecutions of Catholics by the Korean government and its repeated refusal to open the country to international treaty relations and commerce, which culminated in French and American expeditions in 1866, we notice the conflict between the traditional, self-contained culture of Korea bound to its Sinocentric worldview and the modern culture of the West, which had its own parochialism and ethnocentric attitudes.

During this encounter with foreigners, the yangban elites' "ethnic learning," which fostered an incipient national awareness, was expressed in "the language of religion" rather than in terms of political ideology.[3] In premodern Korean society, the moral values that prescribed a comprehensive range of specific norms governing the everyday life of the people and social institutions were thoroughly integrated with a religious system. The Korean religious system was made up of a peculiar fusion of neo-Confucianism with Buddhism, Taoism, and shamanism. With the rise of neo-Confucianism as a major belief-system of the Chosŏn dynasty, the rules of proper conduct stressing the "five relationships" of ruler to subject, father to son, husband to wife, elder to younger brother, and friend to friend were considered the most important means of obtaining harmony with the cosmological order. Particularly the rules governing the relationships of ruler to subject and father to son, which stipulated the virtues of loyalty and filial duty, asserted a connection with the sacred to relate the believer to a transcendent power. Because religion and social order were thus thoroughly integrated without any differentiation between the levels of religion and society, there was little room for an individual to express opinions on social and political matters that differed from the official line. Anyone who advocated divergent opinions was destined to become a religious heretic, invoking ultimate sanctions for any modification.[4]

Korea was the last East Asian country to enter the family of nations. After French and American ships moved into the Kanghwa Strait in 1866, it became increasingly apparent to the Hermit Kingdom that it was no longer possible to remain in seclusion. It had to enter the family of nations by discarding the Confucian concept of tributary relations with the Central Kingdom. Faced with the issue of opening its doors to the outside world, established officials and conservative Confucian literati clung to the traditional Sinocentric worldview without any modification until 1882, when it became necessary for Korea to open its doors to the United States. The inability of the Chosŏn government to keep the barbarian Japanese and Westerners from defiling the sacred soil of Korea, deemed to be the last bastion of the glorious civilization of Confucian China, enraged the conservative literati. With the slogan *Ch'ŏksa wijŏng* (Reject Heterodoxy and Defend Orthodoxy)—the standard way in which the Confucian literati had branded Buddhism and any deviant thoughts and activities that posed a threat to the existing power and the orthodox ideology of the Chosŏn dynasty—the conservative literati, especially those who belonged to the School of Hwaso (Yi Hangno, 1792–1868), rose to defend the old order.

Faced with a fundamental disruption upon contact with Japan and the West, Korea had to make major modifications in its worldview and institutions in order to survive. But the literati of the Ch'ŏksa wijŏng school persisted with the old symbolism of the center and the periphery. They still interpreted the reality of modern international relations according to the Chinese cosmology. Fueled by the xenophobia that had developed after the invasions of Hideyoshi Japan and the Manchus, the literati adopted the typical attitude that they would rather see the state destroyed than go through the humiliation of making peace with, or surrendering to, the barbarian invaders.

For Yi Hangno and his followers, to "revere China and to expel the barbarians" *(chonhwa yangi)* was the axial principle, or propriety *(ye)*, or the Way *(to)* to guide proper action. The distinction between Chinese civilization and the barbarians paralleled the distinctions between principle *(i)* and material force *(ki)*, *yin* and *yang*, the Way *(to)* and materializing force *(ki)*, and righteousness and profit.

According to Yi Hangno, *i* is a formative or structural principle that accounts for what things are and how they should be, while *ki* is the material force that accounts for physical form, material substance, plurality, and change in all things of heaven and earth. The two are interdependent and inseparable in Chu Hsi's thought, although he emphasized *i* more than *ki*. Like Yi Hwang (T'oegye, 1501–1570), who was often referred to as the Chu Hsi of Korea (although Yi Hwang stated more clearly than Chu Hsi that principle is prior to material force in respect of value), Yi Hangno emphasized even more than Yi Hwang the monistic *nature*, priority, and primacy of *i*.

Why was there such a shifting of attention to the primacy of principle? The Ch'ŏksa wijŏng movement that Yi Hangno spearheaded arose to defend the old values and society from the challenge of the West, particularly Christianity. It was essentially ideological and political in nature. Yi did not understand, however, that ideological and political matters do not necessarily go together; instead, he took the challenge of the West as a fundamental attack against the basic metaphysics in Chu Hsi's philosophy that claimed religious ultimacy for itself. For him and his followers, there was only one principle behind the myriad things, and no other cosmological system could oppose it as a rival. Once this axiomatic philosophy was challenged by a rival system of meaning, everything would fall apart, and the latter would gain ascendancy over the former. Therefore, with religious commitment, they maintained that only principle could lead and material force had to follow. Material force, synonymous with the West, was clearly defined as a heterodoxy that challenged the absolute principle which symbolized the Confucian morality and society.

> The Westerners' causing injury to morality is to be worried about the most. Between heaven and earth there still remains a line of yang-element in our Eastern land [Korea]. If this were to be destroyed, how in the world could the Heavenly Mind suffer this? We should, therefore, establish our minds for heaven and earth and manifest the *Tao* in haste as though quenching a burning fire. The being or not being of the nation is rather a matter of secondary importance.[5]

Yi grasped the problem of coping with the threat to external invasion, or external defense *(weyang),* not so much as a problem of consolidating political control and military defense but as a matter of achieving an internal unity of the people by rejuvenating their morality. With the moral revitalization of the ruler and people *(naesu),* all other problems would be solved; the political independence of the nation-state was seen rather as a matter of secondary importance. Clearly Yi Hangno and his followers perceived the world in the language of religion or culture.[6]

Yi Hangno's stance on the threat of external incursion was heavy with moralizing and metaphysical rhetoric, but in Ch'oe Ikhyŏn, who studied under Yi Hangno from his early teens, we find a grim determination to live up to the moral principles of his mentor.

In 1876, Korea was forced to sign an unequal treaty with Japan, opening the long-closed country to the outside world. On the eve of the conclusion of the treaty, Ch'oe memorialized the throne while prostrating himself before the Royal Palace with an axe in his hand—a highly symbolic gesture that he would rather die than see his country suffer inroads by the Japanese. In the memorial, he insisted that Japan was no longer the same country that Korea had known in terms of the traditional policy of *kyorin* (intercourse with a neighbor) and that it was now one and the same with the rapacious West. Branding Japan as a precursor of Western capitalist expansionism and a renegade from the Confucian ecumenical world, Ch'oe reaffirmed the traditional China-centered worldview.[7] Admiring things Chinese, he understood Korea as a small-scale replica of China—"the Eastern screenwall to the Great Ming"—and the last remaining custodian of Chinese culture after the fall of the Ming before the barbarian Ch'ing.[8]

After the ratification of the Kanghwa Treaty in 1876, the changing times made it necessary for the Korean government to take certain measures of reform in the state and society if it was to survive as a nation. In 1880, Kim Hongjip, a Korean envoy to Japan, came home with a painful awareness that Korea had to open its doors to the outside world, discard the old and adopt the new, and launch a "self-strengthening" program by selectively learning things Western. The case for opening up Korea was persuasively presented in the famous political treatise, *A Policy for Korea (Ch'ao-hsien ts'e-lueh)*, written by Huang Tsun-hsien, a councillor of the Chinese legation in Tokyo, which Kim brought home with him. However, the call to do so enraged the conservative Confucian literati in the school of Yi Hangno and their fellow travelers, prompting them to struggle against opening Korea to Japan and the West.

In the main, the Confucian protest movement took the form of present-ing memorials, warning of the erosion of the moral base of the society, and reaffirming the traditional isolationist policy. In these numerous memorials, including the well-known *Memorial of the Ten Thousand People of Yŏngnam (Yŏngnam maninsŏ)*, the leading themes of the Ch'ŏksa wijŏng were reiter-ated. To the literati, "to revere China and expel the barbarians [*chonhwa yangi*]" was the great principle of *Ch'un-ch'iu* (witnessed in *The Spring and Autumn Annals*). Among others, Hong Chaehak's memorial, actually written by Kim P'yŏngmuk, one of the disciples of Yi Hangno, made a profound impression on the country by forcefully arguing that Japan was one and the same with the West and that Christianity and Western encroachment should be expelled to safeguard Confucian orthodoxy as the foundation of tradi-tional society.[9]

For some twenty years following the opening of the country in 1876, the dynasty was obliged to "start again" *(kaengsi)*, or to initiate measures to adapt to the modern world, emulating the Chinese "self-strengthening" and the Japanese striving toward "civilization and enlightenment" *(bunmei kaika)*. The idea of "opening" *(kae)* the country to "transform" *(hwa)* things traditional with advanced, modern Western civilization was a very difficult idea for the Koreans to understand. For the recalcitrant China-centered literati of the Ch'ŏksa wijŏng persuasion, this was a particularly difficult idea to accept. Even Kim Yunsik, a moderate statesman, who was disposed to accept such "timely matters" *(simu)* as commercial transactions, treaty relations, technology, and so on, while preserving the traditional Eastern morality, wondered as late as 1891 how Korea, already a civilized country, could come under the influence of "enlightenment" like the countries in Europe had.[10]

Such had been the dominant influence of Sinocentrism on the Koreans. The Chinese defeat in the Sino-Japanese War in 1895, however, forced the

Chosŏn dynasty not only to discard its traditional tributary relationship with China but also to push toward overall changes in the government and society. Yet, in the midst of this transition, the conservative Confucian literati remained firmly unchanged, opposing fundamental social and political reforms at any cost.

From the summer of 1894 until the beginning of 1896, the pro-Japanese Korean cabinet introduced a series of radical political and social reforms known as the Kabo reforms. Japanese sponsorship and the abolition of traditional practices such as early marriage, the prohibition of widows to remarry, and the civil service examination discredited the reforms. The decree to adopt the Gregorian calendar and the new era was rejected too. But the decision to reform the garment was an affront to traditional culture.[11] Worse, the cutting of the "topknot," the traditional male hairstyle that symbolized traditional culture and personal identity, infuriated the yangban, who wished to conserve their inherited culture by all means. Ch'oe Ikhyŏn, for one, lost the will to live and was imprisoned for disobeying the edict to cut off the topknot.[12] In 1904, he reconfirmed his grim determination: "Better to continue to have a topknot and to die for it than to have it cut and survive; better to be a man of China [i.e., a civilized man] and die, than to be a barbarian and a beast and survive. This is the intention to which this subject has always adhered."[13]

Why would Ch'oe and many others similarly minded rather be beheaded than have their hair cut? The old and familiar symbols—the topknot, traditional garments, the lunar calendar, and so forth—had served to symbolize the totality of the beliefs, sentiments, traditions, and collective practices common to the members of a society. This is what Emile Durkheim meant by the "collective or common conscience," that which has to be defended as the sacred against the enemies within and without. As Susanne Langer pointed out, no matter how fantastic may be the "living rites" and dogmas one holds sacred, interference with those that have "ritual value" is always "the most intolerable injury one man, or group of men, can do to another." When Ch'oe and the like-minded literati were forced to go against their familiar symbols and single-minded principles, they readily chose to fight passionately for those old symbols and principles.[14]

Above all, the brutal assassination of Queen Min at the hands of the Japanese in 1895 angered the whole nation, provoking particularly the literati and peasant guerrilla bands into organizing the "Righteous Army" (Ŭibyŏng) to avenge her death. Attacking pro-Japanese Korean officials and leading guerrilla-style raids against Japanese garrisons in various parts of the country, the Ŭibyŏng under the leadership of such (Ch'ŏksa wijŏng) men as Yi Soǔng of Ch'unch'ŏn and Yu Insŏk of Chech'on manifested the spirit of resistance to defend the traditional state and society against foreign encroachment.[15]

The activities of the Ŭibyŏng were resumed in 1907 when Japan proceeded to make Korea its colony by establishing the 1905 Protectorate Treaty and by tricking Kojong into relinquishing the throne in 1907. When Japan proceeded to dissolve the Korean army in the same year, troops in Seoul and in the provinces formed the "righteous armies" to continue armed resistance against the Japanese. Under the leadership of the literati, these soldiers from the disbanded Korean army joined with the peasant guerrillas, attacking Japanese garrisons and facilities all over the country. After peaking in 1908, the armed struggle against the Japanese began to decline. After the annexation in 1910, the Ŭibyŏng fighters tenaciously continued their fight against Japan as independence fighters in Manchuria and the Russian Maritime Territory.

The spirit of the struggles of the Righteous Army that manifested the will of the Korean people to oppose Japan was best represented in the person of Ch'oe Ikhyŏn, literatus turned military leader, a heroic and high-spirited, upright man, who led Ŭibyŏng resistance against Japanese from around such towns as T'aein, Chŏngŭp, Sunch'ang, and Koksŏng. His concept of heroism—the patriotic scholar-warrior—found its example par excellence in Fan Ching-wen and his forty men of the Ming, in Ti I of Han, and in Wen T'ien-hsiang of Sung China. Each of these heroic scholar-officials had willingly died for his own endangered country even when it faced seemingly unsurmountable odds.

The five hundred years of Chosŏn Korea and its three thousand *ri* of territory had been ruined. The king had suffered the disgrace of being a displaced person in his own land, and the people had faced the misery of being devoured not unlike fish and meat. Describing these conditions, Ch'oe declared that he did not measure his own strength, but that he cared only for the promotion of justice *(taeŭi)* in all-under-heaven. He was above "success and failure and profit and loss," devoting himself "single-mindedly to the country" and setting his eyes only on death, and not on life.[16] It was ironic that Ch'oe's comparatively meager force was readily put down by the puppet Korean government, on whose behalf he would have gladly died. Arrested and exiled to the lonely island of Tsushima, Ch'oe died of hunger in prison in 1906.

In a summons to war, explaining the cause for the war of resistance to Japan, Ch'oe characterized Korea as "Small China" and the last remaining country in East Asia where the beauty of Confucian culture was still preserved intact from defilement by the heretical teachings of the West:

> The four oceans have been filled with foul smelling barbarians. Nevertheless, only our country, situated in the Eastern corner, could preserve a piece of superior, pure land; and it looked as if what was said of yang—that at the extremity of its wane it would wax again and that yang would alternate yin—really became a reality. Who would have reckoned that inferior icy element would now make its way and overwhelm the superior,

Pure Land? This is to be likened to the single topknot remaining atop of the head, becoming the sole target for all of the arrows in all-under-heaven.[17]

The impulse of Ch'oe was for Korea to preserve its Confucian tradition. He believed that without the Confucian ideas, values, and symbols which constituted the national essence of Korea, the Korean people would have nothing in common to hold them together. For Ch'oe and his fellow literati, the culture, not the nation or the people, demanded the highest loyalty from the individual, for without the former the latter would cease to exist. One finds in Ch'oe an anxious concern to preserve and reaffirm the value of the Korean Confucian tradition, which would eventually result in the strengthening of nationalistic feelings among the people.

The idea of democratic, popular participation in the political process, a concept central to liberal Western democratic life, however, was incompatible with the kind of elitism to which Ch'oe subscribed. The *Tonghak,* or Eastern Learning, was a "nativistic" movement that emerged in Korea in the early 1860s as a counter to the Western incursions, especially Catholicism, and the disintegration of the traditional society and culture.[18] By 1894, the Tonghak, with its millennial, populist, and xenophobic message, became involved in open rebellion among the peasants in Chŏlla Province. But the ill-equipped and inexperienced rebels were no match for a combined force of Korean and Japanese troops, and they were defeated and dispersed.[19] In 1907, many of the former Tonghak peasant soldiers joined the rank and file of the Ŭibyŏng. But the literati, including Ch'oe, could not quite overcome their condescending attitude—a mixture of anxiety and fear—toward the peasant soldiers, despite the great need for cooperation between literati and peasants. Martin Luther's vehement tract *Against the Murderous and Thieving Hordes of Peasants,* in which he urged everyone who could to "smite, slay, and stab, secretly or openly" the "poisonous, hurtful, or devilish" peasant rebels of sixteenth-century Germany, comes across to modern scholars as cruel and extreme. Ch'oe's antipathy to the peasant rebels was not as harsh, but it was there in a mitigated form. The Tonghak soldiers' violent uprisings were not marked by such extreme hatred and proneness to bloody violence as we notice in Thomas Müntzer's call to revolution, but there were similar elements of rebelliousness in their acts.[20]

Ch'oe Ikhyŏn branded the Tonghak soldiers as "a group of robbers and thieves like the [earlier] Tonghaks."[21] Between 1898 and 1910, the *Hwangsŏng Sinmun* (Royal Capital News) served as an influential forum of ideas for the promotion of "new learning," the broad educational and intellectual reform movement also known as the modern enlightenment of Korea. Published by Namgung Ŏk, its editorial board included some of the most prominent Confucian scholars, such as Chang Chiyŏn, Yu Kŭn, and Pak Ŭnsik, men committed to forming a new Korean nation by reconciling the Confucian tradition with Western civilization. Even so, in an editorial titled "Beware of the Tonghak rebels," it compared the new religious social movement of the Tonghak to those of the Boxers and the White Lotus of China, condescendingly identifying it with "a sort of magical charms and wicked incantations" which "seduce and beguile the ignorant masses."[22]

The typical elitist attitude of the older conservative literati comes into view more distinctly in, for example, Ch'oe's reaction to the ideology and activities of the Independence Club (*Tongnip hyŏphoe,* 1896–1898), the short-lived, modern voluntary association that played a decisive role in fostering a new nationalistic consciousness and in laying a basis for the wider political participation of the general public. The activities of the club ranged from publishing a newspaper in the Korean vernacular and promoting patriotism and political participation to the manipulation of patriotic symbols and the presentation of an idea for reforming the political system, using the concept of the Western nation-state as a model. The ideals and activities of the club, which marked the beginning of modern nationalism in Korea, however, were too radical in the eyes of the conservatives. Especially the idea of emphasizing the role of the people in representative government and the unprecedented use of public rallies for democratic public manipulation were too heterodox to be accepted by conservative Confucian elites.

Calling the Independence Club Min'gwŏndang (People's Right Party) or Mindang (People's Party), Ch'oe Ikhyŏn identified it with "the ignorant masses in the street" who banned together in boisterous rebelliousness under the pretext of loyalty to the sovereign and love of the nation.[23] "Alas! From now on political power and influence will all be transferred to the people. The king would neither be able to utter a word nor do a thing."[24] Expressing his fear of their growing strength, Ch'oe continued, "If something like this were not to be prohibited, how in the world could there be law and order (*pŏpkang*)?"[25]

Thus Ch'oe betrayed a profound fear that the commoners might take over everything and that Korean society would progressively become a society of vulgar equals in naked competition with each other for wealth, influence, and social status.

> This subject has heard that foreign countries have so-called free representatives (*chayu ŭiwŏn*) and parties for people's rights (*min'gwŏn chi tang*) and that they have instances of people voluntarily electing their own lord. When these party members have already blackmailed and expelled their ministers time and again, would they hesitate to do anything to gain their ends? Suppose these followers had true loyalty to the king and love of country, even so, judging them from the perspective of moral principle (*tori*), we cannot let them continue their plans. Moreover, they are like a multitude of birds gathered together; they are undisciplined mobsters. How can they know the proper ways to govern a country? Granted that they have a word or two that is worthy to be adopted [by the government],

how can they be forgiven for their crime of blackmailing the king? The ministers of the government themselves have not bowed down to die for the country. They divided the people into disparate factions. The king's government, therefore, ought to reflect upon itself, for the people alone should not be blamed.[26]

Ch'oe's fear of a revolt of the masses was only a reflection of the general consciousness of the literati that had been manifest in their condescending and hostile attitude toward the reformers of 1884, 1894, 1895, and 1896.[27]

The idea of people participating in decision-making and governing processes is a central aspect of Western representative democracy. Also essential to the democratic process is the idea that it is the people who can put the rulers in and out of office by popular choice. Democratic ideology such as this was quite repugnant to Ch'oe Ikhyŏn and other orthodox Confucian leaders. Ch'oe firmly disapproved of the democratic forms of free expression and criticism as irresponsible acts. He charged that they did not have the built-in character of "restraint" (panghan) and "temperate control" (chŏlche) which had featured the various traditional ways of criticizing the rule of government such as: pibangmok (the tree on which anonymous protest by the people could be hung); sinmun'go (the drum hung on the palace gate since the year 1401 for people to beat in order to make a plea in an action at law); pokkak (the system of literati presenting memorials in a state of prostration); and kwŏndang (the resident students at the Four Colleges—Confucian academies for higher learning—going on strike in remonstrance to the king). Traditionally, people had the right to speak out and criticize the rule of the government, but they had never expelled its ministers. Although memorials had been presented as remonstrances and pleas, Ch'oe argued, the king had neither been intimidated nor restrained.[28]

Sin Kisŏn, Minister of Education, had also expressed the fear in 1896 that the rights of the people guaranteed by the constitution would overshadow and even usurp the power of the king.[29] Yu Insŏk, a disciple of Yi Hangno, assumed that there was a hierarchy of beings in nature and society. In terms of correlative cosmology commonly accepted in Chinese philosophy,[30] Yu rationalized that the traditional social hierarchy was based on the homology between the structure of the human body and that of a society:

Heaven and earth have differences of high and low; the myriad things have the differences of great and little; mountains have high peaks and lower hills; water has ocean and gutter. How, then, can they all be equal? Likewise, human beings discriminate between ruler and minister, father and son, husband and wife, old and young, high and low, and superior and inferior. There are distinctions between the sage and the commoner and between the wise and the ignorant. If so, how can there be equality?[31]

Equality and freedom would result in disorderliness and the spirit of no yielding, which would in turn lead to the conflict among vulgar equals that characterizes modern society. Therefore, Yu condemned the modern Western values of equality and individual freedom as subversive values, "the worst doctrines in all ages under heaven and earth."[32]

The value conflict between yangban elitism and democratic populism is quite evident. Now the Confucian paternalism, which held that the elite are, and should be, the guardians of the general good of the ignorant masses and that the masses should be kept in line, had begun to be openly questioned. One can sense in the old elites a genuine anxiety that they were no longer able to restrain the nonrational urges and primordial passions bursting forth from among the masses below them. In a tone of militancy and hatred, they antagonized the intellectuals and officials who had been awakened to the reality of the ever-increasing forces of modernity.

It is not difficult to point out how the cultural assumptions of Ch'oe and similarly minded men about the state, monarchical authority, and elitist political leadership were incongruent with the political ideology, institutions, and social system that prevailed in the Western nations. Nor did they have any ideas about how to help their country come to terms with the changing, modern world. By merely clinging to the ideal of a moral community in the imaginary past, these spirited people consciously defied the modernizing forces that required their quick and efficient adaptation. Nevertheless, they colorfully embodied in their lives the traditional values and worldview of Korea and spoke for the deeply felt collective sentiment of the people against Japan's incursions, the importance of a common cultural past and sense of community, and the ardent yearnings of the people for the sovereignty of Korea under the old monarchy. For them, loyalty to the king and his dynasty was actually the same as the preservation of national sovereignty and independence.

The Limits of Confucian National Consciousness

Ch'oe Ikhyŏn and his fellow literati had hammered home, again and again, the point that it was absolutely necessary to resuscitate the traditional culture, restore the moral legitimacy of the government under siege, and expel the Japanese. Acting on his beliefs, Ch'oe's final attempt to cope with the crisis arising from the Japanese encroachment was to lead the military uprising against an invading force that held enormous odds against him. The king, the topknot, the traditional habiliments, the *sŏwŏn* (Confucian schools), the lunar calendar, and so forth—these entities that he had so zealously wanted to protect—were manifestations of the sacred which he held in extreme respect: the sacred principle that underlies humanity, society, and the world.

However, with the turn of the century the course of history changed. With a rapid expansion of interest in the outside world among intellectual circles, small coteries of more realistic and open-minded Confucian scholars joined the growing intellectual and educational movement of the nationalist-minded intellectuals with their bent for the *kaehwa* (enlightenment) of Korea. This movement could trace its origins back to the progressive movement of the 1880s and the Independence Club of the late 1890s. In the case of Pak Ǔnsik, one of the leaders of the enlightenment movement, however, the visions and the example of such Chinese reformers at the turn of the century as K'ang Yu-wei, Liang Ch'i-ch'ao, and the leaders of the Meiji Reformation of Japan had also greatly influenced the formation of Pak's philosophy. Pak, like other enlightenment thinkers such as Chang Chiyǒn, Sin Ch'aeho, and Yi Ki, came to believe that the issue of the time was not the conflict between Confucian culture and Western civilization but the survival of the nation-state. The "old" Confucian tradition was too outmoded to cope with the challenges of the times. These challenges could be met neither through direct political action nor through the military Ǔibyǒng resistance, for which the Ch'ǒksa wijǒng literati had opted; instead, these men thought they could help their contemporaries know themselves and the future directions of Korean politics and society by means of books, study societies, newspapers, journals, and the establishment of schools for the "new learning" of the West.

With the aim of narrowing the distance between the intellectuals and the masses and advocating the necessity to "self-strengthen" *(chagang)* the nation through the development of modern education, science, and technology, these reform-minded Confucian intellectuals published the *Hwangsǒng Sinmun*, mentioned earlier, the *Taehan Maeil Sinbo* (Korea Daily News, published between 1904 and 1910), and a monthly of a provincial study society, *Sǒu Hakhoe Wǒlbo*, in mixed Chinese and ǒnmun, the national vernacular. To achieve the goal of strengthening the nation, various national and provincial organizations were formed. Most active of such organizations was the nationwide Great Korea Self-Strengthening Society *(Taehan chaganghoe)*, founded in 1906 by such eminent leaders as Chang Chiyǒn, Yun Ch'iho, and Yun Hyojǒng, to help build the basis for national independence through the attainment of self-strength. Believing that education, the civilized arts, and technology formed the basis for the wealth and power of the nation and were therefore necessary for the self-strengthening of the nation, these men worked to develop the kind of education that would nurture the intelligence of the people, promote industrial growth for the attainment of wealth and power, and reform the nation through the cultivation of the spirit of love for the fatherland.[33]

Drawing on the new learning and the political and social thought of the West, which came through the filter of Japan and China, the reformist scholars investigated the reasons why the West had achieved power and wealth; why Korea, like China, came to lag behind the West; and how Korea, like Japan, could revitalize itself by reconciling its traditions with the civilization of the West. Among others, the Western theory of social evolution and the concepts of struggle for survival and the survival of the fittest associated with Spencer, Darwin, and Huxley threw light on the predicament of Korean society.[34]

During the period of 1906–1910, the reformist ideologues came to grips with the key issues of national identity and independence. The emergent national consciousness was embodied in the movement spearheaded by Chu Sigyǒng to use *han'gǔl*, the national vernacular, as the natural tongue of Korean people so as to overcome the age-old cultural subservience to Chinese culture *(sadaejuǔi)*.[35] The emergent national consciousness was also expressed through the writing of Korean national history by such scholars as Pak Ǔnsik and Sin Ch'aeho, who sought to promote a national consciousness and a patriotic spirit, rejecting the traditional Sinocentric or Confucian historiography.[36]

Korean independence and survival were contingent upon the formation of the national character of the people. In the final analysis, if the people could not commit themselves in the defense of the larger cultural community, the nation could not be defended from foreign aggression. By comparing the Korean national character with the national spirit of other nations—for example, Japanese loyalty, the American spirit of independence, and the British love of freedom—Yun Hyojǒng, one of the leading figures in the Taehan chaganghoe, noted that these attributes were absent in Koreans.[37] Yun Ch'iho, another well-known leader of the Taehan chaganghoe, also believed that the reason why Korea was "bobbing on the sea of disgrace" was because each individual was full of "a dependent spirit" and was devoid of an "independent and subjective will."[38]

One of the crucial questions facing the Korean state and society was how to free the individual from the shackles of tradition while at the same time harmonizing the needs of the family with the interests of the larger collectivity.[39] The lack of public-spiritedness and the narrowly circumscribed attitudes that divide the peoples of high and low class origins and the inhabitants of Seoul from provincials stood in the way of bringing the people together in a common bond of national solidarity. It was imperative that Korea form the moral basis for a new social order, one that valued individualism, public-spirited citizenship, principles of law rather than Confucian patrimonial relationships, and, most of all, a responsible government.[40]

Yun Ch'iho charged that the absence of "altruism," or "public spirit,"[41] and the patrimonial and oppressive hierarchical system,[42] which tied the people to family, village, and the monarchical state, eroded the very ideas of autonomous, participatory citizenship for the common good. Therefore, cutting himself off from the fossilized and irrelevant Confucian tradition, Yun opted for Protestant Christianity as a new and dynamic ideology that would help Korea to create an independent, free, and modern society. The road to national independence, Yun believed, lay in the cultivation of knowledge, intelligence, moral integrity, and patriotism of the people. "Only Protestantism," not the corrupt government, he declared, was fit to "restore the spiritual fibre of the people."[43] Sŏ Chae-p'il (Philip Jaisohn), the founder of the Independence Club, had also made a great point of this earlier.[44]

The fact that Christianity inspired nationalistic consciousness in Korea, although it remains to be more adequately studied, is a phenomenon that is quite interesting when we compare it to the role of Christianity in the expansion of Western imperialism elsewhere in the world. Many Christian converts led the attack upon Confucian values and norms as corrupt, fossilized, and irrelevant to the needs of the contemporary society. But there were also reform-minded Confucian scholars who refused to remain sheltered in the hackneyed tradition. Many of the values, norms, and customs associated with Confucianism became favorite targets.

The Confucian scholar Pak Ŭn-sik, in his famous editorial "On the Quest for the Confucian Reformation" *(Yugyo kusin non)*,[45] and in other writings, made a severe attack upon his inherited tradition.[46] With a painful awareness of the erosion of the Confucian tradition, Pak wanted to adopt selective values from the West so that the inherited tradition might be renewed and not displaced by the new values. Thus he was not an iconoclast but merely a neotraditional reformer. Pak criticized aspects of Confucianism which repressed individual rights, freedom, and initiative, and these included the inertia of the Confucian community *(yurim)*, the legacy of the civil service examination system *(kwagŏ)*, the hollow discussions of ceremonies and righteousness and neglect of practical life and economy, the elitist orientation of the literati, the old learning *(ku hangmun)* devoted to excessive exaltation of letters, the neglect of "timely" education *(simu kyoyuk)*, intellectual dogmatism and suppression, and the lack of public spirit and social responsibility. Pak looked at Martin Luther's Reformation and Liang Ch'i-ch'ao's reform movement in China to find clues to salvage his own obsolete tradition. He also discovered ideas in the philosophy of Wang Yang-ming, the greatest Chinese thinker since the twelfth-century sage Chu Hsi, which opened a way to fresh moral meaning, critical and creative spirit, dynamic action, and individual freedom. This came as a welcome alternative to Chu Hsi's orthodox philosophy.[47]

For Pak, the nation and the happiness of the people, not the Confucian tradition, were his ultimate concerns. To achieve his goals, Pak would dispose of the tradition if it became an obstacle. In comparison to universalism in Buddhism, and especially Christianity, he found the Korean Confucian heritage to be devoid of popular concerns because of its "majestic" or elitist orientation. Preoccupied with ceremonial propriety and status distinction, Korean Confucianism had ignored the people. In an age when the survival of a nation was dependent upon intelligent people having the right and the willingness to participate in the political process, Confucianism had to transcend the literati tradition and become a general tradition for all. Therefore, Pak sought to discover elements in Confucianism that had certain affinities with the Western universalist ideologies of Christianity, Enlightenment liberalism, and democracy.[48]

Pak's reformist vision of a renewed Confucianism serving the cause of national independence was also shared by Sin Ch'aeho.[49] As Han Kwangho, a sympathizer of Pak's vision, lamented however, the conservative literati of the country largely ignored Pak's call to reform the "dogmatic" and "despotic" authoritarian tradition of Confucianism.[50] Likewise, the eleventh-hour attempts of the enlightenment ideologues to assert national identity and autonomy in the face of the impending annexation of Korea by imperial Japan faced a hostile ruling elite in a tottering government with little popular support among the masses. Isolated from political leadership, the language movement, the new history writing, the affirmation of the nationalistic spirit, and the search for Confucian reformation by the enlightenment ideologues all could not stop the tragic denouement of the kingdom. The fall of the dynasty shattered the hope of the enlightenment ideologues to retain national sovereignty. The patriotic guerrilla resistance of the Ŭibyŏng led by the Confucian literati and ex-officers and soldiers of the disbanded royal army of Chosŏn Korea was no match for the modern Japanese army. It now became apparent that the passing of the old kingdom indeed marked the end of an era for the Confucian tradition which had undergirded it.

Estrangement from History in the Making

As Japan's conquest of Korea and its consolidation of colonization proceeded according to plan, many Koreans, even those who compulsively defended the fossilized tradition in the midst of the changes that were taking place around them, found the old Confucian symbols increasingly hackneyed and barren in coping with the various problems of modern life. Those who cast their lot with the crumbling old social order and morality came to feel that they were stranded in their own land, as displaced people with their permanent homestead occupied by the troublesome presence of foreign marauders.

In 1905, Japan forced the Korean government to sign a protectorate agreement, surrendering control of Korean foreign affairs to the Japanese. This prelude to formal annexation aroused vehement protests from the Korean people, ranging from a torrent of memorials and letters of protest calling for the annulment of the treaty to a number of high government officials committing suicide. Song Pyŏngsŏn, a highly respected Confucian scholar and the ninth descendant of Song Siyŏl, the indomitable leader of the established Noron faction of the seventeenth century, stood for the cause of Ch'ŏksa wijŏng. Despite the epochal changes that were taking place around him, Song rigidly clung to the Confucian symbolic paradigm of principle and material force (i-ki), yin-yang, and China versus the barbarians (hwa-i). Like Yi Hangno, Song insisted that the axiomatic moral basis of Korean society was i, or principle, and that once the universal and absolute axiom was compromised by an ideology which put forth ki as the alternative, things would begin to fall apart.[51] As late as 1903, this Confucian interpretation of reality still provided Song with a vital frame of meaning, evoking a sense of loyalty and awareness of Korea's mission as the last remaining Small China that had a responsibility to set a moral example for the world.

Emile Durkheim writes that the collectively shared moral ideals and values of the group to which one belongs can evoke deep, unselfish sentiments of devotion and love, and that people cannot be separated from those ideals and values without experiencing a severe disorientation of life and even a diminished will to live.[52]

A person who is deeply attached to the ideals and values of the society can "actively" commit suicide "at the command of . . . conscience," violent emotion being "controlled by reason" and by "the will" to die for something which is loved more than life itself. In "a burst of faith and enthusiasm," a person wants to die in obedience to "the command of . . . conscience."[53]

Song Pyŏngsŏn committed suicide when the passing of his country became a reality and the end of the traditional morality (to) and society (illyun: human relations) were foreshadowed. The disintegration of the traditional values that had provided meaning to his life gave him a severe psychological jolt, and it meant the loss of "the courage to live." He could not face the coming destruction of his beloved country and the moral bankruptcy of his society. Nor could he tolerate the disgrace of surviving in his own land as a disinherited alien. At the same time, he felt the weight of moral obligation to die for a cause greater than himself. Through his own death he wished to persuade the king to return to the Way, to call for the punishment of the treasonous subjects who had sold the country, and to reinforce the collective conscience of the society and hold the rapid moral disintegration at bay. His own death seemed to him a noble moral act that would conform to the great classic moral principle of dying for the duty (as specified in The Spring and Autumn Annals) of saving one's traditional morality and humanity from degenerating into a barbarian and beastly state.[54]

Min Yŏnghwan, a close relative of Queen Min and one-time minister of education and minister of home affairs, committed suicide under similar circumstances. Song and Min were only the better-known cases of those who chose to die in "a burst of faith and enthusiasm." In his will addressed to the nation, Min expressed his state of mind, which attached little value to life: "Those who want to live would surely die, and those who pledge themselves to die would surely be able to live on." In his last words to his people, he called upon them to be firm in their will to do their best "to restore" their "freedom and independence."[55]

In August 1910, Korea was annexed by Japan, which thus acquired complete control of the peninsular country. The series of events that culminated in the death of the nation filled the minds of Koreans with anger and bitter-

ness. The heavy-handed takeover of the country by militaristic Japan naturally evoked considerable opposition on the part of Koreans.

Kwak Chongsŏk represented another style of Confucian resistance to
Japan's seizure of the country. In 1903, Kwak was appointed to the State
Council as well as being offered the post of Reader of the Office of the
Royal Lectures, but he declined the appointments, preferring rather to
remain as a scholar-recluse.[56] In 1904, Kwak protested in his memorials to
the king the increasing accommodation of the government to the rising
influence of Japanese imperialism.[57] A year later, when the protectorate was
established, he again submitted a memorial to the throne requesting annulment of the treaty.[58] But he could neither commit suicide like Song Pyŏngsŏn nor unleash his anger in a stormy uprising against the Japanese as Ch'oe
Ikhyŏn had; nor could he go into exile overseas in the aftermath of the
annexation, like Yu Insŏk, Yi Siyŏng, and Yi Sŭnghŭi, to join a long march to
regain Korean independence. In despair and suppressed anger, he simply
chose to live a cloistered life in his home in Koch'ang when the Japanese
conquest of Korea became a reality in August 1910.[59]

Kwak was the doyen of the Confucian community of literati in the
Kyŏngsang provinces, the home of Korean Confucianism. He was a disciple
of Yi Chinsang, who lived in the eighteenth century and stressed even more
than Chu Hsi and Yi T'oegye an extreme, monistic philosophy of the priority
and primacy of principle (*i*). Injecting a more defensive note into the philosophy of T'oegye's School of Principle (*Churi p'a*), Yi Chinsang, along with Yi
Hangno and Ki Chŏngjin (1798–1879), represented a turning point in the
history of neo-Confucian thought in recent Korea. The latter two were not
members of the so-called Yŏngnam School (*hakp'a*) of T'oegye, and the
intellectual backgrounds of these scholars were not the same. Nonetheless,
all of them insisted upon the primacy of principle as a defense against the
rising threat of Western incursion, which they grasped in metaphysical
terms as the threat to principle by material force (*ki*).[60] Kwak closely followed his mentor's view of the monistic primacy of principle and highly
esteemed Yi Hangno's belief in it, even though he was not a member of Yi's
intellectual and social circle.[61]

It may be presumed that these literati ideologues became convinced that
belief in the primacy of principle could be successfully utilized as a system
of ideas to rationalize the moral basis of traditional society, to interpret the
current situation, and to indicate the best future course of action for the
members of society. The theory of the primacy of principle became an ideology to define and interpret the given situation in respect to the achievement
of specific goals: the preservation of traditional morality and society from
both internal and external sources of change.

Earlier, Ch'oe Ikhyŏn explained that his mentor, Yi Hangno, had grasped
the challenges of Christianity, the culture of the West, the philosophy of
material force, and the thought of Wang Yang-ming as the challenge posed

by a belief in the primacy of material force, and that his mentor advanced his own theory of the primacy of principle as a counterideology. According to Ch'oe, his mentor considered the will "to save the corrupt conditions of the times" of utmost importance.[62]

Likewise, in *Yi Chinsang's Conduct of Life (Haengjang)*, which Kwak later wrote about his mentor, the disciple observed that diverse heterodox doctrines all have one thing in common—namely, they invariably begin and end with the belief in the primacy of material force.[63] Following in the footsteps of his mentor, Kwak reconfirmed that the heterodox teaching of Wang Yang-ming, the incursions of the West and Japan, the rationale for accepting the technological methods of the West, and the special danger of Catholicism were all attributable, symbolically speaking, to the fact that the primacy of material force was gaining ascendancy over the primacy of principle. And so Kwak maintained that it was absolutely necessary to arrest such a trend with a counterideology of the primacy of principle.[64]

Kim Ch'angsuk, another eminent Confucian scholar noted for his role in the nationalist movement at home and abroad, affirmed, in the inscription he wrote on the tombstone of Yi Sŭnghŭi (Han'gye, ?–1916), the son of Yi Chinsang and a nationalist exile in Siberia, that Yi Sŭnghŭi had stood for the primacy of principle "in order to save the world from the disease of studying the primacy of material force."[65]

Kwak spelled out what it meant to defend principle against the onrush of material force:

> First, the orthodox learning should be respected. . . . In the teachings of the former sage-kings constant moral duties and virtuous conduct were of primary importance and utilitarian matters and technical skills and art were of secondary importance. . . . Our Korea's literary education approximated with distinction the glories of the "Three Ages" but in the course of gradual passing of time education came to be degenerated. And false scholars without any knowledge of moral duties appeared. . . . Until at last in Your Majesty's time, with the opening of relations with foreign countries, they were startled at the competence of the utilitarian functional skills and art [of Westerners]; and they came to fear the strengths of the Westerners' military and national influences. . . . Your Majesty, you no longer show your presence at the royal lecture, and His Highness, the royal prince, too, does not come near his teacher. And the entire nation has gone with the fashion; and the places where music and chanting [i.e., the classic learning] used to be found are now reduced to places of drinking and eating. Scholar-officials do no longer read writings of Chou and Confucius. In trim clothes and with short haircuts [i.e., symbols of departure from the old customs], they are discussing utilitarian doctrines, and halls for worship of gods and demons and for spells and incantations [i.e., Christian churches] are scattered everywhere in the country. . . . Alas! China has been swallowed up [by Western nations] and the [Confucian teaching] has disappeared. And yet only one place, our Korea alone, has

preserved the last remnant of it. Is not this the case because heaven would rather save this last portion of yang from yin that has been waxing in this world so that it [i.e., Korea] might become the master of the religion of all-under-heaven? In this subject's humble thinking nothing is more immediate than the cultivation and enlightenment of the teachings of former sage kings.[66]

In this memorial, Kwak reasserted the Confucian ideal, urging the king to set a moral example for the nation by his own conduct. He also reaffirmed the inherited belief that Korea was the only country in the East chosen to hold onto Confucianism when it had disappeared even in China, thus exhibiting his national pride. His appeal to the Confucian notions of self-cultivation, virtuous government, moral education, national pride, and Confucian ecumenism were the reverberation of the themes that are familiar through Yi Hangno and fellow thinkers. It is easily imaginable that the same memorial might well have been written by Yi Hangno more than a generation earlier.

Perhaps Kwak was the last major advocate of the theory of the primacy of principle *(churi sŏl)*. During his self-imposed life of exile in his final years, away from the unfolding of the modern world, his theory of the primacy of principle became largely forgotten, like Kwak himself. The theory provided the cognitive principle for the dominant values of the orthodox Confucian literati, who had remained steadfastly loyal to the emperor, the Yi monarchy, and the traditional social order. The more universal nation-state as a community of shared history and destiny never came to the fore as the object of their larger loyalty.

Premature and abortive as they were, the reform attempts of the Independence Club, the Taehan Chaganghoe, and other educational and religious movements, and the activities of the Ŭibyŏng and the exiles, had paved the way for the emergence of modern nationalism, individual freedom, and equality. One could say that 1905 to 1919 was the period in which a new consciousness about national sovereignty and the unity of a nation as a community with a common destiny was produced, culminating in the historic birth of modern nationalism—the so-called 1919 March First movement to regain Korea's lost independence through a nationwide mobilization of the people in which previously neglected elements in society participated, including women, the masses, and the provincials. During the first decade of life under the harsh colonial rule of Japan, the Korean people learned the reality of modern imperialistic politics and the sorrowful burdens of life as an oppressed people. They soon realized the necessity for national unity and resistance to imperial Japan at home and abroad.

Spurred on by the doctrine of the self-determination of nations enunciated by American president Woodrow Wilson, a response to the burgeoning nationalist movements that had arisen in Europe after the end of World War I, Koreans rose to usher in the new "era of justice," putting an end to the "age of force." The unarmed and peaceful movement that "proclaimed the independence of Korea and the liberty of the Korean people," however, was ruthlessly crushed by Japan's military force. Korean leaders were disappointed when the movement failed to win the anticipated support of the Western powers. But the tragic case of Korea and the yearnings of the Koreans for independence did receive wide publicity abroad.

The leadership of the movement came mostly from the various religious circles, including Protestant Christianity, Ch'ŏndogyo (Religion of the Heavenly Way, the post-1905 development of the Tonghak movement), and Buddhism, among others. Although highly visible, both the Christian and the Ch'ŏndogyo groups represented only a small minority of the population and had to gain legitimacy as newly rising social groups. The fact that they became the vanguard of a new political movement was due to the broad appeal of their relatively more modern, egalitarian ideologies and organizational structures.[67]

The Confucian community and the leading literati remained lukewarm and aloof toward the movement, reflecting their hesitation to shed their accustomed feelings of superiority.[68] Chŏn U, leader of the Yurim in the Chŏlla provinces, would not have anything to do with a movement led by those who had their hair cut or accepted the modern world.[69] The literati were reluctant to associate themselves with initiatives designed to increase the power and political participation of the boorish masses. In contrast, the uneducated masses, who had been alienated for centuries from yangban-dominated society through stringent status and regional barriers, could not identify themselves with the elite and the nation-state. It was out of the question for them to have a national consciousness unless the elite were to learn to look up to "the people" as true equals who shared the common destiny of the same community.[70]

From then on, the ideology and leadership of nationalist movements were to come neither from the Confucian yangban, who were representative of the cultural heritage of the past, nor from the uneducated masses, but from those who had exposure to Western learning. Birth, status, classical education, and moral integrity were no longer the bases for social, intellectual, and political leadership. Ability, modern education, and personal resourcefulness became more important assets than morality and the ascriptive social status of the old society. But the literati adhered to the past too "obstinately" to adapt themselves to the changing times.[71] Still another reason why the literati were hesitant to join the movement was that its Declaration of Independence did not mention as one of its goals the restoration of the Chosŏn dynasty.[72] The road to national independence did not lead to the restoration of the tradition-bound society but rather to a break with the old tradition, so that Korea could be infused with the explosive power which had revolutionized the West.

When the March First movement suddenly erupted over their heads, the

Confucian literati were caught off balance and were deeply embarrassed by the event. Actually, the Confucian community was the one recognizable social force that was left behind by the social current in the national movement for self-determination.[73] Deeply ashamed by the apolitical attitude and passive posture of the Confucian community, Kim Ch'angsuk, a noted scholar-patriot, took the initiative and persuaded Kwak Chongsŏk, who was living as a recluse in his home in Koch'ang, to represent the Yurim community, along with Chŏn U, and to join in the nationwide march for independence. Chŏn U declined Kim's plea, saying that "Confucian literati should only preserve the Confucian Way without having anything to do with the rise and fall of the nation"; he preferred to hold on to the hackneyed Confucian tradition than swim with the current of the times in order to save the nation. Kwak, however, found in the movement "a cause to die for." By the end of March 1919, some 137 literati in the middle and southern provinces signed a petition (primarily written by Kwak), which was submitted to the delegates of the Paris Peace Conference through Kim Ch'angsuk.[74]

"We—Kwak Chongsŏk, Kim Pokhan [leader of the Yurim in southern Ch'ungch'ŏng province], and others comprising 137 men who represent the Korean Confucian community—cordially petition your excellencies in the Paris Peace Conference." With this salutation, the petition affirmed that before the unjust annexation of Korea by Japan their country had been an independent nation. Japan, while at first promising the guarantee of Korea's independence in the treaties of 1876 and 1895 respectively, and again in 1903 (in her declaration of war against Russia), had taken advantage of Korea's internal weakness, blackmailed Korea internally, and reduced the nation to the status of protectorate, finally turning the protectorate into an annexed territory. These, observed the petition, were acts that violated international justice *(kongŭi)* and trust *(sinŭi)* among the nations of the world.[75]

It went on to affirm that the principle of self-determination of nations should be practiced by all nations and that Korea should be independent from Japan.

> Though our Korea is small, throughout its 3,000 *ri* [of land], there live some 20 million people. She has not lacked those who had the ability to cope with the affairs of the country, and so why should she be ruled by a neighboring country? The customs [of the people] are not the same even if they be separated from each other only by 1,000 *ri* or even by 100 *ri*. Nevertheless, in saying that our Korea is not capable of being independent, Japan wants to force upon Korea, with its various different customs, the methods used in governing its own country. Custom cannot be altered abruptly, and, therefore, the so-called governance by Japan can well lead to disorder [in Korean society]. Hence it is evident that such governance should not be enforced [upon Korea]. Nevertheless, it is widely advertised in public assemblies that the Korean people have for a long time been

resigned to dependence upon Japan. Korean people are Korean people not only because they were so determined by its territory and climate but also because they attained it by heaven-endowed nature *(ch'ŏnsŏng)*. Therefore, even though they may bend themselves temporarily and suffer its oppressive power, in their own minds they will never for tens of thousands years forget that they are Korean people. How in the world could they deceive their own essential minds *(ponsim)*?[76]

The petition went on to say that the attempt by Japan to suppress international opinion by force of sheer power was not advisable in this new age. Appealing to the civilized sense of equity and justice for all the nations of the world, the spirit of independence was expressed most poignantly, "Chongsŏk and we would rather be executed in a batch, and we hereby make a solemn vow never to become Japan's slaves."[77] For this act of defiance, Kwak was arrested by the Japanese authorities and in August of the same year he died of illness.[78]

Korean Confucian social and political thought ever since the beginning of the Chosŏn dynasty did not posit God as the first cause and designer of society. Neither did it support the idea of society as a social order subject to coercive laws, nor the idea of humanity as bound to objective social forces and shaped by human institutions. What it upheld was a metaphysical conception of human nature (rooted in neo-Confucianism) that has nature-shaped and inherent characteristics. It maintained that there is something recalcitrant and unchanging about human nature, Heaven-endowed nature *(ch'ŏnsŏng)*, and so culture and society reflect this state. It was believed that, by ch'ŏnsŏng, a Korean was Korean, and that it could not be otherwise. This mythical cosmology, which described the nature of the world as fixed and predetermined, provided remarkable stability and continuity in Korean history and society, counteracting opposing ideologies both from inside and out. Social action was not dependent upon the volitional capacities and deliberate choices of the individual. It was neither individual initiative nor personal achievement that counted, but rather the fixed, predetermined nature of a given person and his ascribed privileges and duties based on birth. The notion of the modern democratic society, with its evolutionary and optimistic faith in the malleability of human nature and the possibility for free self-expression, had never been a visible element of Korean Confucian social theory. The belief in *La Loi naturelle* in Confucianism thus served as the basic philosophical justification for national patriotism.

Kwak Chongsŏk was a man with deep roots in the steadfast, conservative tradition of the philosophy of the primacy of principle (churi sŏl) and in the resilient traditional normative system. In his final years, he painfully realized that the Korea of his cultural and historical understanding had come to an end and that the country in which he would now spend the remainder of his life was an altered one under foreign domination. In the quotation above, one finds a beautiful expression of the spirit that fervently professes the primacy of principle in its last public stand. Kwak wanted nothing but heaven-endowed nature to prevail. Yet the broader social and political forces of his time quickly gained widespread support in spite of his unrelenting belief and commitment. Obstinately clinging to his faith in the primacy of principle out of defensive compulsion, he was symbolic of the modern destiny of the Korean neo-Confucian tradition.

Conclusion

The spirit of Confucian national consciousness that Kwak had embodied in his life was largely carried on by scholar-patriots who chose exile over living under Japanese rule and joined the Provisional Government in China or participated in various nationalist activities abroad. Among others, the life and thought of Kim Ch'angsuk, who epitomized this uncompromising spirit of Confucian national consciousness, deserves more serious study.[79] As imperial Japan stepped up programs for the assimilation of the Korean people from the late 1930s, the Confucian spirit of resistance took the forms of resisting Japan's pressure to change their surnames to Japanese forms, evading the conscription of Korean young men for military service, and opposing the rule that prohibited Koreans from wearing their traditional white costume.[80]

"Loyalty, patriotism, and national consciousness are ingredients in nationalism and precede it in time."[81] Nationalism grows out of these, as well as other ideas and conditions, but they alone do not constitute modern nationalism. In order to be loyal, patriotic members of their country had to cherish deeply their cultural heritage and be prepared to die for it rather than to see their way of life change—this was the limit of Korean Confucian national feeling, or "cultural nationalism."[82] Martin Buber once fittingly clarified the baffling variety of uses to which the term "nationalism" has been put, in this way:

> Being a people is simply like having eyes in one's head which are capable of seeing; being a nationality is like having learned to perceive their function and to understand their purpose; nationalism is like having diseased eyes and hence being constantly preoccupied with the fact of having eyes. A people is a phenomenon of life, nationality (which cannot exist without national feeling) is one of consciousness, nationalism is one of super-consciousness.[83]

Nationalism as superconsciousness should eventually involve an effort to cure the disease of the nation, but Korean Confucian intellectuals as a whole could not go beyond the reaffirmation of their "community of destiny and culture" to present workable solutions to cure the disease.

Major ideological strains in the climate of opinion of the 1910s and the ensuing decades included the ascendancy of such radical ideas as modern nationalism, communism, Christianity, the Western ideals of democracy and liberalism, nihilism; and, during World War II, even fascism developed in the wake of the breakdown of the traditional political and moral authority grounded in the unitary and elitist Confucian culture. Even Shinto was imposed upon the Korean people by imperial Japan as an essential part of its colonial assimilation programs. The Confucian morality, hierarchical society, and culture, which had been discredited, all came under increasing attack by the Japanese and by Korean modern intellectuals. There was no way back to the old tradition. The collapse of the old Korean state and society was now directly attributed to the fact that Confucianism had become morally bankrupt, ceremonious, and barren, losing its original, authentic moral "Way."[84]

After 1919, a flare of hope for national liberation and independence kept a sizable segment of Korean people going through a quarter-century of despair and suffering under the yoke of foreign bondage. Among a variety of alternative stratagems Koreans adopted for national independence were efforts to strengthen the nation, such as various educational endeavors, programs for economic enterprise to raise the standard of living and protect the native economic bases, and the publication of daily papers and magazines for popular education. The emergence of numerous organizations for intellectuals, youth, farmers, laborers, and women also meant a leap forward in reforming society for the Korean people.[85]

A generation that had been imbued with traditional Confucian beliefs in morality and society was followed by a new generation of nationalists, which included disillusioned cynics, liberal-minded, Westernized intellectuals, and the growing army of nihilistic and revolutionary Marxists. As a whole, however, the period from 1919 to 1945, the year that marked the liberation of Korea from Japan, did not produce any tangible political results or programs, and Korea's intellectual scene during this period was as sterile and discordant as the political scene. Korea was in desperate need of political leadership and spiritual force to unite the people. Sadly, there was no common ideology to unite and uphold the nation, giving it a sense of common purpose and destiny. At home and abroad, conflicting ideas and diverse social groups vied with each other, enabling the Japanese government-general to divide and rule their colonized people.[86] Liberated Korea after 1945 inherited this legacy of ideological, social, and political fragmentation. The division of Korea into North and South is only a more tragic upshot of this dissonance. After more than forty years of wandering in the wilderness, the problem of reintegrating and readjusting the fragmented society still remains unsolved.

The fundamental problem in Korean society today consists of a serious crisis of meaning. The task of moral, social, and political reintegration of society calls out for immediate attention. Korean society today is torn between persisting loyalty to the Confucian tradition and the strong challenges posed by the contemporary world. Efforts to use traditional virtues such as loyalty and filial piety to induce conformity and unquestioning obedience to superior authority, as with the New Community movement (*Saemaŭl undong*), National Ethic (*Kungmin yulli*), and the Education Charter (*Kyoyuk hŏnjang*), have often been at odds with the contemporary drift toward democracy. History, or the traditional persisting claims of Confucian culture—those beliefs and values associated with the network of consanguineous ties and obligations to which people are still emotionally attached—is in conflict with new values such as democracy and modern development. As Joseph Levenson aptly put it: "History and values are worlds apart, but men are drawn to both, with an emotional commitment to the first and an intellectual commitment to the second; they need to ask the two incompatible questions, and they yearn to be able to answer 'Mine' and 'true.'[87]

Today Korean people are faced with choices about the future direction of their society and the development of their national spirit. These choices must be made neither in a cultural vacuum nor as members of a universal humanity but on the basis of their own inherited cultural tradition. In the process of this intellectual choice between conflicting values, will they break with the historical claims of the Confucian tradition that has largely lost its value, or will they find a middle ground between old Korea and the new modern world? This is a larger problem that calls for another major study.

5

Growth and Limitations of Minjung Christianity in South Korea

Donald N. Clark

MINJUNG nationalism in general is a secular phenomenon in Korea. Nevertheless, religious communities are an important part of the movement, Catholics, Protestants, and even Buddhists being visible as minjung activists.[1] This chapter is about the Christian minjung community and the religious ideology it has developed as a call to action in the political and economic spheres. It is concerned in particular with what is called "Minjung Theology,"[2] its tenets and its development and overall place in the movement.

Minjung Christianity began in the 1960s as an expression of the concern of Korean Protestants with the plight of the dispossessed in South Korea. It was conceived more or less simultaneously with the movements of Protestants in other countries who were seeking ways to minister to the urban poor and of Catholics around the world seeking to practice the lessons of Vatican II. For the Catholics, such efforts were a response to Pope John XXIII's call for the church to realize its responsibility toward "those who are poor or in any way afflicted."[3] At Vatican II, the church declared its duty to pass moral judgment on political matters and to stand up for the right of workers to organize in quest of justice. Vatican II and the 1968 General Conference of the Latin American episcopacy (CELAM II) in Medellin, Colombia, set the tone for a much more activist Catholic church internationally. One well-known expression of this new emphasis was liberation theology, first articulated by the Peruvian scholar-priest Gustavo Gutierrez the year of the Medellin conference.[4] On the other side of the world, in South Korea, the Catholic church reexamined some of its positions and began working harder as a body to show solidarity with the dispossessed.

Korean Protestants likewise responded to the plight of poor people, but because of their fragmentation into numerous subdenominations and factions, their response was not as clearly focused. In time, however, the National Christian Council, influenced by social activists in the Presbyterian Church of Korea, developed programs and political positions on issues of social justice for farmers, industrial workers, and urban settlers.[5]

The Emergence of a Minjung Christianity in Korea

Historical Development

The Yushin era of the Park Chung Hee regime saw a series of episodes which forced varieties of minjung Christians to forge a community and develop a common ideology. One of the early incidents was the Easter sunrise service in 1973 on Namsan, when the Seoul Metropolitan Mission group was charged with plotting to overthrow the government because they displayed placards reading "The resurrection of Jesus Christ is the resurrection of democracy!" and other such political messages. Two leading churchmen were detained for trial, including the Reverend Pak Hyŏng-gyu, pastor of First Presbyterian Church in Seoul and destined to become one of the main actors in the Christian resistance. Hardly anyone took seriously the charges of subversion: it merely seemed like a case of "killing the chickens to scare the monkeys," and the government received even more criticism.

In 1974, however, came the case of the so-called People's Revolutionary Party (PRP), in which twenty-one men were charged with being a cell of North Korean agents fomenting student demonstrations on orders from North Korea. The defendants were the same group that had been charged with the same crime in 1964, in a case that had been bungled by government prosecutors. The second PRP case was the government's attempt to justify the mass arrests and summary trials of political dissidents taking place under the new Yushin constitution. Again, the charges seemed trumped up, and this time there was a powerful reaction from a variety of church leaders who were convinced of the men's innocence and wanted them freed. Support groups for families of the PRP prisoners were formed.[6] These, in turn, were harassed by the police and Korean Central Intelligence Agency, as were any others who protested the PRP case. In the eyes of the Park regime, defending the PRP was one of Kim Chiha's gravest transgressions.[7] In fact, the PRP case was so sensitive an issue to the Park regime that it led to the actual deportation of a foreign missionary, George Ogle, for abusing his status as a religious worker. Ogle, who had been annoying the regime by his strident assertions that the church must speak for the poor and disenfranchised in Korea and had helped organize the Urban Industrial Mission ministry, had called publicly for the release of the PRP members, "who have been sentenced to capital punishment without having committed any crimes or without clear evidence against them."[8] His deportation over the PRP matter was an indication of the regime's determination to press the issue;

and, in the end, eight of the men were executed—apparently to prove that dissent was tantamount to treason.

In the PRP case, all the elements of the confrontation between the South Korean state and minjung Christianity were apparent: the movement's ecumenism and identification with the poor against the state, along with its refusal to be intimidated and the state's determination to taint the movement with the label of "Communist" in an attempt to make labor advocacy itself a national security crime. In the midst of this, the National Council of Churches issued a statement decrying the imposition of dictatorship in South Korea, calling for broad resistance, and challenging Christians in particular to "renew our churches by deepening our theological thinking, by our clear stance and solidarity with the oppressed and poor, by the relevant proclamation of the gospel of the Messianic Kingdom, and by praying for our nation; and we should prepare ourselves for martyrdom, if necessary, as our forefathers did."[9]

This statement was to be the charter, in effect, for the Christian church in Korea to become involved in politics as a matter of faith in action. By this time, too, the term "minjung" was in use in connection with Christianity, and the evolution of minjung theology was under way.

Catholic Participation

Korean Catholics were relatively inactive in politics until the late 1950s, when their membership more than tripled in a period of only nine years.[10] In 1962, along with Vatican II, the Korean Catholic church was liberated from missionary control and Kim Suhwan became its first archbishop. In the early 1970s, prominent Catholic laymen became involved in the opposition—presidential candidate Kim Dae Jung (Kim Taejung) and poet Kim Chiha, to name two. Both of them suffered greatly and even came close to losing their lives during this time, and the church responded by creating networks of support for their families, in the process of which their fate became an issue of church concern.

The Catholic church itself became permanently identified with minjung Christianity on 1 March 1976 at the Myŏngdong Cathedral in Seoul, when a gathering of minjung leaders issued a manifesto opposing the Park regime at a mass celebrating the anniversary of the Samil Independence Movement of 1919. The manifesto, titled "Declaration of Democracy and National Salvation," automatically violated the president's emergency decree outlawing criticism of his regime. Its signers included Kim Dae Jung, former president Yun Posŏn, former foreign minister Chŏng Ilhyŏng, National Council of Churches secretary-general Kim Kwansŏk, the Christian human rights activist Yi U-jŏng, the great Quaker leader Ham Sŏkhŏn, and three who shortly emerged as primary theoreticians of minjung theology: Sŏ Namdong of Yonsei University, and An Pyŏngmu and Mun Tonghwan of Han'guk Theological Seminary.[11] From 1 March 1976 forward, all of them—even the aged

Yun Posŏn—were continually harassed by the Korean CIA. Several were more often in prison than not.

The Established Pattern

The pattern of Christian activism, sometimes on behalf of the downtrodden and sometimes simply protesting the government's actions, and the Park regime's repression in response to it, was repeated many times. The YH Incident, a labor action in 1979 in which the churches' Urban Industrial Mission (UIM) was involved, was a particularly nasty episode that cost the life of an organizer. Later, under the Chun Doo-Hwan (Chŏn Tuhwan) dictatorship, things grew still worse. Scores of opinion leaders in the media, churches, and universities—all of whom opposed Chun—were forced out of their jobs, and some were imprisoned.[12] Others were under virtual house arrest and forbidden to discuss politics with anyone.

Minjung Christianity, therefore, grew in the 1970s along with the rest of the minjung movement. In the process, Christians in the movement struggled to draw a connection between their faith and what was happening to them. As Sŏ Kwangsŏn, who was dismissed from his position as Dean at Ewha, writes:

> The "theology of minjung" is a creation of those Christians who were forced to reflect upon their Christian discipleship in basement interrogation rooms, in trials, facing court-martial tribunals, hearing the allegations of prosecutors, and in making their own final defense. They reflected on their Christian commitment in prison cells, in their letters from prison to families and friends, in their readings of books sent by friends all over the world, in their unemployment, in their stay at home under house arrest, while subject to a twenty-four-hour watch over their activities, and during visits with their friends.
> . . . [It is] a socio-political biography of Korean Christians in the 1970s.[13]

Eventually, the growing opposition in the 1980s rallied around this community of dismissed professors. It was not an easy time for them personally or professionally, and yet they coped. Professors preached; preachers wrote; reporters lectured. In spite of the restrictions, many found ways to travel and even to study abroad, where they enriched their ideas. Minjung theologians overseas sought international support and attention at conferences and raised funds to help support the families of the dismissed. It appears that interest from overseas in some of the cases helped to restrain the regime from even worse abuses of human rights.

Back in Korea, meanwhile, there were serious confrontations and disruptions within the Christian community. One of the best-known instances was the government's intervention in a congregational rift at the First Presbyterian (Che'il) Church in 1983–1985 over the outspoken ministry of Pastor Pak Hyŏnggyu. The government used plainclothesmen (read: hired thugs) and

Army Counter-Intelligence Corps (CIC) agents to evict the Reverend Pak from his own pulpit, leaving the building to a faction in the congregation which supported the Chun regime.[14] Pak and his followers thereafter took up the custom of holding Sunday services on the sidewalk in front of the Chungbu District Police Station in Cho-dong 2-ga, with Pak presiding when he is not in jail. The Che'il Church is the classic example of what is called a *hyŏnjang* (on the spot, ad hoc) church, a minjung Christian type of organization that represents a community of persons engaged in the struggle for justice. Other hyŏnjang churches are comprised of families of political prisoners and persons still on blacklists. An example of this is the Galilee Church, a community which began as a gathering of dismissed professors and reporters, former prisoners of conscience, and the families of political prisoners. The Galilee Church meets and acts out a defiant joy in their services:

> If asked how they bear all the troubles they confront on the way, they will say to you:
> "We have not chosen this. No one really did. We were all somehow pushed into this by God. As we walk along with other friends, however, we experience the spirit of minjung embracing us, enlightening us, and strengthening us. As we work together and pray together, we experience God living in our midst and we experience joy swelling within us. So we keep marching along believing that it is Christ who leads us, granting joy on the way."[15]

Participating Elements of the Church

Many elements of the Christian community participate today in social action activities that might be called expressions of the same spirit of minjung Christianity. There are many *koinonias*, groups which study issues and support each other like the Galilee Church. Youth koinonias include branches of the Korean Student Christian Federation and the Christian Ecumenical Youth Council. There are koinonias of university and seminary intellectuals. Catholic koinonia groups include the Priests' Corps for the Realization of Justice, the Catholic Young Workers Organization, the Catholic Farmers Association, and the Justice and Peace Commission. The Catholic diocese of Kwangju has been especially active since the 1980 Kwangju Massacre. Not all of these would call themselves "minjung theologians." But minjung theology has become an important subject in their discussions, as questions are raised about the relevance of orthodox Christian thought to the political and social realities of South Korea today.

Minjung Theology

Tenets

In the first place, minjung theology defines *the people* as the *subjects of history*—meaning that they ought to claim their function as the people who *shape* history rather than settle for being shaped *by* it. In other words, it is an activist ideology that challenges people to take their destiny into their own hands. This is a departure from traditional Korean Christianity, which has always encouraged believers to accept the history God has given them: that is, a kind of Christian fatalism. Minjung theology would not deny that God's will is what determines history; but it would add that God wants things to change and that Christian believers are the instruments of his will. They are therefore called to fight evil and to position themselves between oppressive political and economic structures and their victims—namely, the working poor of Korea's cities and villages.

So it is, in the jargon, a theology of praxis. It acts out its beliefs, which are shaped by experience. It draws its knowledge of God from the experience of the minjung—that is, all those who are excluded from privilege or are alienated in contemporary society—and stands with them against oppression in an unabashedly political way. They get their energy from *han*.[16] The four noble truths of Minjung Theology are: (1) that *han* comes from being victimized by oppressors; (2) oppressors oppress because of greed; (3) oppressors must cut *(tan)* their greed; and (4) when the oppressed finally succeed, they must cut their natural tendency to become greedy oppressors themselves. They must exorcise their natural envy of the powerful. This exorcism has to be performed by a messiah, and the messianic expectation in Minjung Theology taps a stream of Korean folk tradition (for example, in literature, in the *Chŏnggamnok*, in Tonghak teachings, and in shamanism generally.) In fact, *mudang* (shamans) are the role models for this kind of messiah-hood, for they share the pain of the minjung, listen to their problems, and try to dissolve the bitter han that afflicts them. As David Suh relates it:

> When Christianity was accepted by the Korean people and the Korean minjung, it was accepted within the mind-set of the Korean people and the Korean minjung. For the powerless minjung, the power of the . . . Holy Ghost is most respected and awed. To become a Christian is to believe in the power of the Holy Ghost, which is much more powerful than their shaman spirits. Korean Christians have made their Christian worship service more casual and freer than traditional Western-style worship. They sing loudly and well, like in a mudang *kut* [shamanistic rite]. There is a sense of joy in their service, and even the sense of restivity they experience in the mudang kut. They share their sorrows, suffering and pains as the poor and deprived and oppressed, and they also share a sense of liberation and salvation in the act of sharing. The mudang pathos is embodied in Christian worship and Christian pastoral care. A young Korean Presbyterian pastor who works in a Seoul slum church once remarked that he is not ashamed of being called a "Christian mudang." He would be with the people, suffering together with them in the midst of their everyday existence and sharing their tears and laughter. He would exorcise the evil in people and the evil spirits in the politics of society, to set free the oppressed and deprived, the poor and the sick.[17]

The Biblical Basis

If minjung theology were merely Korean shamanism in Christian dress, it might be dismissed as an interesting heresy. Indeed, some orthodox Catholics and Protestants do precisely that. But minjung theology claims roots in the Bible. As an ideology of an afflicted people, it draws on the Old Testament experience of the children of Israel. One of the favorite traditional stories of Korean Christians under Japanese rule was the liberation of the Israelites from captivity in Egypt, their suffering during forty years of wandering in the desert, and their deliverance into the Promised Land. It was the fate of the "Israelite" minjung to suffer, and yet they remained close to God and were eventually saved. This was very comforting in the 1920s and 1930s.[18] "Korean Christians understood the story of Moses not only as a literal event in the history of Israel but as a literal event in the history of the oppressed people of Korea."[19] The subsequent exodus from North Korea repeats this experience of the Old Testament, acted out in Korean history, and helps to explain the charismatic appeal of such North Korean refugee figures as Han Kyŏngjik.[20]

Minjung theology speaks to this experience of Korean Christianity. God permitted the Hebrews to be oppressed, but when they finally *took action*, he delivered them. Later on, in the New Testament, when the children of Israel were once again under the domination of Rome, Jesus, a carpenter and man of the minjung who was surrounded by han-ridden people, lived a life and died a death expressive of tan through which others were liberated. In the end, in the resurrection, he triumphed over death itself.

An Pyŏngmu believes that early Christian churches took the form of communities of Jesus' minjung expecting him to liberate them, and that the church today must recover this original expectation. As in ancient Israel, God has been working in Korean history and has a special concern for his children—in this case, victims and underdogs. To believe otherwise is to deny Christianity's relevance to Korea, as Korean history *is* such an obvious parallel history of oppressors and underdogs. When you merge Christianity and Korean history, the minjung theologians argue, you *necessarily* produce an ideology of liberation, "not only from physical slavery or suffering, but also from exploitation for political and economic purposes."[21]

Religious Nationalism and Kijang Presbyterianism

The history of Protestant Christianity in Korea reveals continuous threads of religious nationalism, of which the identification with the Israelites in Egypt is but one example. It is commonly understood that Korean Christians sometimes used membership in the Christian church as a form of political dissent during the Japanese colonial period. What is less well known is that there also developed within the church a resistance against missionary control and the dictation of Korean theology by foreigners. This was particularly

acute in the case of the Presbyterians, by far the majority among Protestants, whose seminary in Pyŏngyang was a factory for the kind of conservative theology to which minjung theologians now object.[22] In fact, the
godfather of minjung theology, Kim Chejun, broke away and founded his
own seminary in 1940 expressly in order to become liberated from the baleful influence of conservative Presbyterianism. One early form of religious
nationalism, therefore, was a distancing from foreign missionary influence,
something that continues in the minjung theology tradition today.

In the 1930s, when Kim Chejun began objecting to the conservative
orientation of his church, he was under the influence of Canadian missionaries, theological liberals who tended to be less certain on the issues of salva-
tion-by-grace as well as several other theological points of contention. The
Presbyterian seminary, however, was dominated by American conservatives
from a denomination in the United States that had just been through a
bruising theological war between social gospellers and conservatives. The
conservatives, who were premillenarian and very much concerned with the
spiritual future, took the Bible completely literally and gave no credit to
human intelligence or free will. Everything that happened was God's will,
they said, and man's place was only to try harder to understand God, not to
change what he willed. Conservatives believed in salvation by grace; that is,
there is nothing a person can do to *earn* salvation. This rules out human will
or action as a means to salvation. Certainly good works were the mark of a
godly life, but one could earn nothing by them. A Christian could be in politics as an earthly calling, but nothing theological could be achieved by political activity. The realms were separate, and a Christian should not confuse
them.

The right–left rift in American religion in the 1920s is a fascinating study
in American sociology, but what concerns us here is that the Korea Mission
of the Presbyterian Church U.S.A., were "pre-mils," and that they scrupu-
lously threw the social gospel baby out with the modernist bathwater. As
David Suh explains it: "The attempt of the missionaries was to spiritualize
the Christian message and thus to depoliticize and even denationalize
Korean Christianity. . . . The revival meetings set the subsequent tone of
Christianity in Korea as emotional, conservative, individualistic, and otherworldly." But then—naturally, unavoidably—this theology got translated,
until "today, the average churchgoer follows the fetishistic belief that Christianity is a mere religion for material success in this world and for spiritual
success in the other world. . . . Such a religion also has its roots in Korean
shamanism."[23]

The trouble with this religious messianism is that, in its concern with the
next life, it acquiesces in the oppression of the here and now. Minjung theology calls people to a prophetic witness against injustice, not to subservience
to unjust authority; and inasmuch as the missionaries taught subservience,[24]
they anesthetized the Korean church's impulse to struggle in the world.[25] By
the 1970s, when the need for activism was so obvious, the conservatives'

search for God's will in the present seemed like an abdication of social responsibility. Many young Christians refused to believe that their calling was to accept repression and exploitation and call it the will of God.

Kim Chejun's strain of Presbyterianism today is headquartered in the Han'guk Theological Seminary, where the brothers Mun Ikhwan and Mun Tonghwan have been on the faculty. The Mun brothers are protégés of Kim Chejun and have kept his vision alive in Korea through the years of advocacy and struggle. Although both of them were educated in the West and have many friends in Western church circles and in the missionary community in Korea, when it comes to practice they insist that it is time for the Korean church to confront the situation directly as a mature church, without the restraints of foreign ties. In short, they have taken Kim Chejun's vision a step further, putting their denomination (the Presbyterian Church in the R.O.K./ *Kidokkyo changnohoe,* or *kijang,* for short) squarely in the minjung movement and becoming prime exponents of minjung theology.

Minjung Christianity: Two Modes of Expression

The Celebration of Korean Roots in Ritual

University students in the minjung movement love to act out ethnic themes in music, dance, and drama. No matter what the season at Yonsei, for example, there are students in the woods by the amphitheater practicing *nongak* rhythms on the *changgo* and clanging cymbals and gongs while others practice farmers' dances, often in costume. When there are demonstrations on the campus, they are often led by bands of nongak musicians and dancers carrying banners which paraphrase the banners of the farmers' dance: "Democracy is the root of all!" and the like.

Sometimes, at student rallies, the banners identify the demonstrators by groups, and groups take part in the rallies by singing and performing rituals. Yonsei, ostensibly a Christian university, is a main venue for rallies because of its relatively independent administration, but more, perhaps, because of its five thousand-seat amphitheater. There, in the arena (and sometimes in front of the library), incense is burned and sacrifices offered in ceremonies saturated with shamanist symbols. As the students exorcise the evils they oppose in rituals that would shock the school's missionary founders, there are also Christian prayers offered by Christian student groups in the crowd. Thus the ritual exorcism of the minjung movement political demonstration, which coincides with the *mudang kut* mode, also coincides with Christian supplication and amounts to an expression, or acting out, of minjung theology.

Acting has always been an important mode of expression in Korea. In the 1980s it became wildly popular as part of the minjung movement. Whether it is street theater on Taehang-no or dangerous satires on little stages in cafes in Sinch'on, the themes of han and resistance are always there.

Mask dances are part of this mode of expression. Having evolved from harvest ceremonies into village entertainments poking fun at the rich and powerful, mask dances and mask plays are Korea's favorite form of social satire, and the minjung movement has taken up the genre with gusto. Drums, gongs, cymbals, and banners are all part of it. It is noisy and fun and deliciously vulgar. Through humor, the minjung transcend their suffering and even laugh at themselves.

What does this have to do with Christian theology? Seoul National University anthropologist Kim Kwangok points out that "ritual disguise" is necessary in religion because the already established religious communities are under the control of the state and people have to find other ways to express their ideological orientation.[26] Minjung theologian Hyŏn Yŏnghak argues that if people really *are* the subjects of history, then their emotional expressions are revelations of religious truths.[27] In the messages of han and liberation which well up in the performance of the mask dance, one does discern the message of the Christian gospel; and in the acting-out of roles in the theater, the minjung celebrate their community and rehearse the performance of God's will.

Minjung Christianity in Action: The Yongdŭngp'o UIM

If the rituals of demonstrations and mask dances are symbolic, the work of the staff of the Urban Industrial Mission is decidedly real. UIM was founded in 1960 by a group of Methodist ministers, along with the above-mentioned Methodist missionary George Ogle, to take the Christian message into Korea's rapidly proliferating factories.[28] It soon became clear that the most urgent need of the workers was some form of mediation with their employers and an amelioration of the desperate conditions in which they were forced to work. Thus, by 1970, Urban Industrial Mission had taken on a labor advocacy function.[29] This was taken as an affront by the factory owners and managers and by the South Korean government, which was staking its future on the willingness of docile workers to continue working in abysmal conditions for pitiful wages. In time, UIM was made part of the National Christian Council's social welfare agenda, sheltered to a degree by the size of the NCC; but UIM workers and their families and associates were continually harassed and often arrested, interrogated, and even tortured.[30]

The periodic arrests of their leaders and the eventual cutting off of funds from many of the mainstream churches in the early 1980s left the small UIM staff to fend for itself, being funded by the workers themselves, a few ad hoc church groups, and overseas friends. Yet the need for the organization grew, if anything, more acute. Anyone visiting a Korean factory district would soon see why, like this American:

> We walked by a cutlery factory and . . . [the UIM worker] told a story about how the accident rate is so high that new employees are told that a

bucket full of fingers leaves the factory each month. "I used to work in a factory like that," he added.

I jokingly said, "Well, let me see how many fingers *you* have!" and he held up nine.[31]

In fact, with some of the worst accident rates, hours, pay scales, and labor relations systems in the world, the factories of the industrial districts of Yongdŭngp'o, Kuro, and Inch'ŏn are a necessary testing ground for minjung Christianity. The worst problem, according to UIM, is that the workers have come to accept the way they are treated, to feel that they deserve nothing better than to be exploited and treated like animals or the machines they work with, and to internalize the values of their oppressors.[32]

The task, therefore, is to encourage workers to rediscover their dignity by giving them a hearing; getting them together; organizing them into credit unions and classes for high-school equivalency education; teaching guitar, yoga, and handicrafts; lending them books; and finding them cheap second-hand clothes to buy. Before UIM lost its denominational funding as a result of governmental pressure in 1982, it managed to build a community center in Yongdŭngp'o. Here it still holds Sunday services, and out of a little room in the basement publishes a weekly magazine of articles, poems, cartoons, newspaper clippings, and notices of UIM activities. The center conducts a free medical and dental clinic on weekends. In the UIM basement, there are classes in mask dances and traditional Korean music and songs. In between activities, there are endless bull sessions; and after hours the UIM workers go out drinking with the workers, listen to them, laugh and cry and argue with them, and in general "give body to the news of Jesus Christ in this part of Korean society."[33]

The next step is to expand to other cities, which UIM has done, and to help workers negotiate with their employers. This much—in the 1980s when there was not a single free trade union in Korea—was enough to label UIM as "the spearhead of antigovernment activity." The Chun Doo-Hwan dictatorship was successful in isolating UIM from the mainstream churches. The police still monitor the UIM office, phone, and mail, and armed riot police in green buses are never far away. Visitors to the UIM building are questioned. Workers have been fired for going there. Meetings, worship services, and even weddings of UIM members have been harassed by plain-clothesmen. UIM's history has been built in anguish, yet it is the quint-essential praxis of minjung theology, as well as the practical application of the message of the traditional Korean mask dance.

Minjung Christianity and Latin American Liberation Theology

Liberation theology is an activist religious movement which originated in Latin America in the sixties and seventies. As William R. Garrett has written, "It represents a melange of Christian religious precepts fused with

social scientific categories of analysis, especially as these constructs appropriated from the social sciences have been understood within the Latin
American context."[34] In Latin America, where liberation theology has been
linked with Marxism because of the tendency of Latin Americans to conflate
Marxist and social science categories, the agenda of liberation theology typically carries overtones of anti-imperialism and antidependency, reacting
against the way in which the world economy abuses Latin Americans and
creates vast underclasses among them. Liberation theology freely borrows
certain methodological pointers from Marxism; for example, the importance
of economic factors, attention to class struggle, and the power of ideology—
in this case including religion.[35] This orientation, of course, causes conservative power structures in Latin America, including the hierarchy of the Catholic church, to oppose it. In an attempt to stigmatize it, critics call liberation
theology Marxist,[36] and non-Marxists associated with liberation theology are
forever having to explain the connection. Their lodestar is Matthew 23:10,
"You have only one master, the Christ." But not everyone is convinced that
they do not have a second master, Marx, as well.

Korean Christians in the minjung movement are well aware of liberation
theology,[37] but as citizens of a rigidly anticommunist state they cannot admit
any association with it.[38] Mun Tonghwan claims that liberation theology is
simply irrelevant in Korea and that the Korean minjung can take the necessary interpretations directly from the Bible.[39] As propounded by Ham
Sŏkhŏn and others, an important difference is in the objectives of the two
groups: in Marxism the goal is a dictatorship of the proletariat; in minjung
theology the goal is to abolish structures that oppress and to eliminate,
specifically, the greed and envy that lead to new cycles of dictatorship—and
that includes a dictatorship of their own.[40]

This does not mean that the minjung theologians think they should be
isolated from other liberation movements. As Mun Tonghwan says, Koreans
must compare their experience with the experience of minjungs in other
parts of the world and in other periods of human history; and it is interesting
to note that, in the literature on liberation theology, the Korean minjung
variant is often discussed and Korean minjung theologians often are invited
to participate in conferences on the worldwide ideologies of liberation.

Minjung Christianity and the Mainstream Churches

Relations with the Catholic Church

Although the Korean Catholic Church identifies with the movement for
democracy and human rights in Korea, a distinction has to be drawn
between this identification and support for minjung theology. The church
hierarchy has its own version of social concern and does not take easily to
radical reinterpretations of the gospel in Korea any more than it suffers liberation theology in Latin America. Rather, the high visibility of Catholics
derives from the cast of characters such as Cardinal Stephen Kim Suhwan,

presidential candidate Kim Dae Jung, and a host of lay and religious activists who practice minjung theology but do not discuss it in those terms. Not surprisingly, the hierarchy of the Korean Catholic church will have nothing to do with minjung theology; the discussion is generated mainly by the Protestants. However, Catholics as individuals are highly visible in its practice. In the 1970s, Daniel Chi Haksun, Bishop of Wŏnju, issued a "Declaration of Conscience" against the Park regime and suffered imprisonment. In the early 1980s, Father Ch'oe Kisik of Wŏnju was arrested for sheltering students involved in the Kwangju uprising and massacre (1980) and the Pusan USIS bombing (1982). Through the 1980s, Catholic groups such as Korean Catholic Priests' Association for Justice (CPAJ), the Catholic Farmers Association, the publishers of the Catholic weekly newspaper *P'yŏnghwa sinmun,* and the Korean Catholic Student Council all expressed the church's concern with human rights.

In 1984 and again in 1989, Pope John Paul II visited Korea and spoke eloquently for human rights in light of the gospel. In the months leading up to the democracy movement of June 1987 in Korea, Cardinal Kim Suhwan repeatedly delivered messages directly denouncing the Chun regime.[41] And in 1989 the church was indirectly involved in two of the illegal visits with North Korea: (1) when National Assemblyman Sŏ Kyŏngwŏn confessed to Cardinal Kim that he had broken the law by going to North Korea, and Cardinal Kim kept it to himself; and (2) in the Im Sugyŏng case, where she was escorted back across the demarcation line by Father Mun Kyuhyŏn, representing the CPAJ. These developments make it clear that, with or without minjung theology, the Korean Catholic Church will continue to occupy a front rank in the struggle for human rights in South Korea.

It may be slightly perplexing, however, to note that the Catholic church's theological position on social activism comes from a different source than minjung theology. Indeed, the church in Korea is an authoritarian structure itself, as religious women will be the first to point out,[42] and it is not about to undermine the principles of hierarchy, seniority, and male domination. Nor were the nuns who lined up outside Myŏngdong Cathedral to face the police in June 1987 acting out of commitment to the movement: they were ordered into the street to protect the cathedral from an invasion by gas-bomb-throwing riot troops.[43] Catholics, it should be emphasized, participate in the movement for their own reasons.

These reasons may be found in Catholic documents and declarations from the 1980s. In a 1985 definition of its relation to society in light of its bicentennial, the church set forth certain principles for action toward the community, family, labor, farmers, and so on. Here is part of the section on labor:

> The Church must give voice to the plea of the isolated neighbor and those suffering for justice and in silence. This can only be achieved by a concerted effort. The characteristics of labor problems in Korea are based on

the poor conditions forced on the laborers themselves, hours of labor, poor wages, poor circumstances of work and laborers' strength.

The labor problems are connected with radical and continual development of technology in Korea and the seriousness of the problems is constantly increasing. It is necessary that the ministry of the Church corresponds to the signs of the times. Above all the most important thing is that laborers can banish the unjust treatment they receive themselves and be helped to elevate their position in the economic realm of society. The church must make available to them training and the resources for their development.[44]

The Urban Industrial Mission would hardly have said it differently. But the difference is that the Catholics' efforts remain strictly under the control of the church, and the religious workers serving in the labor ministry are subject to church discipline. From the point of view of the church hierarchy, social and political activism is strictly a matter for the laity, "a responsibility of Christians insofar as they are citizens of the earthly country."[45]

Relations with the Major Protestant Denominations

As mentioned above, because the largest Protestant denominations are so theologically and politically conservative, they keep a wary distance from the theological speculations of the minjung theologians. They are, however, committed to the mission of service and social welfare and so support such organizations as UIM in principle. But in practice, when the rhetoric tends toward themes of class struggle and confrontation with the government, they become uncomfortable and the support melts away. Minjung Protestants, therefore, have learned not to expect mass support from their denominations. The major exception is the Presbyterian Church in the R.O.K., which has always been the liberal wing of the Presbyterians.

To the right of the mainstream Presbyterian and Methodist denominations in Korea are the fundamentalist evangelicals who are allied with the international theological community, which eschews the World Council of Churches as a communist front and concentrates on ecstatic experiences of conversion. Of these, the most commonly remarked-upon is the half-million-member Yoido Full Gospel Church, whose pastor, Paul Cho, decries minjung theology as a "false teaching." Instead of the "new theology," he says, Korea needs the Holy Spirit,[46] and Korean Christians should not allow themselves to be diverted by it into a preoccupation with politics. In fact, minjung Christianity and the Pentecostal faith of Paul Cho are both concerned with the here and now, but in different ways. Minjung Christians stress the material conditions of the world and the need to change them, whereas Cho stresses the material blessings with which God rewards the faithful. One cannot say that Cho is not involved in social action, for his is a significant social movement with a considerable social welfare component. But the political and economic orientation is entirely different. To the fundamentalists, "godless, atheistic World Communism" is the devil incarnate. This alone makes the anticommunist regime of South Korea a godly force. Paul Cho teaches that Koreans are a chosen people, and that the growing prosperity of Korea is proof that God loves Korea the way it is. Cho's thousands of bourgeois members are on the verge of making it themselves, and his juxtaposition of God and Mammon is most reassuring. Their devotion and obedience may be the extra ingredient in the formula for success; and so they follow devotedly and obey Cho and the state. To oppose or criticize church *or* state would be dangerous morally as well as politically. This is diametrically opposite to the mind-set of minjung theology, which *mandates* opposition. As minjung theologian Mun Hŭisŏk [Cyris Moon] explains it:

> Presently, there is real tension in the Korean churches between two types of Christians. One group is still holding on to the fundamentalistic belief of Christian life, continuing the "Egyptian Captivity" of the years between 1920 and 1945. While these Christians are not interested in the social and political affairs of life, they are enthusiastically evangelistic. They fervently believe in prayers and hold daylight prayer meetings daily. Afterwards, they fast and listen to high pressure preaching. Their prayers are filled with personal petitions and requests for the conversion of relatives. . . .
>
> It appears that the main reason these Christians still cling to their beliefs is that many of them are all too aware of the risk involved in a struggle for freedom. . . . However, one of the major criticisms of these churches is directed at their naive understanding of the Christian truth, . . . [for] they have failed to fully understand the meaning of [the principle of separation of church and state], neglecting their duty to prophesy and follow the exemplary life of Jesus Christ.[47]

In short, there is no love lost between minjung Christians and the practitioners of the evangelical gospel in South Korea. They come from the same background, but their visions are very different.

The Limitations of Minjung Theology

Once the stories of the minjung have been told, the han of the minjung has been represented in ritual, and action has been taken to stand with the minjung, what makes minjung theology a theology? Or perhaps the question ought to be: what makes minjung Christianity Christian?

This is not merely a word game. Sŏ Namdong, one of the founding fathers of minjung theology, was troubled by its material emphasis, especially when interpreted as a Korean analogue of liberation theology. "Liberation Theology," he wrote, "is concerned with the struggle against unjust political and economic systems and structures. . . . In other words, [it works] at the level of the infra-structure and [deals] with material issues. . . . For me, however, the most important task of theology is to deal with the relationship between the revelation of God and the social and material infra-structure."[48]

Of all the minjung theologians, it was Sŏ Namdong who seems to have expressed the most concern for keeping the ideology in touch with basic Christianity, putting the practice of minjung theology clearly in terms of *acting out* the life and suffering of Jesus, with martyrdom as one possible consequence: "The task for Korean minjung theology is to testify that in the Mission of God in Korea there is a confluence of the minjung tradition in Christianity and the Korean minjung tradition. It is to participate and interpret theologically the events which we consider to be God's intervention in history and the work of the Holy Spirit. [The minjung theological tradition] . . . asserts that I imitate the life of Jesus and repeat in my life the events of the life of Jesus."[49]

Professor Sŏ's concern, therefore, was that Christians using minjung theology as the religious basis for political action bear in mind the sacrifice implied by the history of both the Jews and the Koreans, and to act fearlessly, then, as extensions of Christ's own life. He taught that it is a matter of the spirit in which one engages in Christian political action that distinguishes it from Marxism or simple rebellion against oppression.

Minjung theology automatically places its practitioners in a political role. Its very essence is conflict and struggle against authority. For this reason its political program seems a bit naive. Minjung thinkers look forward to the day when wielders of power will not be greedy, and if they ever take power themselves, they pray that they will be cleansed of the human tendency for revenge through *tan*. History, however, cautions us to be skeptical, for it gives us little reason to believe that ideologues of *any* kind can so easily let bygones be bygones. Indeed, Christian ideologues have been some of the bloodiest butchers in history. The level of anger in the Korean minjung movement today is reason enough to wonder whether the genuinely nonviolent Christians in the movement might not be pushed aside in favor of activists seeking to be the "sword of the Lord." Minjung Christians are to be admired for their commitment, courage, and sheer capacity to survive so much abuse and degradation with their humanity intact. This alone is eloquent proof of the power of the Christian gospel as they see it. History, however, should make us wary of their zeal.

The Challenges Facing Minjung Theology

In order for minjung theology to grow, it needs a broader definition. The work of UIM in the factory districts of southwestern Seoul has earned its workers and their commitment a good reputation. The stress on Korean tradition has earned it a following among students, who are looking for affirmation and an end to the years of what is seen as *sadaejuŭi* (toadyism) under Japanese and American imperialism. But these are products of an "anti" ideology. To succeed in the long run, minjung theology must develop the positive aspects of faith for the individual. The spectacular success of the Pentecostals' going into neighborhoods to listen to and speak to families and show concern for people where they live (not to mention the continuing success of shamanism as a response to the individual needs of ordinary people) suggests that minjung Christianity needs to transcend its class-struggle bias and speak to the middle class, who, after all, are no less Koreans and, according to some definitions, no less part of the minjung. This will both validate its message and increase its power.

Although Koreans hardly lack for missionary zeal in their churches, it usually takes the form of the "Chosen Koreans" teaching the rest of the "Third World" how to create a church growth explosion. In the din of self-congratulation for its growth and success, the Korean Christian mainstream does not seem to listen very well to the experience of other peoples. This lack of interest in (really ignorance of) the wider world spills over into minjung Christianity and can stunt the capacity of minjung theology to identify with and empower the minjung of other countries. It might be useful, for example, to embrace liberation theology—both to learn about the minjung of Latin America and to assist in the development of a worldwide minjung theology. Yet the student wing in particular is so obsessed with uniquely Korean themes that it is difficult to generate much interest in the experience of other minjungs. Older leaders in the movement should know better than to be so self-absorbed. They should do more to understand and explain those features which they share with the neighboring minjung in China (and—yes—North Korea, Japan, and the Soviet Union), as well as the classic "Third World" lands of Africa and Latin America. Without linking up with minjungs in other places, how can minjung theology claim to be anything more than a flash in the pan in South Korea?

Nevertheless, minjung theology has already done much to challenge the mainstream churches to examine their own social consciences. Moreover, in a culture which encourages conformity and orthodoxy (and is so bitterly hard on deviations), minjung theology's emphatic reinterpretation of the Christian gospel can serve as a model for "thinking about the same things differently." In the fourth of its "four noble truths," that Christians should exercise power with forgiveness and toleration, it might help to heal the endless hurt that comes from theological hairsplitting in South Korea and, as Korea approaches the issue of reunification and reconciliation with the north, to provide a new fund of moral ideas to reshape the future Korean state.

6

The Minjung Culture Movement and the Construction of Popular Culture in Korea

Choi Chungmoo

> I am yet a trainee
> I want to drive a sewing machine
> Sitting at a sewing machine
> With a general's proud face
> . . . I want to sew together my torn life
> Riding a sewing machine
> With the dream to sew together
> All that are divided in the world. . . .
>
> —Pak Nohae,
> *Nodongŭi Saebyŏk* (The dawn of labor)

> To articulate the past historically does not mean to recognize it "the way it really was." It means to seize hold of a memory as it flashes up at a moment of danger. . . . In every era the attempt must be made anew to wrest tradition away from a conformism that is about to overpower it.
>
> —Walter Benjamin, *Illuminations*

National Unification and Minjung Culture

The preparation of this volume on Korea's minjung nationalism coincided with one of the most dramatic moments in recent world history, the massive counterrevolution in Eastern Europe where, from Poland to Romania, socialism was effectively challenged. As a result of the changes there, the major strongholds of socialism are now found in the Third World. In addition, the unification of Germany left Korea as the only divided country, and nationalism in Korea focuses intensely on the unification issue.

Korean minjung nationalists hold that the incorporation of multiple nations into a state with artificial borders, such as India, South Africa, and the former Soviet Union, is the consequence of some form of colonialism. Although the national division of Korea runs counter to the arbitrary incorporation in these countries, to the eyes of minjung nationalists, national unification is coterminous with decolonization. Their discourse contextualizes Korean unification in this sense of world history and attempts to overcome the division of a people with a common culture and history. It aims to fulfill the will of the people. Minjung nationalism resists blatant political negotiations motivated only by the interests of individual rulers, political parties, or even by the vested political and economic interests of powerful members of the international community. In fact, minjung nationalism denounces the authority of the two superpowers, which divided Korea against the will of the people, and their Cold War ideologies. It also denounces the absorption of other countries into satellite states and blocs. In other words, minjung nationalism resists any form of imperialism.

In this expanded sense, the unification effort of the minjung nationalist movement in South Korea is a struggle against a capitalistic world order that attempts to maintain the status quo. As such, the minjung discourse often criticizes capitalism and seeks alternative visions of society. Certain factions of the movement actively incorporate social democratic ideals into their vision and strategy of social reform. In the coming years, this discourse will add its contours to the global ideological map.

In the broad historical context of the Third World, the emergence of such a populist movement as the minjung, combined with nationalistic ideas and symbolic strategies, is part of the decolonization movement still in progress. In fact, for the last few years nationalism and the decolonization struggle have become ever more vibrant as the world's economic and political power centers have begun to shift.

Benedict Anderson, in his germinal work on the origin of nationalism, *Imagined Communities,* identifies two major types of nationalism, inspired by two opposite motivations: the imperialistic and the anticolonial. Anticolonial nationalism arose as a consequence of episodes of imperialistic nationalism, itself a by-product of European capitalism. However, Anderson's study of anticolonial nationalism ends with the nationalist movements led by what Franz Fanon labels the "national bourgeoisie" and overlooks the grass-roots populist movements. Franz Fanon contends that the national bourgeoisie identify with the decadent bourgeoisie of the imperialist West and with the allegedly most enlightened sector of the new state, thus actively transmitting and reproducing the colonial legacy.[1]

Song Kŏnho argues that such distorted bourgeois nationalism in Korea offered a basis for the political legitimacy of the Rhee regime (1948–1960). It enabled the regime to incorporate colonial administrators into its government while forcefully advocating an anti-Japanese policy. Song identifies another brand of nationalism—namely, militaristic, fascist nationalism. This nationalism justifies the colonial invasion by the weaker capitalists through oppression and terror. In some developing countries, Song contends, the specter of this fascist nationalism is once again raised, especially in conjunction with the development of state capitalism. By this, Song Kŏnho is obviously referring to nationalisms like that of the military government of Korea.

As an alternative to the nationalism endorsed by the Korean government,

Song Kŏnho advocates minjung nationalism.[2] This he offers as an antidote to cure a nation still suffering from the consequences of a fascist colonial experience and the liberation by military forces of a third party.

The minjung culture movement, the cultural practice of minjung nationalism, attempts to heal the nation's wounded history by reconstructing a popular culture common to all. Based on the strong bond of cultural commonality, they argue, national unification in the true sense can be achieved. Although Franz Fanon is not the only source of inspiration to the movement, his emphasis on the necessity of reconstructing national culture for the postcolonial nations has left a deep impression on the discourse of the minjung culture movement. Fanon believes that the reconstruction of national culture will not only awaken national consciousness but also provide a breeding ground for native sensibility. However, he warns against the danger of creating a culture by utilizing techniques and language borrowed from the dominant other. A culture so created, though meant to be national, emphasizes exoticism and makes its purveyor a stranger among his or her own people. In its stead, Fanon proposes a reinvigorated indigenous culture. Through participating in such a reactivated culture, Fanon argues, indigenes will grasp expressions and themes that are imbued with power: these will serve no longer as mere invocations but as the empowerment of the people. This, Fanon sees, is conducive to political struggle in both an actual and symbolic sense.

In this spirit, the minjung culture movement properly begins with the dismantling of the colonial discourse on indigenous culture. In Korea, that includes identifying the cultural nationalism of the 1920s as a hegemonic nationalism coopted by the colonial government.[3] Minjung nationalism criticizes the 1920s movement as a passive culturalism based on Western ideas of enlightenment, the subtext of which valorized Westernized Japanese culture and devalued Korean culture: it was a fetishization of the culture of the colonial masters. Minjung historians argue that the 1920s elite culturalists placed themselves in leadership positions and classified the Korean people as objects to be reconstructed. For instance, Yi Kwangsu's "Thesis on National Reconstruction" is considered to be a prime example of such distorted nationalism. But in this influential article, Yi Kwangsu failed to acknowledge the health of the Korean people's indigenous culture, which is created from the life-force of the people. Consequently, his argument was effectively coopted by the colonizers to justify racial denigration of the putatively inferior Korean culture. The minjung culture movement differentiates itself from 1920s culturalism in that it aims to reconstruct the people's culture not only as a way of creating a field of discourse but also as a social praxis.

In the early 1980s, Koryŏ University students produced a reader for its underground study group. It is one of many such texts and is titled "Towards the Establishment of a New Culture Movement." This text envisages the contours of the minjung culture movement for the coming years and states that the goals are not only to revive Korea's indigenous culture but also to incorporate it into everyday life, so that it will be reinstituted and disseminated in the life of the people. The advocates of the culture movement argue that cultural unity should precede national unity and, indeed, that the spiritual realm of national unity cannot be achieved without it. They hold the view that cultural unity is only possible when it is based on indigenous culture, which is thought to be shared by all members of the society. The polemics of the movement call for cultural resistance to foreign culture, especially the commercially marketed, mass-produced culture of the West.[4] This market-oriented foreign culture, it is argued, alienates those who do not have access to the education necessary to cultivate a taste for, and the skills to appreciate, the culture of those considered advanced (and therefore superior) in the enlightenment narrative of the West. This imported and imposed Western culture widened the expanding gap between classes and certainly between Koreans separated by the Thirty-Eighth Parallel. Based on this logic, the culture movement aspires to create a new culture that will appeal widely to all members of the collective, classless community and be conducive to the spiritual unity of the people from both sides of the divided nation. The minjung culture movement, as a political movement in this sense, hopes not only to open up a space for discourse but also to raise popular consciousness so that people's voices can become a critical part of the unification process. It signifies a specific interpretation of popular culture and therefore infers its empowerment, leading to national unification for the people and by the people.

The Construction of Popular Culture and the Carnivalesque

In the late 1980s, South Koreans became accustomed to loud percussion music as students danced to farmers' music, dressed in traditional farmers' white clothes, and battled with riot police. No longer alien to the postdivision Korean public was the mask-dance drama, with its characters who struggled against the exploitative company owners during labor strikes. Koreans also understood the singing of humorous protest songs by university women expressing their wish to marry muscular North Korean laborers in an attempt to conjure national unification. The general public now recognizes social and political protest staged in the form of reconstructed folk culture as a part of the minjung culture movement.

The students' use of popular culture as an instrument for raising critical consciousness or mobilizing the masses, as I shall describe shortly, resulted from their engagement with rural life through the *vnarod* movement of the 1960s. The 1960s vnarod movement took place following the student revolution that toppled the United States–dependent Rhee regime in 1960. The end of the Rhee regime could have signified the end of colonial dependence in Korean political culture. However, the student revolution was, according to Paik Nak-chung (Paek Nakch'ŏng),[5] an incomplete one in the sense that the actors were students with a limited power base. Consequently, the task of nation-building was transferred to the weak interim government, which allowed a military coup in 1961 and thereby perpetuated military rule in Korea until the present time.[6]

In the following years, the legacy of the student revolution continued in a number of campaigns for reform. Among them were national unification campaigns and a native land development (hyangt'o kaech'ŏk) movement. After the 1960 student revolution, the students identified the final goal of the revolution as national unification, a subject that had been taboo throughout the twelve years of the Rhee regime. The students' National Unification Union called for a South–North students' meeting. However, the campaign was quickly repressed as the 1961 military coup gained momentum, and its leaders were eventually sentenced to lengthy prison terms. In the ensuing period, instead of participating in state-building, the students devoted their energies to helping the farmers restore their life-style, which had been devastated economically and psychologically by severe colonial exploitation (1910–1945) and the Korean War (1950–1953).

When in 1963 it appeared that the military junta was preparing to install itself permanently, a number of Seoul National University students began staging shamanic rituals to revive the depleted spirit of the nation. When the military government announced a plan to normalize diplomatic relations between Korea and Japan, intellectuals concluded that this new relationship would bring in Japanese capital to finance the military government, which would help consolidate military rule in Korea—a foreshadowing of military dictatorship. Painful colonial memories aside, being troubled by the potential neocolonial exploitation implied in the conditions of the treaty, students and intellectuals poured out into the streets appealing to the public to halt this new form of colonization. A poet, Pak Tujin, protested this treaty in his poem "We cannot become slaves again." Journalist Song Kŏnho predicted that the treaty would legitimize Japan's economic invasion. Ecclesiastical leaders foresaw that the treaty would materialize Japan's neocolonialism in Korea.[7]

In this moment of crisis, a form of folk culture was invoked to awaken the critical consciousness of the popular masses. The now legendary Ritual to Invoke Native Land Consciousness (hyangt'o ŭisik ch'ohŏn kut)[8] was performed as a part of the students' massive protest rally at Seoul National University in May 1964. The "funeral of national democracy," the symbolic funeral of the military government, concluded the ritual, in which approximately fifteen hundred students participated.[9] Such symbolic funeral processions have since thrived as a part of the protest movement. The widely publicized shamanic ritual dance performed by Yi Aeju during the public funeral of Yi Han'yŏl in the spring of 1987 documents the flourishing tradition of protest ritual: Yi Han'yŏl died from a wound caused by a pepper-gas canister during student protests earlier that year. The protest ritual became a catalyst for a month-long mass mobilization of the people, which eventually brought about the demise of the Chun Doo-Hwan (Chŏn Tuhwan) regime.

Efforts to empower the oppressed and marginalized people thus began to take shape in the form of symbolic resistance. In 1967, a folk-theater research association was formed and named the Malttugi Association, after a character in the Pongsan mask-dance drama, who is both slave and antihero. In this style of theater, the slave, Malttugi, ridicules the ruling yangban class (aristocracy) with exuberant, bawdy puns and obscenities, using bodily substrata, and defames the very authority of the rulers. The lowly slave also profanes the sacrosanct Confucian morality of the yangban and exposes the falsity of their moral superiority, the foundation of the existing class hierarchy. By way of poetic transgression, the drama suggests the possible reversibility of the hierarchical social order. The members of the Malttugi Association selected this character to represent the critical characteristics of the organization and its subversive activities. Presumably the members of the Malttugi Association were not aware of Mikhail Bakhtin's work *Rabelais and His World.* However, we may note the similarity between Bakhtin's idea of carnivalesque inversion and the subversive notion embodied by the characters of mask-dance drama. Bakhtin argues that a folk festival (carnival) "celebrates temporary liberation from the prevailing truth of the established order. It marks the suspension of all hierarchical rank, privileges, norms and prohibitions. Carnival was the true feast of time, the feast of becoming, change and renewal. It was hostile to all that was immortalized and complete."[10]

In this light, naming the folk-theater group after Malttugi was a political statement pronouncing the group's revolutionary ambition: the inversion of the power hierarchy, the triumph of subordinated people over the dominant and oppressive rulers. This symbolic inversion suggested to the oppositional groups a populist, utopian vision, the culmination of the minjung movement. Cho Tongil, a former member of the Malttugi Association, took on the unprecedented task of analyzing this aesthetic principle of the mask-dance drama which offered a theoretical ground for the symbolic inversion. He located the power of the mask-dance drama in ribald humor and satire, which detonates the minjung's energy in confronting the dominant and subverting the hierarchical social order.[11] This aesthetic theory implies the revolutionary potential of counterhegemony and offers a subversive strategy for politically disenfranchised people.

Based on this revolutionary aesthetic of folk theater, the mask-dance drama became an icon of the people's resistant spirit and a mark of minjung identity. In less than five years—that is, by the early 1970s—most universities in Korea had mask-dance theater groups. However, at the beginning of the movement there were different layers of understanding of popular culture among the participants. When folk-theater groups were first formed on university campuses, the term "minjung" was not familiar to most Koreans. When a few literary critics used the term, the meaning of minjung was loosely defined as "popular masses." Members of the folk-theater groups had only a romantic notion of the folk and their culture. According to a former member of the mask-dance association, the members had a genuine sense of mission: to revive the lost art of the people and "return" the revived folk-culture items to the people, their true owners. Fulfilling this mission, the mask-dance association of Sogang University in Seoul did reconstruct the art of the Hahoe mask-dance ritual and returned it to the Hahoe villagers. This static view of culture leads to the total objectification of popular culture.

In fact, such objectification was initiated by the military junta in 1962 with the legislation of the Cultural Assets Conservation Act. Under this act, numerous items of lost popular tradition have been "excavated," preserved, and disseminated through mass media, public exhibitions, and performances. These items are designated Important Intangible Cultural Property.[12] Now the objectified Hahoe mask-dance ritual is permanently museumized as Important Intangible Cultural Property No. 69, as are many other genres of performing arts and rituals. In other words, in the early stage, the minjung movements displayed little awareness of the need to mount a critique of the dominant construction of culture. Rather, what inspired the students was the fact that the Japanese colonial administration had repressed Korea's cultural past through the discourse of modernization. It was precisely this criticism of colonial erasure that was the selling point of the cultural policy of the military government.

Nevertheless, in dancing the ancient dance, which was thought to have been "systematically erased" under colonial rule, the students were celebrating becoming-one-with-history and the establishment of the historical context. The language the students used in the performance pamphlets describes the discovery of self in history and conveys a rich symbolism. For example, dancing often signifies "breathing together with the ancestors," "reclaiming oneself by becoming one with the spirit of the ancestors," "discovery of oneself through the rhythm of the ancestors that is embodied." One pamphlet succinctly stated that performing mask-dance drama is an effort to discover one's identity. It says further that the student mask-dancers are responding to the call of history.

Resituating the present in the past was a technique of allegory some of the writers, such as Kim Chiha, chose to practice. In his lecture delivered at the Anti-Japanese Nationalist School (hangil minjok hakkyo) in 1970, Kim Chiha argued that the most important mission of young Korean poets was to discover the value of oral literature and adapt it creatively to express contemporary situations.[13] He particularly treasured humor and satire. His *Five*

Bandits (Ojŏk) appeared in the spring of 1970. His reconstruction of the traditional oral tale-singing genre, *p'ansori,* is one of many subversive cultural practices. In his *Five Bandits* and *The Rumor,* Kim Chiha restores not only the form and rhythm of p'ansori but also the technique of subversive satire. The genre arose in the eighteenth century with the growth of a market economy. This new genre celebrated the life of the common people and the ideology of the newly rising commoner and merchant classes over the declining gentry class.

In Kim Chiha's critique of the ruling bourgeoisie and their exclusive access to wealth under the protection of the military government's state capitalism, he effectively recaptures the mode of p'ansori production: the language of the illiterate commoners who were denied access to education in the privileged language, Chinese. In the *Five Bandits* and *The Rumor,* he dismantles and radically bastardizes Chinese characters to suit the sound of the Korean language in his carnivalesque critique of the bourgeoisie as ravenous, simian creatures. Indeed, Kim Chiha's pungent satirical writings awakened the critical consciousness of his readers, and his vision of social reform contributed to the ideology of the minjung movement. However, this temporary liberation was far from the remedy needed to deal with the realities of the time.

History and Magical Realism

The utopian project of treating a nation's wounds by reaffirming its cultural past inevitably involves recuperation and remembrance of a self-identifying history. To Koreans of the period after national division, colonial experiences are inscribed in their memory and embodied as habitus. Epistemologically, the minjung culture movement is a movement to liberate people from the psychology of the colonized, their self-pity and degradation, which Abdul JanMohammad refers to as a Manichean struggle to overcome their subalternity.[14] It is the ending of alienation by reconciliation with essence. It is "thinking the unthought," as Foucault describes it, and voicing the history of the subaltern[15] who has been silenced in the official state history. It also means liberating the domesticated (both by the state and the family) culture of the carnivalesque in general: the ribald humor, parody, grotesquerie, and so forth, which were incompatible with the official elite culture.

History thus remembered is, as I shall illustrate later, not the history "the way it really was." It is referential history for the purpose of redeeming the present. In this history, past is often surrealistically grafted onto the present. The supratemporality, or magical realism, in this strategic history is the very fountainhead of popular imagination about revolution.

Sin Tongyŏp's epic of the Tonghak Peasant War, *Kŭm River,* was one of the first steps taken to remember the unthought by unleashing the hushed-up memories of that war.[16] The poem begins with the poet's memory of a folk song, an agent of social memory:

When we were little
in the dusty village on a hill,
on the back of my grandmother,
my sister and I learned
the song of a blue bird.

Bird, bird, blue bird
dare not sit on the mungbean patch.
If the mungbean blossom falls,
the beancurd seller will leave in tears.
We did not know then
that this song would bring
the needle pusher to take us away.

The folk song, "Blue Bird," invokes the peasants' wish for the success of the Tonghak revolution, which is metaphorized in their wish for the mungbean blossom to seed. Mungbean was the nickname of the commander Chŏn Pongjun of the Tonghak Peasant Army. As metaphors are polysemic, this song also powerfully invokes the picture of economically and socially devastated rural communities at the threshold of Korea's modernization. The livelihood of the resourceless peasant, represented here as a beancurd seller, is so precarious that one crop failure may force him to leave his land.[17] Here Sin Tongyŏp also protests the oppression that silenced even a folk song about a peasant's simple wish to remain on his land. To the powerless peasants, the Tonghak War might have been the only chance to realize their simple dream. However, as the poem unfurls, we learn that the Peasant War was brutally trampled with a violence perpetrated by the firearms of foreign forces.

The poet sarcastically points out the fact that the memories of terror and violence were effectively repressed with the threat of a mere acupuncture needle. By extension, Sin Tongyŏp also protests against the contemporary Korean situation, in which people's voices are effectively muffled under the military rule fostered by the guarding presence of foreign forces.

In this poetic reconstruction of the Tonghak Peasant War, Sin Tongyŏp collapses linear time into a contemporality to make a point-by-point comparison between the realities of the 1890s and the 1960s and to suggest the imminence of a popular revolution. He interprets the Peasant War as a peasant's struggle against both the corrupted ruling class and the encroaching imperial powers. Sin Tongyŏp thus locates the Tonghak War in the history of world capitalism and defines the devastated situation of postdivision Korea as a repetition of that war.

In *Kŭm River*, the hero, Sin Hanŭi, is at once a day laborer in Seoul in the late 1960s and a warrior of the Tonghak War. The poetic strategy here, as mentioned above, is to equate the devastating economic and political conditions of the 1890s with those of the 1960s. Through the insertion of the poet's autobiography into the body of the epic, it is hinted that the hero Sin Hanŭi is also Sin Tongyŏp himself, who spiritually joins this utopian peasant war. The politics of Sin Tongyŏp's magical realism warns readers that Korea is under the threat of a new colonialism and prophesies the imminence of a people's revolution. Like the novels of some Third World writers, such as Cuba's Alejo Carpentier, Sin Tongyŏp's *Kŭm River* contains the revolutionary future in the memories of the past. The late Sin Tongyŏp, who grew up in colonized Korea and whose history had been denied and distorted, could only write an alternative history, with its own transgressive time. Sin Tongyŏp's magical realism and the new interpretation of Tonghak opened a new door to historical and social consciousness.

As Sin Tongyŏp had predicted, already in 1970 the disconcerting experiences of transnational capitalism and a subsequent labor-intensive industrialization had begun to permeate the everyday life of Koreans. In the fall of 1970, a young factory worker, Chŏn T'aeil, committed self-immolation, protesting subhuman working conditions and pleading for the workers' right to unionize. Chŏn was a laborer in the garment industry at the Peace Market in Seoul, and his numerous attempts to unionize the workers failed. In his will, Chŏn appealed to the students, his contemporaries who were the privileged recipients of a university education, to help the uneducated laborers unionize. This incident shocked and stirred many students, especially those who had been involved in the various types of student movements, and they began to reorient their movement and reexamine Korean realities. In the following decades, they actively involved themselves in the labor movement, raising critical consciousness, educating laborers, and organizing labor unions.

However, for the purpose of transforming Korean society, symbolic protest was no longer effective. It became increasingly apparent that mask-dance drama was a passive medium seeking a temporary liberation. A new kind of form was necessary—a form that would have more persuasive and lasting effect, a medium that would articulate the newly developing problems and point to the means to transform the realities. While Kim Chiha explored the possibility of revitalizing the revolutionary religion *Chŭngsan'gyo*, an offshoot of Tonghak,[18] Ch'ae Hŭiwan examined the historical background of the mask-dance drama and developed Kim Chiha's idea of *madang*, a courtyard or a space within the wall around the house. However, in the farming community, *madang* also means a shared space where people carry out communal activities (*ture*), such as harvesting. According to Ch'ae, the very root of the mask-dance drama during the precapitalist period lies in the collective activities of ture. It was at this madang that the mask-dance drama and the shamanic ritual festivals had been performed for the well-being of the community. This was the space where tenant farmers communally harvested, but their year's work was ruthlessly taken away by the landowners, mostly of the ruling class, the yangban. There, it is imagined, the collective will to struggle arose and solidarity was attained. In an expanded sense, the communal ritual-festival is coterminous with the people's struggle against the ruling class. The landowners connived at and even helped finance the festival to ease farmers' discontent and thus rule them more effectively.[19] In this sense, the struggle between the ruling class and the oppressed cannot be seen as black-and-white. The complexity of resistance can be detected at every level of practice, as was implied in the case of the Cultural Assets Conservation Act and the students' reconstruction of popular performing genres. Nevertheless, this complexity does further revolutionary imagination.

Kim Yŏlgyu had argued that during the shamanic ritual-festival, community members experience shared ecstasy;[20] following this idea, Ch'ae Hŭiwan asserted that, through this collective ecstasy *(chiptan sinmyŏng)*, members of the community achieve not only a sense of communal solidarity but also the energy to struggle together against the exploitative ruling class.[21] In his reading of the communal space, we detect the notion of collective activity and collective unity *(kongdong ch'e)*, which was later developed into the key word for national unification, national unity: *minjok kongdong ch'e.*

In this communal sense of the word "madang," Kim Chiha created a new drama genre, *madangguk,* adapting the aesthetic principle of mask-dance theater. The polyphonic open structure of the mask-dance theater rather than a linear narrative structure, and the incorporation of shamanic ritual, are two of the crucial elements of madangguk. These ritual techniques allow the theater to function as an open forum anticipating audience participation and communication. Unfortunately, a number of Kim Chiha's madangguk, which problematized various social and political issues, were either performed underground or banned from public appearances until 1980.

The introduction of the term "madang" demarcates the beginning of a theoretical development in the minjung culture movement. By constructing madangguk, Kim Chiha poses a critical question: where is the madang in today's Korean life? He rhetorically proposes that the minjung culture movement should turn to history to reread contemporary reality.

In an article "From Theater [*madangguk*] to Ritual [*madang kut*]," Ch'ae Hŭiwan and Im Chint'aek suggest that the future madangguk must turn to ritual enactment to realize collective life. The authors argue that by transforming theater into a ritual act, the actors and the audience together share ecstatic moments and experience oneness with each other.[22] A ritual presupposes reconciliation and transformation. Based on this assumption, the ritual that Ch'ae and Im envisioned implies the transformation of Korean society; the contradictions which divide the lives of Koreans need to be abolished and conflicts reconciled. Ch'ae's and Im's idea of the ritualization of theater challenges divisions: the division of work and play, of production and consumption, of haves and have-nots. The theorists of the minjung culture movement who work within the framework of Wallersteinean theories of political economy attribute these social divisions to national division, the imperialistic powers that partitioned Korea, and the forces that perpetuate such division.

Kim Chiha catechistically identifies this nation-dividing force as a devil. This devil, he argues, should be exorcised through a collective shamanic ritual *(kut)*, and thus existing divisions will be eliminated, be they class or national. As briefly mentioned earlier, Kim Chiha thus turns to Korea's millenarian religions, especially Tonghak and Chungsan'gyo, for historical references for social reform. Both religions syncretized *chŏnggamnok,* an indigenous belief in the coming of a just king, and the elements of Buddhist Maitreya tradition into new millenarian religions and prophesied the coming of the second perfect cycle of the world. Kim Chiha incorporated this millenarian idea into his vision of a "revolutionary religion." He suggested that the revolutionary ideas of popular religious movements may help the underclass to lead the world. Kim Chiha learned that Chŭngsan'gyo adapted shamanic ritual as a symbolic form of social transformation. Noting that ecstasy is quintessential to the shamanic transformation, Kim applied the notion of collective ecstasy to the ideas of minjung culture as a principal force of transformation. Through collective ecstasy, the oppressed people reach a certain state of *communitas;* in this state, a collective will to struggle is formed, and energy is drawn to break through the social and political impasse—a revolution.

This millenarian idea of social reform and the strategic interpretation of ecstasy as a method of channeling collective energy into revolution gives a semantic turn to the issues of national unification. The radical reading of ecstasy and the idea of ritual bringing together what is divided merge into yet another form of syncretic ideology through the mystification of shamanism. Paek Kiwan, director of the National Unification Research Institute and a presidential candidate during the 1987 national referendum, is also an adviser to the National Kut (shamanic ritual) Association. Paek expands the meaning of ritual to encompass the people's struggle to overcome and transcend national conflicts. To put it simply, the kut is a metaphor of the struggle for national unification. He maintains that unification can be achieved through collective ecstasy. Paek divides ecstasy into two types: religious fantasy and historical experience. He argues that religious fantasy is a metaphysical concept that ignores the reality of people. As a religious practice, it is concerned mainly with accumulation of material. He warns that this capitalistic aspect of ecstasy is subject to manipulation by a hegemonic ruling ideology.[23] He goes on to contend that ecstatic experience in the true (not distorted) history of the minjung has been the culmination of the struggle to break loose from the coerced reality and an individual's effort to encounter his or her real self as a human being. Ecstasy, Paek continues, is a momentum through which each individual experiences true transformation of self. It becomes an aesthetic moment when individual experience merges with social praxis. Ecstasy in this sense should become the very momentum from which history "develops."[24] Paek suggests that shamanic ritual is a historical experience through which one learns the history of a people's struggle and revolution.

Paek Kiwan identifies *history* as the knowledge of the contradictions in people's realities and the process of creating a world where such contradictions are resolved. Hence, the development of history is a process of struggle to realize this contradiction-free world. Paek attributes all the contradictions that Koreans are experiencing to national division and calls for a national unification ritual, whereby each individual learns the minjung's realities and experiences a transformation of consciousness. That ecstatic experience will be energized into a collective force, which, in turn, will be channeled into the unification of the nation.

The methodology of the minjung culture movement is essentially a rereading of history as history of the oppressed minjung's struggle and a representation of that history as a paradigm of change. In the history thus reread, hitherto marginalized people enter the central arena or become agents of history. In this process of historical evolution, minjung culture, that is, the politicized folk culture, no longer lies on the periphery. Strategists of the cultural movement believe that folk culture, with its latent subversive and transformative power, can lead the movement through the reform process and into the postrevolutionary era once the minjung become the subjects of history. Minjung culture is, in the word of one reform activist, a methodology of redemption.

The minjung culture movement has indeed left an indelible mark on modern Korean history, not in that it achieved its revolutionary goal, which is implicitly utopian socialism, but because it opened up an alternative epistemological space. For the first time in Korean history, a large number of elite and members of the oppressed class found common ground for solidarity in the name of cultural nationalism. So powerful was this phenomenon, that the movement mobilized massive numbers from the middle class that had grown up in the wake of South Korea's ruthless industrialization.

However, as has been suspected, since the "demise" of socialism and rampant globalization of capitalism, the once powerful minjung movement now faces the deflation of its revolutionary energy. The decline of socialism, I would argue, is only a convenient cause of the decline of the minjung movement. Rather, I suspect that the shortcomings of the movement stem from its inherent weakness, the problematics of the minjung movement. As a noted political scientist, Ch'oe Changjip, once observed, the minjung movement is the politics of *han*. Han is an aesthetic concept denoting bottled-up resentment and sorrow. This han, unless released, will explode into a destructive power causing harm to life. Curiously, Korean aesthetics does not provide the methodology for sublimating this han. If we imagine that the minjung movement, a collective ecstasy, was a releasing of the han of the oppressed nation, then how to achieve sublimation and the transfor-

mation of a nation is left unanswered. (To be sure, minjung christian theology attempts a solution, as Donald Clark observes in chapter 5 of this
volume.) When the revolutionary han seemed sufficiently released and the
next stage of thinking was required, South Korean oppositional intellectuals
found a vacuum, which was exacerbated by the decline of socialism upon
which they belatedly relied. This is the limitation of the politics of aesthetics
and, to a large extent, of critical thinking without an informed agenda.

This Korean experience may be instructive to postcolonial theories. As
Robert Young pointed out in his critique of Said's *Orientalism*,[25] such theoretical releasing of resentment toward European imperialism opens up a
critical discourse. Yet, criticism of colonialism does not deter or impede
imperialist practices. Recent discourse about Korea in the Western media
occasioned by the "nuclear crisis" in North Korea attests to continuing
orientalism even after decades of the most vibrant critique of imperialism in
Western academia. The task for the next generation, then, Koreans and
other Third World thinkers alike, should be to develop methodologies to
sublimate both this critique and cultural resistance. What good is resistance
without anticipated transformation?

7

Minjung Movements and the Minjung: Organizers and Farmers in a 1980s Farmers' Movement

Nancy Abelmann

THIS CHAPTER concerns itself with the interactions between farmers and so-called external forces, or *oebuseryŏk*, various support institutions and individuals, in the microworkings of the Koch'ang Tenant Farmers movement from 1985 to 1987. The movement was a protest calling for the distribution or sale of the tenant plots of the Haeri landlord estate, or *nongjang*, to its tenant farmers; a purchase agreement was reached in September 1987. The Haeri Estate in the Koch'ang district of the North Chŏlla province dates back to the Japanese colonial period, when a large-scale land-reclamation project was undertaken by the family of Kim Sŏngsu and Kim Yŏnsu, well-known historical figures, who are considered by some to have been Japanese collaborators. In the immediate postliberation era, in spite of a land-reform policy, the farmlands of the Haeri Estate were not distributed to their cultivators. The 1980s protest escalated into a dramatic demonstration when in August 1987 over two hundred farmers traveled to Seoul and staged a month-long occupation of the headquarters of Samyang, the landlord corporation. By the time of the final settlement, however, the movement was polarized, and many farmers returned to the countryside disgruntled.[1]

Here I shall take up competing idioms and ideals of activism through the story of the Koch'ang Tenant Farmers movement. We shall see that this movement, like all movements, was forged in and took its course from these very dissentions. I situate this late 1980s movement in the broader context of social activism and the minjung movement in the late 1980s. For my purposes here, the minjung movement refers to the theories, idioms, and strategies by which a community of activists sought to evoke and mobilize people broadly perceived to be dispossessed, and hence the rightful subjects of history and agents of political transformation. This chapter thus considers the practical exercising and effects of such ideologies in the workings of a single farmers' movement. By extension, however, it suggests the broader political climate and praxis of the heterogeneous community of dissent in late-1980s South Korea.

In this movement "external forces" included university students, nonlocal farmer activists, and nonfarmer activists. I regard these external forces as part of what was, in the late 1980s, a rapidly growing community of opposition. The primary external forces were members of the Catholic Farmers Union (CFU), members of the Koch'ang Farmers Union, which was originally a branch of the Christian Farmers movement, and student activists from Seoul's Koryŏ University.[2] I shall discuss the relationship between farmers and external forces, not only over the days of protest in Seoul, but also since the movement's rural beginnings. Although most of the movement's rhetoric reflected the unified voice of both external forces and farmers, at critical junctures apparent and effective resonances between the farmer and organizer communities were shattered. Although neither the agriculturalists nor the external forces in this movement constituted undifferentiated or cohesive communities, I will draw broad lines of contrast between these two communities. In documenting the basic lines of dissent between farmers and organizers, we can identify disparities in their perspectives on history and their conception of the nation. By dissent I do not only mean out-and-out disagreement over what action to take, but a difference in the construction of the meaning of "action."

The relation between these two communities was not one characterized only by dissent. To the contrary, I will argue that, in the late 1980s, although there are lines of dissention worth isolating in the explication of the dynamics of this farmers' movement and of social movements in general, there was growing convergence between many members of the specialized community of opposition and the target population of their organizations: the minjung or the people. The convergence was, above all, facilitated by a turn away from the discourses and practices of ideology toward a discourse of experience, not only among rural organizers but also in South Korea's community of opposition in general.

Contesting History and the Nation

Concerning history, organizers focus on the structure: materialist analyses. In this vein, South Korea was at a historical juncture where politicized individuals—the organizers—were highly engaged in, and articulate regarding, history's deep structure. In contrast, farmers narrated history as experience. Therefore when it came to historical rectification, organizers called for a change in the structure whereas farmers focused on the need for a change in immediate conditions; this is in no way to say that organizers' concern with structure was unrelated to immediate conditions or, conversely, that farmers recognized no structure to immediate conditions. In a sense, farmers were so aware of the structure of experience that it was part of their silent common sense rather than their discourse. In the organizers' focus on structure, they called for a drastic reordering. Farmers, on the other hand, in focusing on experience, did not work with the ideal of infinitely permutable structures but rather within the domain of possible permutations based on their experience.

With regard to history, the convergence I speak of above refers first to the politicization of farmers whereby they were taught to understand, or perhaps merely articulate, their understanding of things in more structural terms. Conversely, in the community of opposition there was increasingly a call for a dialectic between organizers' and farmers' experience which, at least in theory, implied that the status quo of the community of opposition be challenged by different visions of social movements. It is in this context that the notion of subjectivity, or *chuch'esŏng*,[3] was employed in the community of opposition, to refer to the subjectivity of the people or minjung whose lives are most intimately affected by a movement's agenda.

What were the divergences between farmers and organizers on the question of the nation? In the community of opposition, the politics of the nation figured centrally. Discussions of the nation were couched in cultural and historical discourses. The call for a unified state in the name of the Korean people or minjung—the unification of the South Korean and North Korean states—was a political imperative for organizers. For many farmers, however, there was a sense of nation independent of the polity and political agenda. In some sense, the nation has a natural existence as an extension of the land, Korean land. This is in no way meant to imply that unification was not a goal for farmers; it was a profound one, but their aim was a unified space for peaceful "living and eating" rather than prescriptions for an institutional political structure or ideology. Of course, such a call is profoundly political, but voiced in the language of anything but politics.

With regard to the nation, a convergence between farmers and organizers in the 1980s emerged as organizers stepped away from strictly political articulations of nationhood and activism, and farmers developed a sense of the need for politics in programs aimed at social reordering. The community of opposition moved closer to the agenda of farmers with its turn toward experience. It is helpful to think in terms of competing claims for the "authentic national experience of the Korean people." If "subject-oriented" refers to the affirmation of experience, then the aim of the project became somehow to isolate unadulterated experience—that is, experience unadulterated by ideology or by the "wrong" ideology. Considerations of which experience to affirm or which farmers to understand as subjects were central not only in theoretical discussion but in day-to-day decisions in the course of this movement.

In South Korea, the community of opposition's conscientization and the state's indoctrination programs were both justified as bringing people closer to their own experience, that is, to authentic national experience. Experience has been accorded great value on both the political Right and Left as pure, and particularly as purely national. The rhetoric of both nationalisms and counternationalisms searched for the authentic experience of being "Korean" in the twentieth century. The state and the Right in the 1980s operated, at least rhetorically, on the idea that when you strip away "impure" elements—those who force others' experience into evil and foreign frameworks and those who violate the national security laws and are thus part of national and international conspiracies—South Korea is an economically growing, prospering, natural, and national entity. In this formula, "impure" students were contrasted with "pure" students (Dong 1987: 234); impure students threatened national security, while pure students were training to become the minds of the body politic and the engineers of economic development.

Counterhegemonic nationalisms argued, on the other hand, that stripped of the state's policies, programs, and rhetorical tactics, the people are left with the raw experience of colonialism and imperialism and will naturally call for a radical reformation of society. For the people, then, it was the right-statist-nationalist hegemony over experience that needed to be unraveled. The oppositional community made the convincing argument that the structure of life, as well as the hearts and minds of "the people," had been under the sway of national experience as understood by hegemonic institutions and ideologies. They continued that the building blocks of a counterhegemonic national consciousness were the cultural artifacts of a national folk. The peasantry was understood to constitute that folk and thus to provide the repository of a "pure" national and natural culture. Although the details of the relations between farmers and external forces in the Koch'ang movement do not entirely conform to these dichotomies on history and the nation, we do find them undergirding much of the dissention.

The Movement Begins: Farmers Meet Organizers

A review of the early encounters between external forces and farmers in Koch'ang reveals the complex and often fractured human relations that would characterize the entire movement process. The details of this early phase also remind us of the enormous heterogeneity of both farmers and external forces. Furthermore, these early episodes and dialogues demonstrate competing discourses on social activism and ideal social movements. In Seoul the movement divided over the price settlement—whether to agree on a purchase price or to hold fast to a demand for a noncompensatory land distribution; we shall see that these developed from early struggles over the movement leadership and competing ways of reckoning its legitimacy. Judgments over the legitimacy of the leadership reflected judgments

over how, and by whom, history should be propelled. Although these judgments were often couched in terms of notions of subjectivity—arguing that
those most directly victimized should lead the movement—this was often
tricky to reconcile with the practical concerns of expediting the solution to
the land issue at hand. Because movements are self-conscious agents of
change, there were constant evaluations of what constituted a "correct"
movement.

There were several competing versions of the "start" of the movement;
although they were in some sense at odds with each other, these explanations were in no way mutually exclusive. I shall first review these versions,
followed by a discussion of their claimants. The first version claimed that
farmers' accumulated resentment or *han* somehow exploded. In this case it
was the timing—why 1985?—that needed to be explained. This view suggested that a broad-based mass movement would naturally follow. Further,
depending on the nature of that han, it could also suggest a broad political
and social movement as opposed to a more narrowly economic one. A
second explanation focused on the familial vendettas of particular movement leaders against Samyang; in this case it would have been plausible for
the primary actors to be willing to work almost entirely through the political
system to accomplish their task. Samyang, not the system, was the enemy,
and the task—rather than broad-based participation—was the object. A
third explanation suggested that the movement was started by the information bureau of the police agency because of what one officer of the Catholic
Farmers Union called "internal friction and the 'eating quarrel' of the ruling
class"—that is, the power struggles between various business and government elites over the spoils of the landlord corporation, namely, anticipated
payoffs from Samyang for favors. In this case farmers were rendered merely
as objects for elite aims. Finally, there was a range of ideas about the external forces; some suggested that external forces created a consciousness,
while others argued that they sparked a consciousness that revealed hidden
historical continuities. Throughout the course of the movement, various
interpretations of the start of the movement suggested qualitatively different movements.

The Samyang Tenant Relinquish Committee, the steering committee of
the movement, was formed in 1986 by Yun,[4] a fisherman who earned some
income by farming the tenant plots of his older brother. Yun explained that
for years he had harbored a grudge on account of submitting rents and
having nothing remaining: "If we didn't have to pay tenant fees, I would
have been able to go to middle and upper school." In the late 1970s he
began to send appeals to the Ministry of Agriculture. In 1980, he sent a
letter to the then head of a newly established government agency, Chun
Doo-Hwan (Chŏn Tuhwan), who would later become president. Chun
answered that distribution of the land was impossible and advised the
farmers to "continue to devote themselves to agricultural life and develop-

ment." Yun explained that in 1985 when there was talk of democratization of the military government, then Vice President Roh Tae Woo (No T'aeu), in preparation for his candidacy, promised to "listen to and try to solve the problems of workers and farmers." Yun sent tens of letters to various government party and ministry officials and also to the president.

Farmers, farmer organizations, and students initially understood that the Relinquish Committee was farmer-initiated, or, in the language of students and organizers, "self-initiated" or "subject-oriented." Its self- (farmer) initiation made it legitimate, but as we shall see, at another level organizers had to ask not only the seemingly obvious question—"Who is a farmer?"—but also "Who are the farmers? Who are the legitimate agents of change?" or, in some cases, "Who are the farmers most likely successfully to effect the change particular outsiders consider legitimate?" They addressed the question "What kind of historical experience will condition farmers to call for the 'correct' change?" Change is, of course, the key point, because of a consensus that at least a local change needed to be effected along with, for many involved, the shared conviction that history itself needed to be propelled in new directions.

A Catholic Farmers Union official, however, suggested that the movement had not been farmer-initiated. He traced its real start to an information officer in the police department of North Chŏlla province, asserting that Yun began activities on account of such encouragement. He understood that the information officer had provided Yun with printed material, had promised protection, and had even warned him that at some point he might have to feign taking him away. In short, he had provided him with a careful script of how things were to proceed. Min postulates that Yun was selected for this police plan because "he was smart, but not talkative." Min explained the "eating quarrel of the ruling classes," in which Samyang, with its vast political connections, treated local government and police people, such as information officers, "like the dirt at the end of one's toenail." Specifically, he alleged that the police were unhappy that routine bribe payments from the company had stopped. The officer thus planned a movement that would threaten the company so that he would be able eventually to quell it and thus demand considerable payoffs for having brought things under control. Min's calculations were based on a clear calculation of sides: farmers, the company, the police, and so on.

Early on, Yun was skeptical of outside oppositional support forces because of their "left-orientation"; in particular he did not like the Catholic Farmers Union, because they "criticize the government." One officer of the independent Koch'ang Farmers Union, which one year before had broken away from the Christian Farmers Union in the spirit of localizing the movement structure and agenda, heard about the tenant matter and visited Yun, but he described Yun as "focused on the eyes and ears of the bureaucracy *(kwan)* with no mind to talk to him [organizers]," that is to say, he catered to the authorities. Nevertheless, he gave him pamphlets demonstrating how organized farmer groups were prospering in Korea.

A representative from CFU reports that the following conversation transpired with Yun on the first day of their meeting:[5]

CFU: We are not a group that solves problems for people.

YUN: What do you mean?

CFU: In the past, we used the power of our organization to help some farmers in trouble, but it is best if people make efforts to solve the problems themselves—then they become the masters *(chuin)* of the country *(nara)*. If you become great farmers—regardless of whether you succeed or fail in this struggle—then, next time difficult things come up, in this or other regions, you will be people who can join in the fight. But, to become a member is a difficult decision; it is necessary to receive education and to learn how to resist suppression. You, sir—head of the Relinquish Committee—have appeared in a big gambling house. Put down your stakes!

YUN: Stakes!?

CFU: In gambling you put down your stakes. You are the person in charge of a unit, a unit attempting to capture a vast field [the land] now in another's name [Samyang]. Are you ready for the danger and oppression, are you ready to risk your life, to submit yourself to terror? Can you do this?

YUN: Not at all.

CFU: Why can't you risk?

YUN: I'm afraid. What should I do?

CFU: Then go home. If you can't decide to sacrifice then it is impossible.

YUN: But we need to get the land. Since the rents were lowered[6] the residents have become much more courageous. So let's get the land. It seems that I have become the region's hero. They say that Yun [self-reference] did what even a senator [referring to an earlier 1955 struggle] couldn't do.

CFU is a national group at once confident in its political invincibility, or at least in the political power of its umbrella organization, and confident about the fearlessness of its membership, men and women ready to risk their lives for the movement. It stressed education, and more than being concerned with incorporating vast numbers, it was focused on raising a vanguard; as Min put it above, "membership is serious and the stakes are high." For CFU the land question at hand was just a phase in the larger struggle. The primary goal, then, was to train activists who would continue to struggle, becoming the makers of a new society. Yun was firm that he was not cut out for the vanguard, but he was willing to send other men members of the Relinquish Committee. The discussions between Yun and the CFU representative continued as follows:

CFU: If you hate to sacrifice, but you need to find a method to definitely make this succeed, I have a proposal: why don't you go back and send a few other people? I'll give them education and make them part of the organization so that the project can succeed. But you must not disturb what I do. You must also not inform the government or the police. Remember that government institutions and district heads are on Samyang's side.

YUN: Instead why don't you give three hundred people education and then together we can stage a hunger strike at Samyang? That should solve it. I'll take responsibility for bringing people to you.

CFU: That is not so wise. You must try all other ways of fighting, and at the most advanced level—with a well-trained organization—you can stage an organized hunger strike. For farmers who live with physical labor—it's most disadvantageous to have a hunger strike.

YUN: Well, then, let's have a lecture at the Koch'ang Cathedral or somewhere in our district.

CFU: That too would push things ahead, but first we must train—send some lower people for training. It would be best if you also got some education, but if to boot you are afraid of that, what can we do!

YUN: So, what sort of people shall I send?

CFU: First of all, they should be bold, courageous people. Second, they should be people who are recognized in their villages; and third they should be people who aren't unintelligent, but their level of education is of no matter.

Many months later, Yun praised CFU to Kang, one of the people he sent to CFU for training, and Kang asked him why if he thought it was so good he did not join. Yun answered that he did not want to live "intelligently"; Kang challenged him, "Then why are you doing this work?" Eventually women's and men's CFU branches were founded, and Min was satisfied that several people had become "real leaders with an ability to struggle." Cho, another of the people Yun sent, recalls that at first he thought that if he became a member of CFU he would die. Kang, who had never even heard of CFU, explained that Yun introduced it to him as an organization that "criticized the President." As one farmer, one of the youngest village heads in the region, put it, "When people hear CFU they think movement-people (*undonggwǒn*), and that has nothing to do with farmers." The first woman to seek out CFU and who eventually became the head of the CFU Haeri Women's Division, went initially to "find out why the government hates CFU." She concluded: "They tell only good things to farmers and speak about government problems, so that's it [why the government hates CFU] I figured . . . I didn't join, but I agreed in my heart; but the police and the local government officials make it so that you can't live." One of the farmers who became closely affiliated with the CFU was a fan of late-night television seminars on South Korea's agricultural problems. He admired these "great" doctors (Ph.D.'s) on television, saying, "Even if I had to die of starvation, if I could die having received a Ph.D., I would have no resentment *(han)*." He was also impressed with the life-style of CFU professional activists; he was amazed, for example, at Min's consistency, that he didn't drink coffee or coke because they were foreign products.

Over time the Samyang villages became delineated by their CFU or anti-CFU orientations, and it was widely understood—at least by those in the CFU villages—that police and local officials shied away from villages even partly organized by CFU. This was not surprising, given the tenor of CFU's education programs, statedly antigovernment and confident in the power of the opposition and the potential for a new world. However, farmers were not so confident about that new world, and when their confidence began to wane, their world and the CFU world seemed worlds apart. A farmer in his late thirties, firmly committed to the opposition party but residing in one of the non-CFU villages and the home village of Yun, put it this way: "When I go to the CFU education it seems American imports are wrong, but we farmers come home and forget the education and think again of only eating and living." Months later this same farmer, on the eve of the December 1987 presidential election, in spite of his passionate movement and antigovernment activities in Seoul, told me that he was afraid to join the CFU, thinking, "What would happen if Kim Dae Jung doesn't become president?"

Kang, who proved the most consistent, fearless, and enduring CFU member—the prototype of CFU's vanguard leadership—became extremely confident in the CFU infrastructure. This confidence, though, derived not from membership alone, but rather from day-in, day-out contact with CFU. He explained that after he became a member he probably traveled to the Chŏnju regional office one hundred times, and that at the slightest news of the police he would call Chŏnju; in a single month his phone bill was W40,000.[7] Just the same, however, he described a distance between his world and that of the CFU education programs that he periodically would travel to attend. "The professors [lecturers] are so smart, and their meanings *(ttŭt)* are so deep." Here *ttŭt* refers not only to thought or meanings but, more specifically, "to have a perspective on the world," to have some sort of a program in mind. Those "without ttŭt" constitute a residual category of those who live without ideology or politics, or similarly, fall into a natural category in opposition to those who live with thought, intention, and ideology. He was particularly impressed by a university professor and newspaper columnist who had traveled to China twelve times; from his lecture, "Peasant Liberation and National Unification," Kang learned that farmer problems in the south had to be solved before unification could be addressed. He summed up what he had learned from this lecture on detailed global and political trends, particularly in the communist and socialist world, with the Deng Xiaoping maxim that "white or black, all cats are mice-eaters," or "democratic or communist, all countries have to live well." Throughout

his excited report of the meeting, however, he reaffirmed and finally concluded that "people like Pak [another participant in the meeting and silently
present in our discussion] and I can't know what they [the professors] are
truly about."

Farmers repeatedly expressed their respect for highly educated people.
The interaction with CFU education encouraged them to see their experience in the context of broader structures, and although this was in many isolated cases very successful, there were also limitations; as we have discussed
above, farmers tended to see a gap between their "living and eating" and
politics.

Active Protest

As we turn to the early protest activities of the struggle, we continue to witness competing idioms and models of activism. Also apparent are divergences among actors concerning movement platforms and their signifi-
cations.

In the fall of 1986, following the initial spring contact with CFU, some
two hundred farmers signed an agreement not to remit the rents. Those
who signed gathered their harvests, the rent in kind, in village reserves. On
31 January 1987—already months after the rent was due—they assembled
in front of Samyang buildings in the countryside to protest. Min admits that
his presence there served as institutional fortification against the police; he
explains that farmers told them not to leave, "otherwise the police will break
it up." Min describes the demonstration as follows: "The *level* of their demonstration was low. There were no slogans, no songs, and no leaders. They
just stood in no particular form, staring blankly. We told them to bring
drums so that they would warm up and get courage. They nodded 'yes', but
did nothing. Yun and another leader of the Relinquish Committee stood
there as if to say, 'Their being gathered like this is no fault of ours.'"

At nightfall, they made a fire of a rice-stalk stack and sat around, seated
on rice stalks. They were silent when the police came and put out the fire
and pulled the stalks out from under them. Min explains how his example,
though, challenged their passivity. When the police pushed him, Min began
to shout, "Why are you pushing me?" and this shocked the farmers and gave
them courage. Min answered a policeman's request, "We are trying to dis-
perse the farmers, you leave!" with "I won't leave; I have to watch how you
police treat the farmers—I can't leave." Yun encouraged people to submit
the rents, having been promised by the chief of Koch'ang County that there
would be a meeting with the landlords if they paid. Kang and Cho and all
those tightly rallied around CFU only learned after the fact that the rents
from Simwŏn district had been remitted.

At this juncture, an interesting tactical struggle occurred when CFU discussed the question of the relationship of the movement leaders and the

mass. Min ascertained that only a small minority would be willing to hold out in the land struggle and determined that, because their infrastructure was not well formed and by now polarized, officials and Samyang would end up running the course of the movement in most of the villages; he suggested that they pursue education for another year to be able to lead all the people correctly. He summarized, "It is a bit of a problem if the members [of CFU] are entirely different from the mass (taejung)." A higher officer in the North Chŏlla CFU, however, calculated differently, concluding that, because of the pending revisions of land-contract laws in Korea (for October 1987), now was the time to fight; so he encouraged them not to pay. Finally, nine houses did not remit the rents, and by then women's and men's CFU branches had formed in two Haeri villages. Shortly thereafter, the company began to place stickers on the property of those who had not remitted rents, including even cows and television sets. Farmers described this humiliating experience at great length. The CFU counseled them to pay little attention to the stickers and to worry about education; consistently, CFU was concerned with the long term. For many farmers, though, this perspective was far removed from the day-to-day demands of their lives. But CFU logic tended to explain such farmer hesitation as "barriers of consciousness."

CFU consistently acted to turn the world on its head, to activate farmers in an often shocking and empowering fashion. In March 1987 about twenty people participated in a CFU education at the Koch'ang Cathedral. When they gathered in Haeri, the local officials and police intervened, telling the farmers that they were being unnecessarily led astray. Min reports having said to the officials, "You slave bastards—how is it that you ask your masters where they are going?" and another CFU affiliate turned to the police chief, saying, "Is this the achievement of the 'justice-society' [a play on one of Chun's government slogans]; who told you to do that? Did Chun [Doo-Hwan]?"

March was a turning point, as the movement began demanding no-compensation relinquishment of the land. Here, too, it is interesting that farmers who supported the no-compensation demand did so in quite a different spirit from their organizer and student colleagues. For organizers and students the no-compensation claims were the most striking response to the history of the exclusion of this land from land reform assumedly on account of the power and politics of the Kims of Koch'ang. Further, this claim brought to their minds the failed popular and North Korean attempts at no compensation, no-payment socialist land reform after the liberation (1945). Those farmers who supported the no-compensation relinquishment platform, however, did so much more according to "land-to-the-tiller" universal values of work and dignity. Some did explicitly associate this with programs from 1940s People's Committees days, but many more spoke of it as a basic Korean or even human principle. One member of the original leadership insisted that no-compensation was the initial idea of the movement until government officials stated "this was the language of revolutions, impossible in a capitalist society," at which point they abandoned it. In April, four CFU members received a court order for negligence in rent payment; in this way the CFU members had, in a sense, become the subjects of the movement.

The CFU attitude toward court proceedings was that they were a vehicle for unifying the farmers, something to rally around. They also calculated that it would attract public opinion to the side of the farmers. Regarding the strategic decision as to whether to focus resources on the court case, one Christian Farmers Union member was very disapproving of such a tactic, arguing that court struggles lead nowhere. Min reports that he answered such doubts with "I would see this trial as a great success if it went on for twenty years. If they didn't pay rents for twenty years . . . it would be fine, even if they lost. During that time there would be sufficient time for the farmers to organize as they were farming—how good that would be. You can't compare a court case for people who have lost their land and people who now have land—they are different discussions." Few farmers would have seen a twenty-year trial as a success; in voicing this opinion so clearly, Min stood isolated from the time frame and sense of dignity concerning land ownership characteristic of many of the farmers.

Nonghwal in Theory

In the month preceding the August 1987 Seoul demonstration, over two hundred students from Seoul's Koryŏ University dispersed among twelve tenant-farmer villages in Koch'ang's Haeri and Simwŏn districts for "agricultural action" *(nonghwal)*, rural programs for students during their summer vacation. It is widely understood that this facilitated the August move to go to the center of protest in Seoul; farmers largely think that Seoul's demonstrators and the community of opposition are dominated by students. In 1987, students were increasingly concerned with subjectivity and so-called subject consciousness. Not surprisingly, students' action was suspended in self-conscious evaluations not only of others' historical subjectivity but also their own. Thus an integral part of nonghwal was extensive introspection and discussion aimed at drawing out these ideas, attitudes, and consciousnesses. The nonghwal schedule included daily discussion sessions with farmers to reach their consciousness and, in turn, daily self-reflection sessions further to reveal their own consciousness and the progress of this meeting of consciousnesses. Before we continue with the particulars of farmers and outside activists in Koch'ang, we shall consider the late 1980s student programs in the countryside, nonghwal.

By opening themselves up to a consideration of farmers as subjects, students then had to explain farmer passivity and inaction—farmers as objects—as much as they celebrated whatever oppositional activity or culture they found. They thus had to be concerned with farmer consciousness.

This self-consciousness necessitated extensive and impressive production of words, reconciling thought and action in the record of, and reflection on, students' nonghwal in Koch'ang. Slogans on posters that appealed for student participation in nonghwal in 1985 and 1986 revealed the emotional and intellectual logic of nonghwal. Some slogans appealed to an idea of the essence of farming and agricultural life: "We Must Stand Squarely on the Earth (*ttangŭl tikko sŏyahanda)*" (Foreign Language University) or "Let's Go! To Agricultural Villages—All to the Heart of the Earth (*kaja! nongch'onŭro t'anŭn hŭk kasŭmŭro)*" (Kyonghŭi University). Other slogans appealed much more directly to images, not of agricultural essentialism, but rather of the exploited, barren, pathetic and ungiving land crying for help. At Koryŏ University, posters read, "Let's Go, to the Barren Red Earth Where Dawn Hasn't Come Yet (*kaja! ajiktto tong t'ŭji anŭn kŏch'in hwangt'oro!)*" or "Beads of Sweat to the Barren Land (*ttambangurŭl ch'ŏkppak'an nongt'oe)*" or, at Foreign Language University, "The Earth Calls You (*hŭk purŭnda)*." Others focused more directly on a call to the experience of labor: "Let's Go—Let's Find the Meaning of Sweat and Earth (*uri kapssida. hŭkkwa ttamŭi ŭimirŭl ch'ajŭrŏ),*" at Sŏnggyun'gwan University, or "Let's Work with My Land, My Sweat, My Hands (*nae ttan, nae hŭk, nae sonŭro, ilgumyŏ).*" Finally, there were straighter political appeals to the victims of government power: at Kyonghŭi University, "To the Agricultural Village Where the Price of Cows Is Becoming the Price of Dogs" or Koryŏ University's "Farming Village Economics—Oppressed by U.S. and Japanese Capital—Let's Go" (University Students Agricultural Action 1986: 411).

In the middle of the 1980s, the character of nonghwal was openly challenged. In 1986 students were self-conscious that their call for a farmer-as-subject–centered nonghwal was the new call of a new student movement era. The new nonghwal was to stand in opposition to farmer-as-object nonghwal.

The student characterization of the farmer-as-object nonghwal is as follows. First, nonghwal made objects of farmers not by failing to consider them, but because farmers and their communities were understood as the recipients of service, of students' social-welfare activities. As such, the equation was: givers-subjects-students and recipients-objects-peasants. Second, nonghwal itself was an object for the student movement, a way to conscientize, particularly, underclass men and women—a link in the student movement socialization. One senior admitted quite honestly that when he began college he saw no reason for nonghwal, but that in 1985 he came to realize its meaning for the student movement. Taken to its extreme, though, this logic asserted that nonghwal was something that fulfilled a function for the student movement and was otherwise expendable. In this model the consciousness of the farmers is absent; the only consciousness that matters is student consciousness. As such, there was no dialectic between students and farmers, or the student and farmers' movements. Nonghwal, rather, was a useful experience for the student movement, confirming its logic and its reading of the material conditions of Korean history. The particularly important aspects of this experience, then, were students' (often first) encounter with hard physical labor and, for some, with the hardships of lower-class life in Korea. In the case of Koryŏ University, after 1985 most people active in the student movement began to participate in nonghwal.

In fact, many nonghwal teams had been concerned with farmer consciousness, but largely as objects for conscientization, irrespective of farmers' experience of history, without any desire to interact with them as subjects. In this vein, the "new" nonghwal demanded an active dialectic between the student movement and farmers' movements, and between student and farmer, both as subjects. Conscientizing in dialogue, while affirming the subjectivity of farmers, is perhaps the most tautological of the "new" formulas and extremely difficult to realize in practice, as we shall see.

Thus, the challenge for those proposing a new nonghwal was to their own consciousness and to their view of farmer consciousness. The logic of the new nonghwal stressed that nonghwal should be neither for service nor unidirectional farmer conscientization, nor merely an activity for training student-movement activists. A farmer-as-subject nonghwal must be long-term, interactive, and experience-centered. The new equation is tricky, though, because students were fundamentally still committed to service, the training of student activists, and "raising the consciousness" of farmers. "Long-term" refers to forming long-term relationships between students and farmers rather than one-shot, summer vacation encounters. "Interactive and experience-centered" refer to a conscientizing based on an understanding of and intimate interaction with farmers' actual or historical (has-been) and normative (should-be) subjectivity. The primary goal of such a conscientization was to awaken farmers to a realization of their own subjectivity. As one publication put it, "students, through a comprehension of the realities of farming villages, will personally experience the reality of their colonial territory-homeland and build an emotional link with farmers.... While farmers, through [their contact with] the students will plant a consciousness to become the masters of society and get connections with students." Students have high hopes for this meeting between farmers and students—it should "solve the contradictions of history" (Agricultural Action Resource Collection Statement 1987: 1, 4).

Students' "new" commitment raises the following queries. To what extent did these subjectivity considerations challenge students' understanding of the material conditions or structure of history? Did nonghwal discoveries effect any change in the agenda or actions of the student movement? It did seem that the students' above-outlined call for changes in their own consciousness did affect—albeit slowly and in small increments—the very contours of the discourse on Korea as it has been and should be. This very matter—whether students were willing to surrender farmer movements or even their own movements to the course of action subscribed by the min-jung—was central in this movement.

Students at many universities in 1987 considered this a watershed year for nonghwal activities. Nineteen eighty-five, however, marked a low point for nonghwal, as Seoul University students were kicked out of villages in South Ch'ungch'ŏng Province by local officials; but in 1986, with less government intrusion, increasingly students worked through the Catholic Farmers Union for protection from the anti-nonghwal forces in the villages (University Students Agricultural Action 1986: 48). At most schools, includ-ing Koryŏ University, nonghwal decided in 1987 to venture into regions where movements were already raging. This was a significant change from previous nonghwal, which had had little cooperative contact with nonstu-dent organizers. Some organizers found them a menace to their activities; as one put it, "Nonghwal often has a bad influence on peasant movements, as it is not in tune with village life and students often come with disjointed, unreasonable plans, ending in distrust and frustration." Some schools, how-ever, decided to forgo nonghwal that year, based, I think, on their judgment that farmers were not and would not be central subjects of current social movements or of the ultimate achievement of subjectivity at the national level—that is, unification. In this vein, some schools adopted a new cam-paign, sending "conscientization letters" to junior-high-school students all over the country informing them of the social and political ills in South Korea and of the projects and aims of oppositional movements. Students at Yonsei University were at the forefront of this effort (University Students Agricultural Action 1986: 408).

Nonghwal in Koch'ang

The Koryŏ University students' decision to join in the Koch'ang struggles was in keeping with the new commitment to support local initiatives. *Undonggwŏn* was the word reserved for serious student activists. Joining the student movement was for many a painful process, requiring the unlearning of personal and national political pasts. Every student seemed to have an ini-tiation story about feeling deep anger as he/she came to feel that he/she had been deceived, fear at the prospect of unraveling his/her past, and heartfelt celebration of promise and potential. Students reconstruct history based on the powerful idea, as one student summed it up, that "everything [they] learned before college was lies." It is important to remember that the pro-cess of joining in student political activity and eventually entering the ranks of the student-movement leadership was a painful one that required estrangement from family and posed great danger. One student explained that her mother thought of nonghwal as "reds" who were out to make "reds" out of students and farmers.

The process of unlearning history through nonghwal was particularly dramatic in the case of Koryŏ University because of the relation between the Koch'ang landlord family and the campus history. It was not difficult for students to draw a connection between campus democratization struggles—as they struggled with their university's particular legacy—and the struggles of tenant farmers in remote Koch'ang. In 1987, this was particularly fitting, because the student movement was determined to politicize students on national and international issues via local campus issues. One student described her own awakening through her studies of history after entering college. In her reading of a book on the liberation era in an underground social-science club, she was particularly shocked to learn about Kim Sŏngsu's collaborative activities. She explained that the Koch'ang problem arose in her sophomore year in the middle of the protests against the "irrationality" of teaching the national security law in a graduate political science department at Koryŏ University. One student was shocked in his freshman year to see a poster denouncing Kim Sŏngsu as a "man who sold the country."

Another student expressed that only in the late 1980s would she have probably joined in the student movement: "I don't believe in God *(hananim)*, but if there are gods *(sin)* I am grateful that I began university in this period rather than ten years earlier in Pak's Yushin Period [1972–1979]." For this student, the Koch'ang freshman nonghwal was the climax of a spring and summer of student-movement initiation. "You can't believe the world," she exclaimed after she shared this nonghwal memory: "a junior-high-school student asked me how a man who made farmers unable to live and did bad things was able to become the president of a party [referring to Kim Sŏngsu and Hanmindang] . . . I didn't know what to say." Her experiences in Ko-ch'ang seemed to justify historically the new world she had learned about in just a few months of university life. She explained her general skepticism about contemporary South Korea and history as she learned it in school through her new understanding of Samyang's Kim Sŏngsu. Her newfound doubt concerning dominant historical representation called into question the state representation of North Korea; in her account below, she regrets having discriminated against her own people in North Korea.

> [of Kim Sŏngsu] . . . How could an enlightened smart person tell people to go and fight for the voluntary Japanese military units . . . ignorant citizens believed this. . . . And now Roh Tae Woo who participated in the coup d'état [by Chun] and Kwangju still runs for president, calling himself a "regular guy" *(pot'ong saram)*; is it so easy to become a great person? If *he* is a great person, *who* will try and become a great person? . . . When I hear male students who study [in the student movement] say that the people in North Korea live well and fully, I doubt them . . . but since I have seen the distortion and hidden facts [in South Korea] I'm not really so surprised. In Junior High we were asked to write down what we knew about North Korea; I wrote "corn meal soup [i.e., no white rice], forced labor, and reds catching flies and killing them" . . . how deplorable that I wrote that about people of the same nation.

She described that before college she had been "completely unaware," that "things just passed me by." Her first weeks of college coincided with the aftermath of the Pak Chŏngch'ŏl torture incident, and she was encouraged to go to the demonstrations, told that "of course students participate." In early March the Koch'ang farmers gave students pamphlets, and she was shocked to learn that Kim Sŏngsu had extracted tenant rents in Koch'ang, backed by the political power of the Hanmindang; before this she had only known of Kim as a nationalist and textile industrialist who had—as a nationalist—prevented porcelain from being smuggled out of Korea. In April and May, the commemorations for the 19 April 1960 student revolution and the 17 May Kwangju massacre were further opportunities to learn "what really happened." She said that she should have gone to the streets for the 6 June 1987 democratization rallies, but that she was petrified that day; she wished her friends a safe return and went home.

The protests over the arrest of Yi Inyŏng, Seoul University student council president, were the first in which she had actively participated. The front gate was locked and students ran around the athletic field at the front of the campus in so-called *sŭk'ŭrŏm* formation (from scrummage)—that is, linked shoulder to shoulder with arms interlocked around each other's necks and shoulders. She was impressed by television misreporting. Students, unfairly described as "reds," were depicted as needlessly throwing rocks, and no mention of tear gas was made. Her first participation in student demonstrations beyond the campus gates was in a rally against the state's use of tear gas; she trembled as she went, but explained, "Students were calling to get rid of a bad thing—how could I not participate?" "Losing her senses" on account of the military police and tear gas at every corner, she was amazed and thrilled at the warm welcome of mothers and grandmothers who came into the streets with water hoses and edibles for the students. Students surrounded the riot forces, but agreed to disband when the police promised that they would not use tear gas. They were nevertheless immediately fired upon. As she escaped, crying, she saw that a riot policeman had hit a girl a few paces behind her with a small tear-gas bomb. He chanted, "Have a taste of this." As a "powerless female student in that state of not yet having my consciousness awoken," she explained, "I was furious."

Throughout the rest of June she demonstrated, often returning home late and ill, lying to her parents that she had waited at school to "hear the news of the demonstrators." At one demonstration, students ran out of weapons, so she joined those who were breaking stones, and recalls, "I had no theoretical basis, but I felt something [an awakening] at the very thought of the image of myself breaking stones." At another demonstration she recalls riot police using tear gas as the students sang the national anthem. But perhaps what spoke loudest in her memory was being called "radical leftist, extreme student-movement demonstrator." She wondered who they were talking about—"freshmen like me and the neatly dressed students all around me."

During summer vacation, although not a Christian, she went on a retreat with a conservative Christian organization; this experience became another turning point for her. She returned on 10 July to the news that one million people had gathered at Seoul's City Hall for the tear-gas victim Yi Han'yŏl. She reflected that at the retreat she, however, "ate watermelon and drank cola, and oblivious of the strength of the residents [Seoul citizens], only looked for God." Critical of her own indulgence, of religious obliviousness to the political, she decided to participate in nonghwal.

Thinking back to her earliest nonghwal initiation, she was amazed at her own passivity. She recalls, at a nonghwal seminar on agricultural debt, the problem of the importation of agricultural goods, and the methods of farmer movements, thinking, "precisely. . . sure, sure [i.e., an indifferent response]." In the Samyang villages, she was assigned to one home and heard the "objective talk" of a former Samyang tenant, who explained that he got rid of his tenant plots because it was so disgusting and dirty to be treated that way. She asked him about the colonial period, "Had it been that bad?" and realized, "I hadn't been well educated. I had lived unknowing in this fashion." The farmer asked her sarcastically, "Did you think farmers ate white rice?" She cried and cried over her own ignorance and concluded, "Such a thing as tenancy shouldn't exist." Over and over she exclaimed that she had lived knowing nothing. She taught this man the *Farmer Song*, a popular student protest song, and he brought chicken and liquor to the greenhouse where the nonghwal students were staying. She explained that, although the farmers asked the students to fight for them, because students are— she feels—in a "neutral position," "we wouldn't satisfy them [the farmers]." At nonghwal's final self-reflection meeting she was asked, particularly as a freshman, to offer comments, and she remembers having said, "Indeed, you really need to know many things. Reading books isn't enough to understand the inside of problems; you have to come [to the countryside] and experience it directly."

Nonghwal was a turning point for another student, a senior who had studiously stayed away from student-movement activities. This student ended up moving to a farming village after graduation to engage in farming and organizing. He explained that during his freshman year it would have been impossible for him to have been interested in farming villages, because, in "accordance with the Confucian tradition, he couldn't think of separating himself from his parents." He went to the military and, like most students, returned more conservative. In his sophomore year he continued to be preoccupied with "individual desire," but the nonghwal, which he went to thinking "what is this nonghwal anyway?" was the experience that "awakened" his thinking. A student of German literature and interested in law, he had planned a legal career, and he was particularly interested in the Koch'ang case because of its relation to civil law. Not only did he learn about the "contradictions of law in theory and in practice," but the poor farmers who "*live* like duck eggs in the Nakdong River" and "*die* without a name . . .

touched my heart." Here the Nakdong River is a reference to the many who were killed there during the Korean War.

One French major described his rather ambivalent relation to the student movement, and to nonghwal in turn. During high school, he had thought that student activists who sided with the North and incited confusion should be killed. In his freshman year he had no interest in social science; he was only interested in dating. One of his seniors told him to "study," that is, to read social-science and historical materials in conjunction with the student movement, and although he did not like the strong tone of the suggestion, he began to "study." He explained that he and the student movement were like a "Western pot and *ondol* [the traditional Korean heated, paper-covered floor]," that is, like oil and water. An upperclassman unimpressed with his attitude told him, "Get out of here—go away!" which made him determined to continue these studies. As he studied, his "emotional wrath [against the state and system] built up" and his "desire for a logical movement" grew. This time, however, younger students criticized him because he was not sufficiently active in the movement. He fully realized his "responsibility as a youth of the Korean peninsula" and "became more certain of what he should study," so he joined in movement activities more frequently. Yet he hated the way that students harmed each other in the movement, and although he stopped participating as much in the activities, he continued to study in the under-circles, or student-movement study groups.

One student explained that before studying history he had even yelled "Long Live Korea" when Kwangju protestors were suppressed and had thought that South Korea would fall when Park was assassinated. He explained that he learned about skirmishes with Kim Sŏngsu's family in Bruce Cumings' *The Origins of the Korean War* and was therefore optimistic about protest potential in the region. He went on to explain that, in the more stratified villages, the poorer farmers were unified. This was the case in his nonghwal village, where people still used informal language (half-language or *panmal*) to address former farmhands (*mŏsum*). Class, then, is what facilitated the tenants' solidarity in the land movement in Koch'ang. He concluded that you can only know the root cause of activism by "feeling ideological problems and people's actual pain" in one's study of history. He explained that he studied history to find those roots.

For students of agricultural village origins, the nonghwal experience is a very particular one. One student commented: "I grew up in an agricultural village, but nonghwal was like being born again." Several students with rural origins expressed that their "awakening" through revisionist historical studies is very different than that of city students, because they recognize the livelihoods of their families and villages in discussion of the past. One student expressed how strange it had been to feel that he had been living in others' pasts; he explained sadly that the temporally distant childhood described by a teacher at the regional high school was not unlike his own rural childhood in the village he had left to attend the school.

Koryŏ University, and nonghwal in particular, is known for its high percentage of students with humble, rural origins. The nonghwal participation of rural students often strains their family relations. Fulfillment of filial duties would require that such students return to their own homelands to work during vacation. Also, filial duty for all Korean students, and particularly those from poor families, demands academic success and "rising in the world." This, of course, relates most fundamentally to their decisions to participate in the student movement in any way. One history major, the ninth child of ten, himself from a North Chŏlla tenant farming village more rural, mountainous, and impoverished than those in Koch'ang, stated: "I am very happy to have continued studying at college. I like history; but after graduation I will go to my countryside, but in the countryside they hope I will rise in the world [and not return]."

As rural youths who have left the countryside, these students are in an awkward position when they champion the continued vitality of the rural sector. One student reported that the contradiction was brought home to him when a junior-high-school student approached him with the question, "Isn't it a contradiction that you tell us to stay in the countryside, but you yourself left?"

Nonghwal in Practice

In student–farmer interactions we find the most self-conscious reflections on the complex relationship between the theory and praxis of minjung movements. Here we witness that the realities of village life and social organization posed challenges to the minjung imagery. We also see, however, that in the late 1980s—at least upon reflection—students aimed to redirect their minjung theory in accordance with local realities.

The nonghwal teams, like the chapter headings of a village ethnography, were divided into committees attending to subpopulations of the village according to age and gender. Students were often torn between theoretical assessments of which village group was or should become central historical movers or subjects and the realities of village life. Students had to face the competing structures of legitimacy in the village, whether to work through the official hierarchy of the village or through other competing systems, including the rank of civil servants (often linked with Samyang) or the movement leadership. No single student formula of subjecthood or historical legitimacy made for a perfect fit with farmers' lives on the ground.

The general custom of nonghwal is to focus attention on the *ch'ŏngnyŏn*, young and unmarried men who do the full labor of adults but are not tied down by the family duties of married men. Students figured that married men, consumed by household concerns, are unable to engage in the frequent gathering and drinking of young, unmarried men. Students' interest in this group were based on several calculations and miscalculations. They expected that their closeness in age would facilitate exchange; but it often produced tension, because this proximity underscored their different lots in life, either by chance of birth or by feats of achievement. Students also figured that young men would be unfettered by the historical experiences that engendered cold war perspectives. On the contrary, they found that many young rural people, even more than their urban counterparts, were still steeped in the physical and social geography of their locale's Korean War experience; lineage, in all senses, is clearer in the countryside. Finally, their calculation that young men are freer than family men also proved to be misguided. They were surprised to find many of them intimately involved with extended families and bound by rigid requirements of filial behavior; this was particularly the case because, often, they were the only sons who had agreed, by force or by choice, to stay in the countryside. One team reported that the "problem consciousness" of young men was insufficient, particularly compared with older men, because of lack of "organic, active" communication, and that their "feudal" relations with older men had precluded the formation of young men's groups. Students were also disappointed to discover that because many young men had worked as laborers in the city, it was impossible for them to become stable farmers.

In keeping with the above miscalculations, students who were assigned to young men reflected on the importance of interacting with them without being constrained by considerations of their "historical role." Students often criticized themselves for having attempted to direct conversations toward particular topics, hence precluding freer exchange. Also, they reflected that it would have been good to match the number of young men and students; often the students far outnumbered the young men, making it uncomfortable for the villagers and ironically objectifying them as historical actors. Repeatedly, students asserted that interactions should have been arranged more informally, making them more conducive to the development of friendship. One team, however, organized a young men's group and reported that they "played together in the water, catching pigs." In a sense they called for naturalization of the process. They did not, however, want to relinquish all control. In one reflection session, students announced the prescription: "listen to their [farmers'] opinions with a humble attitude and guide them to conclusions." One student echoed this maxim, explaining that "there was one farmer who agreed with us so completely, that we stood him up as a leader to actively go forward." Similarly, one team was particularly content that at the festival or demonstration the young men from their nonghwal village had been a "progressive force" in the denunciations and slogan chanting. Also, they were excited that these were the very young men who came up with a plan to enter Samyang forcefully, that they had been at the forefront of the violent activity of the day.

The issues for teams assigned to other age groups were entirely different. Teams assigned to younger teenagers explained that "we should help them make their opinions scientific and theoretical because they have no individual or group vision of their future." The university students regretted that their preparation was insufficient, because "we don't know what to talk to them about."

Across the board students seem to have been happiest with the children's group; it proved a convenient way to link up with entire households, and because it is sanctioned to "play" with this age group, the most desirable relations were achieved. They set out to "grasp reality" through the children, and the meetings were more frequent and spontaneous than they had even hoped for. As for the women's group, nonghwal teams unanimously agree that they should have paid more attention to women. They understood that women were "exploding" under the weight of "double oppression"—that of landlords and men—and that their efforts to overcome this oppression emerged vividly through this movement. For instance, many groups commented on the ease and enthusiasm with which women learned songs.

Student self-reflection appraised their own group organization as a metaphorical "student village" that they had modeled after their mind's-eye vision of an agricultural village. One team reflected on its insufficient harmony and direction. Another team similarly noted, "the ability of the team leader to bring people together was insufficient, but this is also the responsibility of nonghwal team members." Several nonghwal teams decided that they had been passive and lacked a "subject-oriented appearance." They understood this problem in part to stem from a deep compulsion to maintain fastidiously the senior–junior hierarchy among students. South Korean clubs uphold this age hierarchy not only through language differentiation that reflects status and rank, but also through the division of labor. The self-criticism of one team included such comments as: "Despite constant reflection, we have seen no change in our actions"; "we need more criticism of each other, more criticism with love"; and in order to achieve successful community life, "the individual needs to be diminished."

One widespread nonghwal principle was completely to refuse food and drink from villagers, including the *saech'an*, snacks customarily prepared for those providing labor services under any circumstances. Their logic for not eating the food was twofold: they wanted to be careful not to be an economic drain on village resources; and, understanding that villages are stratified, they did not want inadvertently to invite a hierarchy of hospitality. This nonghwal principle to refuse food, however, was nearly impossible to execute in practice. As educated people, students are considered precious guests, who furthermore provide a service free of charge. It is inconceivable for villagers, at least those villagers inclined to establish rapport with the students, to imagine breaking this most basic rule of communication, and farmers often say, "Food and drink is the only thing we have to give." By refusing this food, students denied farmers the ability to extend the only thing they could count on giving: foodstuffs. On the third day, one team, already recognizing the impracticality of this measure, decided that the problems they were running into reflected a larger concern: they had neither made their principles clear among themselves nor sufficiently communicated them to the villagers.

Nationwide these food conventions were being put to the test. One Foreign Language University student visited a village as part of an investigative team and was told earnestly, "Don't come if you don't plan to receive food for your labor." A Seoul National University team decided that they would accept simple things that farmers had made themselves, but no purchased goods, such as cola or juice. In Koch'ang also, in some villages, students informally received food.

Although I have highlighted some of the barriers between farmers and students, there is no question that the students largely endeared themselves to the farmers. Somewhere between the farmers' "That could be my child" and nonghwal students' "This could be my homeland," there was a powerful sense of nation. One village woman said she was particularly "moved" to know about parents of student activists who had formed a committee while attending their children's trials: "When I heard about that my heart hurt, but I thought that these mothers are so smart with such smart children and I was envious. I thought that if all the people in our country were that understanding and united together that well, there wouldn't be affairs like this one [the Samyang tenant struggle]."

Students on Farmer Consciousness

What, then, is the student and general understanding of the realities of farmers' consciousness, and how in turn do they understand it historically—that is, understand the factors and processes which have produced it? The unwritten and often unspoken query is: why have they revolted less, changed their circumstances less, and why still do they revolt less and seek less change? They speak of farmers' consciousness "of defeat," "of conservatism," "of damages," and "of anti-ideology." "Consciousness" is loosely attached to nouns, and in this vein I have also heard of the "master [i.e., master–slave] consciousness" and the "insufficient solidarity consciousness."

Over and over I heard about farmers' "defeatism," or *p'aebae ŭisik,* a persistent fear and belief that things will come to naught. One student pointed out that it was epitomized in farmers' fear of even a phone call from a policeman: "Isn't it our [students'] function to get rid of defeatism?" he asked. Another student explained this defeatism as being engendered by a reality whereby support by the ruling party brings real benefits to individuals and villages, such as loans or opportunities for employment. Yet another student observed that, "Exploited and pushed down for decades, they are overcome by defeatism . . . even though the movement has awakened them to injustice they are still not confident that they can triumph." Another explained that the students decided that the movement had liberated farmers from the defeatism engendered by their historical experience, which "had enslaved them to the illegality and injustice of remitting tenant rents." Samyang, "which they had breathed like air, they now thought of as their enemy."

The historical passivity of farmers has been attributed to their lack of class consciousness; as one student put it, "History severs it." Similarly, some students attribute farmers' "fear of ideology" both to the politics and education of the "red-complex" and to their historical experience. One student with rural roots, a history major, explained that, in postliberation history, the government got rid of the Left and made people afraid of ideology, so that "people just do what they have to do."

Perhaps the greatest challenge for students was to reconcile farmer passivity with their desired changes and the requirements for subjectivity in movements and history. Students understood the situation in this way: farmers are the subjects of history, but history has often left them blind to their subjectivity. And to create a society where farmers are subjects, first, there must be education to rescue them from the blindness that has effectively kept them from historical subjectivity, and second, there is a need for movements in which they are subjects striving for changed material conditions.

Students and the oppositional community are thus passionate about moments of light in history's darkness, interludes of farmers' political action. Or again, more subtly, they are interested not only in political movements, but also in the much less self-conscious oppositional moments, "blind vestiges" that reveal consciousness untold in history's annals—consciousness that has not been exercised strictly politically because of the weight of the repressive powers and structure of material conditions. In this equation, cultural expression (songs, dance, oral tradition, and so on) was understood as the repository of such consciousness. It is not surprising, then, to find cultural revivals—based on peasant culture—clearly articulated for nonghwal's cultural agenda.

The opposition community in general, and particularly student activists, appropriated peasant culture for their oppositional practice. Students asserted that the "community" culture of farmers had been destroyed by "individualistic materialistic culture and administrative force" under the false name of modernization (Agricultural Action Resource Collection 1987: 131). They called for a revival of "healthy minjung culture" to "realize a national community where humans are liberated" (Agricultural Action

Resource Collection 1987: 131). They understood the cornerstone of traditional farmer culture as the integrated nexus of work and play (Choi, 1989:
12). The nonghwal paradox is that, while the "subjects" of production, farmers, have turned away from "traditional" culture, students have been maintaining it. Students, then, want to have these subjects of cultural production
recapture their "healthy" culture. As they put it, "The real problem is to
draw out their unknown healthiness through doing minjung culture . . . it's
not showing or teaching our thing, but showing them their own thing." Students assumed that participation in unified work and play, epitomized historically by the *ture* or traditional labor cooperatives, would help farmers
"realize their own value and raise their consciousness as farmers."

Students, however, found their encounters with labor and play confusing.
In their reflection sessions they often expressed dismay at how difficult it
was to meet with young men after a day of work; the men were exhausted
and would fade away into private lives beyond the students' reach. Students
were also frustrated to find that while they worked alongside the young men
they could find nothing to talk about, no common ground. The students discussed their desire to establish a routine structure, feeling that this was the
best way to mimic laboring lives: "If we live loosely then it will seem that it
isn't that we came here to learn, but only for the purpose of confirming that
we are university students." For one group, the chance to clean the out-
houses was a meaningful experience that "helped to change farmers' understanding of us." Students felt very strongly that they should be doing natural
labor—namely, not tasks dreamed up to appease their requests, but rather
necessary work which they discovered for themselves "with a subject consciousness." Further, students discussed the need to labor more in conjunction with farmers. They cautioned each other that they should work
diligently and try to avoid being "caught napping." Labor was considered to
be crucial to farmer consciousness and likewise to any formation of student
consciousness. During this particular nonghwal, it rained incessantly, making it difficult to labor in any way. The students were also jarred by the fact
that it was usually the richest villagers who could provide sustained labor
activity for visiting students. Finally, labor was, students found, hard to
endear themselves to: "In seminars we frequently hear the words that labor
is the prime mover in human history, but I still don't really understand. Our
goal is to obtain a minjung character. But when a leech attached itself, I
flung it off so quickly."

For the source of a revolutionary spirit, many students found it helpful to
refer to the historical subconscious of farmers. One student remarked,
"I had learned that everyone has a revolutionary spirit," but after his first
nonghwal experience in Kangwando Province he came to doubt this; in
Koch'ang, though, "the disappointment of last year completely disappeared
as farmers' potential was revealed through the movement." Another student
explained that it was difficult to politicize farmers in Haeri because they

had yet to break through the oppression of Samyang to wake up the sub-conscious.

We can see, then, in students' revisionist perspective, that they turned to cultural expressions and the historical unconscious, thus calling for farmer mobilization. Still, in practicing nonghwal, it was hard for students to recon-cile the realities of contemporary rural life with the above-described histori-cal and cultural character of farmers.

Farmers on Farmer Consciousness

What, then, is the farmers' view of ideology, or *sasang?* Recalling the above-outlined construction of the farmer burdened with various conscious-nesses—of defeat, submissiveness, fear of damages, and so on—in the farm-ers' discussions of ideology they do not appear as submissive defeatists, but rather as astute actors who have carefully evaluated their situation histori-cally. That is, apparently passive onlookers, in fact farmers are careful read-ers of the material constraints affecting their lives.

It is impossible to divorce the farmers' view of the movement and of the outside organizers from their historical experience with what they under-stand as ideology and the people they associate with ideology. Regarding ideology, most prominent in farmers' minds was the Korean War, the time when, as one farmer put it, "people died over ideology." Another farmer said, "People died right side up and upside down, but what do we village guys *(nom)* know about the world?" For people who lived through the Korean War period, ideology referred mostly to communism, which was in keeping with the state's cold war framing of the Korean War. Thus, for farmers, "ideology," or sasang, refers to political thought over which people have fought and died.

In talking with farmers it became clear to me that anything having to do with a stated set of ideas, anything other than those thoughts and practices that are at once part of nature, an extension of the land—eating and living—is considered the province of ideology. As one man put it when talking about the Korean War, "my life [life-long] is a green life; like the dew on a blade of grass, like a reed; if it goes there I go there; if it goes here I go here . . . we don't have ideology . . . isn't that what we *paeksŏng* [Koreans] are . . . what do people like us know? Life? No one wants to die. . . . I know all about the time of communist rule or *in'gong,* but I don't want to talk about it."

There was a sense among farmers that ideology is reserved for the intelli-gent, those in society who are educated. In this way the contemporary coun-tryside was rendered an entirely residual category. Historically—particularly with reference to Korean War times—all the intelligent people—that is, those "with ideology"—were killed or over time were forced by the govern-ment and by the local stigma attached to such a past, to leave for Seoul. In recent years as well, enterprising and intelligent people—those with a vision of a better life—had also left for the city. As for the Korean War period, one man put it: "Ignorant people couldn't be reds, you had to know something; we [i.e., ignorant people] just went there if they said 'go there,' and the other way if they said 'go over the other way.' " This sort of talk of the ideological and practical intelligence that had been drained from the countryside was a mainstay in my discussions with farmers.

The hegemony of the state is not that the state is understood as a natural order, but rather the fact that it has effectively constituted the entire realm of the political as the domain which farmers have not thought to change. For example, many farmers' versions of good and bad do not accord with official histories or constructions in the government's largely successful casting of the Korean War experience or turmoil in the realm of ideology. They do, however, conform to the government project to cast it all in terms of ideology. For farmers who recast ideology into catchalls of intelligence, politics, and directed action, only the living and eating—the direct extensions of the land—are their domain. It is in this context that the 1980s turn of farmers' movement organizations away from ideology was effective; similarly late-1980s moves to localize movements and detach them from national organizations were a part of this effort. Let us now turn to the events that transpired only a month after the nonghwal, when the Koch'ang farmers ventured to Seoul to stage a protest at the corporate headquarters of their landlords.

The Price Wars in Seoul

The month of protest in Seoul was intensive; developments escalated, and after only a week several violent incidents had occurred. From the earliest days of the occupation, tension was building, and the so-called Leadership Committee of the Relinquish Committee was splitting, largely in accordance with, if not necessarily on account of, sympathy for or antipathy toward the CFU. Specifically, though, the issue at hand was the matter of price: at what, if any price, farmers would concede to buy the land. Here, too, we find divergence between farmers' and organizers' often disparate claims. Above all, organizers underestimated the significance of internal divisions within the movement.

From the very first day, external groups addressed the farmers, proclaiming the farmers' relation to history, announcing that this movement itself was historical. They spoke to legitimize the farmers' movement in two senses, noting both its representativeness and its particularity. First, they affirmed the history of the claim that the tenant land should long ago have been theirs, establishing the fact that the farmers' story was not an isolated anomaly but in keeping with deep historical structures such as the laws of victors and losers in Korea's postwar history. The second way in which they historicized the movement was quite different, noting, not the structures that made for the movement's agenda, but rather the movement's particularity: its prominent, unprecedented, and symbolic meaning.

The first history, then, is the deeply entrenched patterns, class relations, and so on, whereas history in the second sense refers to the rupturing effect the movement is to have on history. Furthermore, the more historical the movement became in these two senses, the more it was located both in the present and the past as being political and social as well as economic. As the movement escalated in Seoul, however, it became clear that farmers did not always impart the same historical meaning to events. Although above I contrasted outsider-structural and farmer-experiential readings of history, let me suggest that the project of constructing legacy or proclaiming historical rule is often an elite vocation. Those people objectified by structures or victimized by systems know that proclaimed changes are often just more of the same, bringing little transformation for them.

For farmers, the most upsetting discovery in Seoul was the lack of media attention they received. They found this lack of coverage shocking; it was as if they had turned the world on its head and nobody had taken note. Visitors to the headquarters were barraged with questions as to whether they had seen anything on television after arriving on August 12. It was not until August 15 that the story was covered in the *Tonga Daily*, the most prominent national newspaper, which farmers referred to later as the "eyes and ears of the nation." The August 15 article, however, was not only scanty and marginally placed but blatantly distorted. It denied the legitimacy of the farmers' claim by negating their historical argument.

The angry response to the *Tonga Daily* article, however, was different on the part of farmers and nonfarmers, although both were equally concerned with history in their own fashion. Nonfarmers were principally concerned with the historical relationship between the Samyang and Tonga corporations; Kim Sŏngsu, Samyang's founder, also started the *Tonga Daily*. They considered this relationship as a revealing structural and historical one: Korea's power elite backing successive authoritarian regimes. As such the distortion represented above all the Tonga connection, a meticulously embroidered web of oppressors. Farmers, in contrast, were most bitter that their protest had been ignored, their history distorted, and their words twisted. A structure, the relationship between powerless farmers like themselves and so-called system powers like the *Tonga Daily*, was clear even without knowledge of the relation between these elites. Most farmers learned of the historical connection between their landlord and the country's largest newspaper through this incident. But it was their humanity that was offended, because no one took note of what was, for them, the most radical of all actions: attempting to overthrow their landlord.

Over time, two conflicting notions of settlement emerged: a contractual version, that is, a price settlement, and a settlement that would rectify historical wrongs, establish legitimacy, and affirm moral principles. In the earliest meetings, the company was willing to argue in historical, moral, and legal terms. Interestingly, during the course of the negotiations farmers learned to talk in the historical terms of the company elite. As the corporation increasingly discussed an in-the-present, realistic financial settlement, the farmers framed their no-compensation claim in historical, moral, and legal terms. Eventually one group of farmers retreated from these articulations in favor of a reasonable settlement, while another group held tenaciously to the platform that had been constituted through the course of debate and confrontation with the company in the buildings, the street, and the negotiations.

By early September, with the imminent farming demands of early fall and because of heavy rains that had flattened much of the rice stalk, the majority of farmers called for a speedy settlement. Organizers and a minority of farmers argued, however, that with two already seriously injured student protesters they could not give up; the majority of farmers asked instead how they could go on endangering the lives of fellow Korean parents' sons and daughters. The discussion at an internal meeting of the farmers after three weeks of protest, one week before a final settlement was reached, was revealing: by that point it was the internal dissension, the split itself, that was most troubling to the farmers. Broadly, whereas some were reconciled to their own weakness, others insisted on employing the full strength of outside forces:

WOMAN: We have come 200 ri [unit of distance], why is the Leadership Committee [Yun and his close associates] split; let's not do this!

MAN: We paid rents till yesterday so we have to buy it.

MODERATOR: How should we fight? It seems like 1,500 won per pyŏng [a unit of land] is possible. They mentioned it at Red Cross.

YUN: The problem is that if we discuss it there will be rumors, but if we don't discuss it, then there will be no basis on which to calculate. Please believe the organizing committee—as we are committed to following the majority.

WOMAN: How long will you persist with 500 won?

LEADERSHIP COMMITTEE: Leave it up to us. . . . We can't say.

OLD MAN: Let's not split up—We came up believing Kim, so let's go down the same way.

OLD MAN: We are so hungry we can't sleep. Hungry people always have difficulties . . . those people [the corporation] eat well and are full. . . . Let's leave it to the leadership committee.

OLD MAN: We can't do it with our own power so let's get other organizations [said very strongly] because the company considers us lightly. [Applause]

COMMITTEE MEMBER: Let's cooperate with as many organizations as possible.

YUN: It is not that I am against that, but without the farmers, other groups can't do anything—our farmers should come up [to Seoul].

MAN: The village representatives should go to Koryŏ University and
'phone from there.

YUN: Six hundred farmers cannot agree on a price, so the Leadership
Committee should do it.

MAN: If we don't have people we can't work. Let's get people from farmers' organizations and be really active.

YUN: First of all we need more farmers.

MAN: There has been a dramatic drop in the numbers since we first
started. Our will and the will of the leaders have weakened. We
should figure out how many people there were and bring the numbers back up to that level.

YOUTH: It is important to ask youth groups, such as the religious youth
groups, to participate . . . those people don't have private
desires. . . . And let's get help from the students also.

MAN: Actually, two students have been injured; if we get more support
there will only be more [injuries] so let's quickly settle.

STUDENT: Let's squeeze the neck of the poisonous snake; if we let it be,
we will never be victorious. Let's strengthen our internal solidarity.
Let's develop better methods of struggle.

MODERATOR: There is the Red Cross protest and various methods; so
let's leave it up to the Leadership Committee.

At about this point, suddenly, education or conscientization activities
waned. Largely these had been lectures on Korean history and agriculture.
One day, on the blackboard usually reserved for song lyrics that were being
taught to farmers and for lecture notes, "NO MORE EDUCATION" appeared in
enormous letters. It is unclear who wrote this declaration, but Kim
explained the turning point for himself and Lee: "I didn't like farmer education—the movement people (*undonggwŏn*) indulge in their greed to have
people become movement people . . . so we decided to have no more education." The final straw for Yun, however, was when he heard Min say at one
of the meetings: "If we just fight for one or two months—even if there are
no results—we will be able to take even the salt fields when we go down."[8]
He explained, "When I heard that I didn't want anything of it . . . I couldn't
put up with it any longer. . . . I thought, we don't need any particular education; as long as we eat, sleep, and stay united, I figured we would win."
Finally, it was the impulse to return quickly, to divorce themselves from the
spiraling politics, and of course to tend to their paddies that triumphed for
the large majority of farmers.

At about that time one farmer told me that things had gone astray
because they had meant it to be a tenant struggle or *sojak chaengŭi*, but
instead it was becoming a movement—that people were trying to make
"movement people" out of them. He contrasted a single movement with a
broader struggle against broader structures. Many farmers did not want to
become members of the permanent community of opposition. Indeed, by
the final days of the protest the farmers were literally split into two camps,

even demonstrating at different sites. Finally they decided to purchase the land at the government set price, 1,881 won per p'yŏng. One woman, a great admirer of CFU who followed its more radical line, said that she was sad that CFU people did not understand why they had had to finish everything so quickly. As she put it, "Since students had gotten hurt, it couldn't help but have ended quickly . . . but the CFU people only thought about cutting the price, not the students . . . money was running out and fund-raising wasn't going well."

Far-Reaching Effects

The settlement of price did little to settle deeper conflicts over the legitimacy of the Relinquish Committee, the external forces, and the movement itself. At the center of these considerations were basic concepts of leadership, activism, and settlement. Although there was variance in protest styles and even strategies, there had been, at least to some extent, cooperation before and during the time at Seoul. Things really came to a head, though, shortly after the mid-September dispersal, when a quarter-page apology from the Relinquish Committee, signed by Yun, appeared in South Korea's four major newspapers. For some, this apology, above all else, undermined the legitimacy of the Relinquish Committee. Stroke by stroke the apology denied the historical legitimacy of the entire movement, negating each and every premise of the struggle and apologizing for having unjustifiably attacked the corporation's good name.

It was not, however, so easy to pinpoint Yun, to label it his personal betrayal, because the final contract—which CFU members Cho and Kang had also signed—stipulated that an apology to the company would be published in the name of the head of the Relinquish Committee. In response to this settlement, the CFU forces were closely involved in mobilizing for an annulment of the contract, reformulation of the leadership committee, and for at least a revision in the terms of the land purchase and, equally important, the terms of the government loan program for the purchase of the land. Min wanted to offer a "new table of distance" or "correct direction" for the vanguard of the tenant struggle: "the main force that rolls the wagon wheel of history—the male and female, old and young tenants who, like the sun, radiate light from the center and fought putting everything on the line."

One student reflected on a meeting that he and another student had organized in order to explain the unfavorable aspects of the contract to the farmers. Thirty-five people came to the meeting in the village hall. Although many farmers showed interest and some got excited, the student reflected critically that "only those who know something," specifically, more prosperous farmers with government connections and often those higher on the village and social hierarchy, "those not directly related to the profits and losses [of this movement], spoke up." He explained that those farmers truly related to the movement, tenants who stood to lose or gain, left the meeting. He commented that they should have held the meeting in a private home.

The countryside was further polarized in the aftermath of the movement because it became the common sense of some of the CFU affiliates and some nonmember farmers that Yun had been paid off by the company with an impressive sum of money. Furthermore, this was published in a pamphlet that was widely distributed against the wishes of some of the members of the non-CFU independent peasant movement organizations, particularly the independent Koch'ang Farmers Union. The accusation seemed to polarize farmers even more. For some it was not just Yun but farmers as a whole whose integrity had been bludgeoned by the heavy-handed denunciations. The debt to outside groups, particularly the CFU and the students, had been universally recognized among farmers, but for many the denunciation canceled the debt; their dignity had been offended. One man who earlier had even contemplated joining the CFU concluded, "if CFU doesn't publish an apology, then they are really not a group which helps weak people . . . if they are truly an organization for us, they should fight for weak farmers." A resident of the same village as Yun, he put his finger on the troubling gap between debt to and denunciation of CFU, the space where farmers had been first propped up and then cut down:

> For farmers to fight like that—in one place—is historically unique . . . we were really exceptional, but that isn't the "heart of farmers"; it was all because the CFU and other groups helped us, but then the CFU circulated that rumor. Of course, the CFU is better than we are, so everyone believed them, but I don't know if it is true or false . . . I don't know whether they said that based on something or whether they wanted to split the farmers. . . . Yun is just a person who catches fish in the reservoir and sells them himself. . . . I've known him since I was a child; he is not someone whose heart would be "badly eaten."

He repeated that it was the split that was the bad thing, but that still he remained grateful for the CFU's help. He explained that of course Min was very smart, but "in terms of character and the things he says, he is really different from us farmers . . . it is hard for people like us, mere land tillers, to talk to him."

Six months after the Seoul movement, Yun explained his decision to end the Seoul activities precisely in terms of farmer subjectivity, "if at that time we hadn't reached some result, the CFU would have become the subject of the movement." His notion of leadership and of the movement centered on "winning" or accomplishing the task at hand, settling the local land matter. Yun was not ashamed, for example, of the assertion that he drank outside of Samyang in Seoul with officials; he explained that this had been negotiation on behalf of the farmers. Nor did he find it incongruous with his notions of the movement to explain that he had—outside of the controversial contract—unwritten agreements with Samyang ensuring that if the appropriate government loans were not issued the company would arrange a payment program over several years.

After several months, those rallying to form a new Relinquish Committee scheduled a large meeting. Although Yun had been asked to come, he was furious that the meeting had not been discussed with him; his "pride and his sense of subject" kept him away, he explained. One student, though, understood Yun's absence as an admission of guilt regarding payoffs, concluding, "It is wrong to think of him as one of the mass (taejung), he is an enemy." Yun's sense of subjectivity was at odds with the sense of subjectivity of the external forces. Many onlookers, organizers in particular, criticized his seemingly self-propelled commitment to the economic struggle and his politically compromising technique.

In December 1987 it was announced that farmers could buy their land with loans at 80 percent for all land under two thousand p'yŏng (approximately 2 acres). For the majority of farmers this was a feasible and reasonable offer; for most it was even more government support than they had counted on. One man claims that it was at this juncture that the CFU erred in continuing to press for a better arrgreement. He explained that if the CFU had then agreed on the purchase, they could have gone on to the next (organizing) task, but instead it became impossible for Min to talk to those who had purchased the land and impossible for them to talk to him. Repeatedly I heard that these strained human relations in the countryside were traumatic, particularly for those who had largely backed the line and decisions of the CFU. One man who decided to purchase his land explained that he felt apologetic to Min and respected him, "but now I can't meet and talk to him because he probably won't understand me and he will probably think I was bought off by Yun and others." For this farmer, Yun's decision to return to the countryside was not at all a matter of ideology or politics, it was merely, "Yun and others on the side of the farmers, knowing that the farmers were exhausted, wanting to speed things up and return home."

Even farmers who settled very clearly on different positions in the course of the Koch'ang Tenant Farmers movement were ambivalent about these dissentions back in the countryside. One active CFU supporter and radical fighter said months after it was over that it was a "shameful thing" that "it had ended up like this"; by "this" he seemed to be referring to the divided state of affairs, particularly embarrassing because of the sacrifices so many outsiders had made. Back in the countryside, sitting in one of the contiguous villages, unity is something that farmers esteem highly. Cho, many months afterward, put it this way: "the police and Samyang are one, but Yun holds his distance from both, although he is close to both." As for his feelings for Yun, he explained almost longingly, "he hates me, so—there is nothing I can do about it—I hate him, I have to hate him." As to the bribe, he wavered, "I have no proof, but it is possible . . . perhaps it cannot help but be so."

Students, or at least the loudest and most articulate of them, settled under the policy and platforms of the CFU. After things became complicated, some farmers resented the fact that the students, too, had become the voice of CFU. The students had originally planned fall and winter nong-hwal, but because of the dissention they met with among farmers and their own internal disagreement as to the seat of legitimacy in the by then splintered movement, they did not return to the countryside. This disappointed many farmers.

One of the long-lasting results of internal dissention was that further political-politicizing activities in this region became more difficult. It is striking, for example, that in February 1989, when 200,000 farmers gathered in Seoul for unprecedented protests over the American exportation of foodstuffs, only three farmers from this region were there, in spite of statistics documenting that participation from the Chŏlla provinces was highest. By that time all the CFU groups in this region had disbanded and only a few farmers remained active. The Koch'ang Farmers Union, in spite of its firm commitment to independent local organizing, in the eyes of most farmers had largely been subsumed by the CFU and the various controversies; at one point rumors even circulated that the local Koch'ang Farmers Union had also been paid off. One of its members echoed Yun's concern that the CFU had become the subject of the movement. What saddened this young, unmarried, uneducated farmer, who would later become an officer in the Koch'ang Farmers Union, was the CFU's lack of understanding of the lives of local farmer activists. He explained that CFU members had spread rumors that it was difficult to meet Koch'ang Farmers Union members because one farmer activist did not make it to an important meeting—"Intellectuals can't understand; he couldn't come because he was busy working in the fields." He pointed out that activists' lives follow the calendar of political events, but that farmers' lives follow the rhythm of work and slack of the agricultural calendar. We were talking after the December 1987 elections, and he commented that elections too were "this way": "although the important thing is to involve the masses, their [outsiders'] focus is always political issues."

Non-CFU activists resented what many called the "CFU hegemony over the movement." One activist particularly resented the CFU's constant allusion to its "organizational strength," that is, the power and authority of the Catholic church, thereby undermining local initiative and strength. She particularly objected that Min had addressed the farmers saying that, if things didn't work out well [in Seoul], because of a "hidden card"—presumably Catholicism—they would triumph.

One of the most instructive lessons for me during fieldwork was running into a group of men at the restaurant at the bus station in Koch'ang several months after the Seoul protest. Gathered there were four men—all acquaintances of mine, men clearly on opposite sides of the political fence with whom, one-on-one, I would probably have steered cautiously clear of any discussion about the other, and probably would even have been afraid to admit my occasional meetings with the others. Yet, here they were, a motley crew—Yun, a man from Samyang, a CFU-affiliated farmer activist, and a policeman, all having coffee together. Such is how the dust of conflict sometimes settles, or at least appears to settle, in the countryside, where "living and eating" are stronger than ideology, as the farmers so eloquently tell us.

Through an examination of this farmers' movement, I have attempted to characterize the dissent between farmers and external forces. At times, various outsiders did not have a realistic understanding of the fabric of rural life or the nature of the astute politics of farmers. As I have indicated, though, increasingly there was a turn in the community toward the experience of farmers or the minjung. Farmers' movement organizations and students were making heroic attempts to localize their campaigns and to follow farmer self-initiated campaigns. These compromises, however, were difficult to exercise inasmuch as, frequently, they resulted in less broad-based political action. The Koch'ang farmers' movement was considered a failure by many in the organizing community and by many farmers as well. For the organizers it was a failure because, first, the final settlement was not comprehensive or favorable enough and, second, because there was no ongoing activism in the region and in fact the region had become, in their estimation, impossible to organize. For many farmers it was considered a failure because of the divisiveness that descended upon the region in the aftermath of the final settlement.

The movement, however, was also considered a failure by some farmers because, although they were pleased to be landowners, they realized increasingly that landownership did not solve the basic problem of agriculturalists in South Korea. In this sense, farmers naturally tended toward more organizer-like structural readings of their history and their world, and ways of linking the matter of individual and national subjectivity. In the 1980s, minjung-as-subject ideas were central to much of the discourse on the Korean past and to prescriptions for the Korean future. Through the vista of this movement we have seen that minjung-as-subject activism posed, albeit diversely, challenges to the community of opposition's general way of ordering experience, to farmers' received practices, and to the South Korean state.

We have seen that the minjung imagery—the ideals, idioms, and ideologies through which minjung others were conjured—was an important agent in the Koch'ang Tenant Farmers movement. In this spirit, we must reflect on South Korea's minjung movement as both the politics and history of this minjung imagery, and on its exercise or interaction with the movements of "the people." It is in the midst of the complex and shifting character of these interactions in the late 1980s that we must ground the course of the Koch'ang Tenant Farmers movement. In so doing, movements emerge not as scripted or coherent activities, but rather as phenomena constantly in-the-making, suspended in the idioms and ideals of diverse imageries.

8

The Iconic Power of Modernity: Reading a Cheju Shaman's Life History and Initiation Dream

Kim Seong Nae

A Painful Story

"Aih, it hurts! Whenever I think about it, my heart aches severely," Kŭn Simbang lowered her voice, drawing close to me. After a pause, she blew out cigarette smoke as if sighing. Her sons and their wives were in another room across the way.

Kŭn Simbang volunteered to relate her life story to the cassette tape. She asked me to write a personal statement applying to the government for reconsideration of her veterans' pension on behalf of her dead husband. The pension was stopped twenty years ago, but the government recently announced that it would reimburse lost or unclaimed pensions to those whose pensions had been discontinued for some reason. If people reapplied with an adequate explanation of the circumstances under which their pensions had been cut, they could be eligible to receive the monthly stipends once again. Kŭn Simbang's husband had been serving with a local militia established to defend the village when a gun accident occurred in 1953. It was "the month of the winter solstice. The second eighth day. The year of the snake. The day of his death. Then he was shot to death during the turbulent times *(siguk)*." I took out a notebook and started to write down what she was telling me.

The story Kŭn Simbang told is not merely the life story of an individual *simbang*, the Cheju native term for a shaman; her story attests to the history of modern Korea as it has shaped her personal suffering and transformed her into a shaman. Just as she begins her life story with her husband's death, so the modern history of the South Korean nation begins with the deaths of soldiers who fought against the communists. This was when Korea began to establish its identity as an anticommunist nation in 1948. Beyond being a personal narrative, her life history parallels the progression of modern Korean history.

155

In this chapter, I present the life story of Kŭn Simbang, a sixty-four-year-old female shaman who lives in Kosalmi, a seashore fishing village in the northeastern part of Cheju Island. Within her life history, I focus particularly on the narration of an initiation dream she had in 1964; she was then forty-two years old. In the dream, the image of an American military ruler appeared as a shamanic ancestor who prophesied that she was destined to be a shaman and indicated the spiritual power this required. This dream occurred at a crucial time in modern Korean history, when the Korean government had just launched the first national economic development plan to help Korea gain economic independence and prosperity. Between 1945 and 1961, the Korean economy had been dependent on various forms of foreign aid, including a great deal of food.[1] There is a question here why a dream in the 1960s would contain the critical experience of the April Third Incident of 1948: could the mythical aura invoked in her dream be purely political?

Kŭn Simbang's religious experience of ancestral revelation, which lasted over two decades (1948–1964), must be analyzed within the particular historical context of Korean national experience. Her dream reflects the political iconography of modernity whose dominant image is the development of the Korean nation under the supervision of American power, which occurred during the period between the 1945 liberation and the early sixties, the dawn of national economic development planning. To interpret this dream, I treat it as a narrative in which elements of Kŭn's life story and the national history could be intertextually construed. I will argue that the redemptive power of the initiation dream—power to transform oneself into a shaman—germinates in the shaman's act of dreaming, transforming immediate events and experiences into a larger social text for personal and historical change. This may be another way of looking at nation and nationalism, as an idea projected on and practiced by people through their experiences of life and death. The key tropes of modernity for Korea in the 1990s with which we are concerned here, namely, *minjok* (nation) and *minjung*, must be understood also from within the vague and mysterious regions of the imagination and experience. In examining Kŭn Simbang's life history, we can witness how these tropes ordinarily acquire an overt symbolic identity that encourages an attitude of secular subjectivity which reorganizes social and epistemological categories according to the metaphysics of progress—that is, modernity.

True Stories

Kŭn Simbang's husband's death in 1953 is related to the April Third Incident, called *sasam sakŏn* in Korea. On 3 April 1948, several hundred communist guerrillas attacked police stations and thus began an ideological struggle that was to last for nine years until the last guerrilla was captured in 1957. According to Kŭn Simbang, the remaining communist guerrillas continued to threaten the islanders even after the end of the Korean War. The civilian militia was mobilized as a secondary antiguerrilla force to supplement the constabulatory army and police. Because the native militia was familiar with the surroundings and knew the possible hiding places of the remaining guerrillas, they were often placed in the front lines for surveillance purposes. In this capacity, Kŭn Simbang's husband guided hundreds of people from several neighboring villages deep into the Mount Halla area to collect reeds in order to repair their thatched roofs and feed their cattle and horses.

Although Kŭn Simbang did not explicitly describe the circumstances surrounding her husband's death, her seemingly offhand and cursory description of the event suggests an unwillingness to share all the facts of the story. In public, she often described the event in a way that suggested that he had been shot by the communist guerrillas, although she always omitted actually saying by whom. "He was shot to death," she stated without specifying the agency of this violence. Given the situation at the time, it was automatically assumed that he had been shot by the communist guerrillas; it was therefore unnecessary for her to name those responsible for her husband's death. On the other hand, her reluctance to discuss the details of this event might stem from a fear of raising questions about her husband's loyalty—that is, whether he had supported the "democratic" or the communist side; and on this issue, none of the islanders would press her for a clear-cut explanation. The Cheju people generally do not talk about the April Third Incident in ordinary conversation; when they do refer to it, it is simply known as "those turbulent times."

Only once, during the tape-recorded session, did Kŭn Simbang tell me the truth about her husband's death. She said that he had been "shot to death" *not* by the communist guerrillas, as in the publicly accepted version, but accidentally by his own machine gun while he was wrestling with his fellow militiamen, who warned him not to load the bullets. The "true story" was a painful one. In fact, Kŭn's personal truth would eventually discredit the official truth about his heroic death as a soldier. It remains a mystery still whether or not the official version was what was actually reported by the authorities at the time of the accident.

According to Kŭn's account, the authorities helped out at the funeral ceremony as well as providing a relief fund every month, which amounted to compensation for the bereaved family members of dead soldiers and policemen. Apparently, the most prominent doctor from the city was summoned to perform an immediate operation, which could only be viewed as a truly honorable gesture to this poor, uneducated, landless widow. The whole village sympathized with the widow; they helped her renovate her dilapidated house and offered her a job at the mill where her husband had worked. In short, her husband was treated as a national hero in the village, glorified in (self-induced) death by the authorities' fictional narrative, in which he was added to the roll of patriotic deaths in those turbulent times. In contrast, the consequence of this honorable death, a casualty in the campaign to build a new democratic nation-state through the repression of communist rebels, was poverty and hard work in the mill for Kŭn Simbang.

In spite of the fact that Kŭn Simbang was given her husband's job after his death, she was left with four children and was forced to live in a state of poverty. Because she subsequently had two more children out of wedlock, she quickly lost her pension. (Unchaste behavior legally disqualified women for such pensions.) It is ironic that the same government which glorified Kŭn Simbang's husband in death terminated her pension when she needed it most. Although Kŭn Simbang seemed to bear stoically the burden of the heroic death of her husband and the popular myth of the independent, hard-working Cheju woman, she suffered greatly as she became more of a social outcast in the community. It was this state of alienation, however, that prepared her for the role of simbang. In describing it, she chose a phrase typically used when referring to the fate of a simbang: "Destiny had been turned upside down *(chŏnsŭng-kŭrŭkch'ida)."* So how is her personal tragedy and self-transformation to be understood in the context of Korean national history? Her dream-story indicates how history is tamed into narrative. The hard times of the 1960s and 1950s she invokes never stride about in the light of day, but roam in the shadows of people's memories, as dream in complicity with collective muteness.

The Initiation Dream

In 1964, at the age of forty-two, Kŭn Simbang had her first healing experience as well as a mysterious dream, which I here call an initiation dream. In the dream, a mysterious man, perhaps the ancestor of a simbang, prophesied her destiny to serve thousands of spirits of dead people. That dream became a reality. As her clientele in the village increased and brought rice and money in payment for her healing practices, her family was able to live securely. At forty-five, she underwent a formal initiation rite.

Kŭn Simbang described her initiation dream with vivid imagery:

> At the crossroads, near what is now the chicken farmhouse, there had been a *ch'ongsal* [a cottage gate made of two wooden poles]. I was hung from that. My hands and feet were swollen and tied to it as if I was praying. Then a giant man who was as wide as a tree trunk, wearing a huge, room-sized hat like an American Military Police helmet, came walking down the street from the southeast. He had a huge iron club, red on one side and black on the other. As he approached me, I saw thousands of people, children and adults, men and women, coming toward me from every direction. Some of them held spears in their hands; some had been working in the fields. The giant [*orŭn*, a respectable person] stood by me and said angrily, "Who bound her? Who chained her?" And he touched me three times with the red side of the iron club. Thereupon I was released from the ch'ongsal. As I turned my face away crying, he held and

comforted me. "Don't cry," he said. "I will offer you a straw-sack of rice and two sacks of barley. Don't cry and go back home." After walking back home in the dream, I woke up.

Next day I told an old woman in the neighborhood about my dream rather cautiously. "I dreamt last night. A big gentleman wearing a half-moon shaped MP helmet on his head approached me and touched me three times with an iron club. He said that he would send a sack of rice and two sacks of barley to my house." The old woman responded, saying, "That sounds really queer!" . . . But next day around four o'clock in the afternoon, special relief food unexpectedly arrived at my house. A gourd bowl of rice flour and two bowls of corn flour! So they were equivalent to one sack of rice and two sacks of barley, exactly as predicted in the dream!

When I first heard this story, I could not figure out why the giant man wore an American Military Police helmet and carried an iron club, nor why Kǔn Simbang was hung at the gate of the village. Usually the gate is located in front of a private house. I wondered if this village gate really existed. And who were those thousands of people, especially those carrying bamboo spears? Later Kǔn Simbang explained to me that they were the *three thousand soldiers* of the shamanic pantheon, the hungry and low-ranking spirits of those who died violently through suicide or murder or in war, and so on.[2]

Kǔn Simbang was not concerned with these questions, nor with a literal interpretation of her dream. She simply took it for granted that the appearance of the giant man was a sign of a revelation from the simbang ancestor. Instead, she put more emphasis on the fact that she was released from the bondage of poverty. Although the actual quantity of relief food was much less than the promised amount, her dream had come true and would never betray her hope for the future. After this initiation dream, Kǔn Simbang had many clients throng to her house. Thereafter white rice or barley was brought as payment for her skills, and she and her children were well-fed. The kind words and promises of the giant gentleman—that is, her spiritual ancestor—were indeed the only sources of consolation for her in the face of poverty and social ostracism as an unchaste widow. It seems ironic that the warmth from her ancestor (and the hungry ghosts) was the only source of hope and welfare. Indeed, this balance between this-worldly alienation and otherworldly compensation represents Kǔn Simbang's sense of justice, which is imbued with the popular perception of a utopian dream. However, questions I raised earlier about her dream images must be clarified.

Redemptive History

Pictures in a book about the April Third event in 1948 provided some crucial clues to the mysterious dream imagery (see Plates 1 and 2).[3] The ch'ongsal, the village gate to which Kǔn Simbang was hung and tied by her hands

Plate 1. The dream image of Ch'ongsal

Plate 2. "An American advisor looks on silently where no advice will help" (*Life* magazine, October 1948).

"Look! Here is our implacable enemy! Look at this Yankee soldier who is standing shamelessly and coldly watching these mourning women at the scene of merciless massacre!" (Kim Minju and Kim Ponghyŏn 1963: 259).

and feet, actually existed during the turbulent times (1948–1953). It was a surveillance gate standing in front of a sentry post temporarily constructed at the village boundary in defense against the communist guerrillas. It was constructed with four three-foot-high, vertical wooden poles on each side, on top of which were placed two horizontal ones. Indeed, the ch'ongsal marked the physical limits of village safety. Each village was surrounded by a protective stone wall. At the gate rose two seven-foot-high, three-foot-wide stone towers, between which stood the ch'ongsal. The village militia ordered curfew between sunset and dawn. When the villagers had to work in the fields outside the fortress, some of the armed militiamen accompanied them. Outside the ch'ongsal, anyone was susceptible to rebel attacks or being accused of collaborating with the communists. Kŭn Simbang was hung there as though she were awaiting public condemnation as a captured communist rebel. In reality, a captured rebel was usually dragged to the village school ground and punished publicly by stoning by the villagers.[4]

The giant man wearing a military police helmet and carrying an iron club resembles the image of American Military Police who came to Cheju Island as military advisors to the Korean central armies. These advisors were often dispatched from the mainland by the police during the war.[5] The image of a big, tall American MP in a jeep driving fast and uninhibitedly on rough roads, or anywhere he pleased (like the giant man walking freely from outside the village defenses in Kŭn Simbang's dream), must have deeply impressed the Cheju natives. Granted their formidable stature as the victors of this internal ideological warfare, how was it that the American MP was here imagined as a savior figure?

The imagery of the MP as a superhuman and nearly divine benefactor (which was actually promoted by pro-American political propaganda) overlapped allegorically with that of the beneficent ancestor (chosang) in Cheju popular culture. Historically, at the deep level of the popular imagination, the divine image of a giant man has its roots in the folktales of divine winged heroes.[6] In these tales, the protagonist is portrayed as a tragic hero, such as a general who fails in battle or a peasant rebel who dies while leading the oppressed peasant class in a rebellion against the corrupt bureaucracy. The common plot of these stories is as follows: although these heroes were born with a sign of divinity or novelty such as small wings under the arms, they could not become noblemen or victors on the battlefield because their wings were discovered in infancy and cut off for fear of their "excessive rebellious spirit" and its likely tragic outcome. They are portrayed as superhuman, very large or strong in comparison with ordinary people. In general, the tragic imagery of these heroes' stories is identified with the historical fate of Cheju Island in the popular imagination. If the heroes' tragic deaths represent the fateful history of Cheju Island's natural devastation, hunger, political neglect, and oppression, their divine births do justice to a desire for freedom from such forces of fate.[7] This island had always been isolated politically, used as an asylum for political exiles, and exploited by corrupt governors. The islanders could identify themselves with the heroes whose intrinsically divine character remains intact forever throughout the oral tradition in spite of the castration of their wings.

Interestingly enough, the divine wings are often discovered *after* the heroes' tragic deaths. Their superhuman abilities on the battlefield are then understood, and they are glorified as powerful ancestors of their native villages or family groups. The case of Yi Chaesu is a good example. In 1901, Yi Chaesu, who was originally the servant of a local magistrate, became a rebel general leading Cheju insurgents against foreign forces, consisting of seven hundred Catholics and two French priests. After he was sentenced to death at a court in Seoul, strange wings were found in his armpits, according to his biography written by his sister thirty years later.[8] This posthumous discovery and the subsequent mythologization of the rebel testify to the power of the traditional narrative to invoke the popular hope for rebellion and the overthrow of the existing hegemonic power.

Going back to the initiation dream-story, we can see the cultural logic depicting the relationship between the giant benefactor and the thousands of hungry ghosts in the background, whom Kŭn Simbang identified as the three thousand soldiers, the low-ranking spirits of the dead in the shamanic pantheon. In the dream, the giant obliged Kŭn Simbang to feed the ghosts; here the ghosts represent the hungry and oppressed Cheju people. The giant symbolically manifests himself as the paramount ancestor and popular hero of the Cheju people. He also helps Kŭn Simbang to reintegrate herself into society in her new role as simbang. In short, we can postulate here the redemptive function of her initiation dream to transcend the immanent reality of poverty and social alienation.

The Iconic Power of Dream Images

However, it is not Kŭn Simbang who inquires into the social and historical significance of the dream imagery. There is therefore no use questioning the intention or reasoning in her mind during the dream. Interpretation may have absolutely nothing to do with the specific images of the dream apart from the interpreted signs.[9] Kŭn Simbang did not see the image of the American MP giant as an American MP, but rather as an ancestor. The fact that the ancestor-figure appeared in the guise of an American soldier does not necessarily imply that the dream offers a specific historical interpretation. (The same caution applies to drawing symbolic meaning from any of the dream's images, and Kŭn Simbang herself could not explain why she dreamt in that way.) The images in the dream are treated here as if they coexisted independently; I see their spurious alliances and configurations like a montage.

In this context, I am concerned with the redemptive function of dream images rather than redemption of those spirits of the dead. By redemptive function, I mean the iconic status and cognitive organization of the dream images that are predicated on otherwise inchoate or ineffable reality.[10] The images are not symbolic objects but representations of reality as well as the represented. Like signs, the images concretize networks of association without necessarily trying to symbolize particular objects. Below the threshold of awareness, they integrate material experience and individual aspirations and mediate social practice. The dream images in Kŭn Simbang's dream not only integrate the personal experience of poverty and the rebirth of a shaman but also throw the spectacle of a political unconscious on the background screen.

To paraphrase Walter Benjamin's notion of dialectical images, "these images are the dialectic at a standstill." Thus they point to the possibility of awakening "knowledge of the past."[11] Dialectical images are both part of a historical process and its arrest, and waking is a metaphor for historical consciousness. I imagine that the dreamer, who at least can remember the dream vividly later on, is *half-asleep* and *half-awake,* and actually stays in the fantastic dreamworld while pondering the content of a dream on an empty stomach.[12]

In Kŭn Simbang's dream, the three central dream images—the ch'ongsal, the giant man, and the thousands of spirits of the dead—are *ideals,* as Benjamin suggested, through which the people seek "to transcend the immaturity of the social product and the deficiencies of the social order of production. In these ideals there also emerges a vigorous aspiration to break with what is out-dated—which means, however, with the most recent past. These tendencies turn the fantasy which gains its initial stimulus from the new, back upon the primal past."[13] The impulse to break with "the most recent past"—a betrayal of modern Cheju history—which Kŭn Simbang would only desire in a dream state and not consciously, fills the gap between the ideal of self-sufficiency and political freedom and the present reality of subjection and poverty. What is at stake in the relationship between ancestral revelation and personal acceptance of destiny is the way the image of the ancestor in Kŭn Simbang's dream embodies the narrative of redemption.

The image of the American MP and that of the ancestor are not precisely equivalent. Literally speaking, one is a victor, and the other a victim. Yet these two images correspond, not in terms of symbolic meaning, but in terms of the iconic power of emancipating benediction and prophecy. Also, in the mythic account of dream representation, their intrinsically tragic language (one as the foreign invader and the other as the native rebel against the former) transforms so as to glorify the future. In waking reality, the two images of the "ancestor" may feed the thousands of hungry ghosts and liberate the Cheju people from political turmoil. This is the revolutionary moment in sobriety that transcends "the deficiencies" of past history, which has been scarred by violent ideological conflicts. The nonidentical images of the American MP and the tragic, heroic native rebels do not hamper a more advanced interpretation of the dream; rather, they stimulate further understanding of the complexity of the history of ideological warfare and its violent effects on Cheju Island.

Despite the fact that the American military presence on Cheju Island was actually threatening to its nationalistic autonomy, the American MP's beneficent posture, ironically associated with the iron helmet and club like a collage, transcends the unforgettable terror of the violent massacre of innocent people together with Kŭn Simbang's husband's death. This transcendence is certainly the popular expression of a utopian ideal in the political unconsciousness of the Cheju people, which is indeed manifest in Kŭn Simbang's unquestioning recognition of the military police officer as the ancestor of the shaman *(simbang)* and also of the Cheju people.

The Signs of Modernity and Minjung

In conclusion, what place does this dream have in the discourse on the minjung? The dream and the narrative that describes it are expressive forms of the minjung's historical experience. Kŭn Simbang's dream of the ancestors—both mythical and historical—was "god-sent," predicting a means of livelihood as well as the ill-fate of becoming a shaman. It is a paradoxical lesson of history as transformative power: the dream brings a miraculous healing force into misfortune and ill-fate. Her dream was a divine remedy.[14] Her life stories of (her husband's) death and poverty prefigured this dream retrospectively.

Story is always synthetic rather than analytic but nonetheless narrates history and politics through images of emotions and ideas that are strictly nondiscursive media. Kŭn's husband's story (national hero) and her dream of the American MP (folk hero) are texts for the minjung's imagining the nation as a reality, existing on the border of premodern and modern history. Ever implicit constructs, story and dream are the signs of modernity that point to an alternative realm of power and redemption. Indeed, the meanings of these sign texts are always prefigured, and current history confirms their significance: Kŭn Simbang began to receive the military pension again and became a great shaman. Like photographs, dream images, which are reproducible imagery, take on an iconic value as near-truths. They forge bonds of intimacy, without yielding their autonomy, between the colonizer and the colonized and remap the body of the colonized subject: the shaman's body hung on the village sentry gate. This dream picture was an insidious and invisible displacement of colonial power through the fragile agency of the colonial subject. Without providing a specific statement about the minjung or the nation, story and dream produce and disseminate signs and meanings of modernity: thus they comprise part of a semiotic battle. These are the minjung forms of resistance without effects. Devoid of ideological premise or political interest, they demystify the dominant discourse of the nation and the minjung. This, at least, I hope to have conveyed: the unconscious, implicit nature of the minjung's, or people's, social knowledge. It might well betray the ideological impulse of the "minjung discourse" should it claim that Kŭn Simbang was not a minjung.

9

Contemporary Korean Literature: From Victimization to Minjung Nationalism

Choi Hyun-moo

Translated by Carolyn U. So

ANALYSIS OF a contemporary movement that is still unfolding is a formidable task. The attempt to trace the development of *minjung* and other nationalist movements within South Korean literature after Korea's liberation from Japan in 1945, through all their manifold political, social, and cultural permutations, involves numerous hazards stemming from the incomplete nature of these movements. Further, if we follow Marcel Granet's classification of historical diversity into "dense" and "not-so-dense" periods of development, then the history of Korea since the liberation in 1945 is a period of unparalleled density, crammed with complex problems, rapid turns of events, and dynamic and unpredictable forces.

In any case, the literature of this era, like other aspects of society, begins with a series of ruptures. The rupture of tradition, and of national identity arising from the division of Korea, demand epistemological adjustments different from previous eras. It is precisely within these adjustments that the new concepts of nationalism and the minjung have taken root, while in the gradual growth of the two concepts one can discover the continuity that synthesizes the complex and conflicting literary movements through their various stages from the 1950s to the present.

In themselves, minjung and nation are neutral concepts. However, as the two concepts merged, the addition of the word "minjung" to nationalism has endowed contemporary Korean literature with a particular dynamic. This term, "minjung nationalism," was then defined, redefined, and revised during the process of political and historical change. A discussion of its linguistic changes is not the aim here. Rather, I endeavor to discuss two aspects of the term in relation to its contribution to the continuity within the changes in Korean literature since the 1950s.

First, the term stands in contradistinction to the "official" nationalism promoted by the government after the 1950s, signifying another type of nationalism that challenges it. Second, the concept of minjung-centered nationalism is not a literary concept, but denotes a practice within literature which has been spawned by a specific social and historical logic. This literature thus simply constitutes one of a variety of actual practices in the broader minjung nationalism movement, by itself not an adequate concept. The corresponding literary concept is realism.

The sine qua non of these two aspects—the avant-garde nationalistic side and the committed teleological view of literature—is a transformative or progressive dynamic. For, on the one hand, to be truly avant-garde, literature must endlessly reform itself, while, on the other hand, it must portray the ever-changing reality on which its commitment is premised. However, as we shall see, certain pitfalls are inherent in the conjoining of these two aspects. One is typification of literary form stemming from the tautological nature of values grounded in goals and intentions. The other is the stagnation of literature due to domination by nonliterary discourses. Before treating these dilemmas, however, I will first address some problems that surface in selected minjung literary works as various changes propel minjung-centered nationalism toward more concrete definition.

Victimization: Historical Fate

The steady development of minjung-centered nationalism has been indicated as an element of continuity in Korean literature since the 1950s. The circumstance underlying this continuity is the division of Korea into two states between 1945 and 1948. Unresolved, this division immediately made "practice" a pressing issue in literature. Kwŏn Hyŏngmin writes: "Contemporary literature, which has been developing over the forty years since the liberation, is perceived as the literary experience of the era characterized by the division of the people and the state. In other words, literature of this period is not some static historical fact, but something alive which functions as a situational condition of the present as it unfolds."[1] Focusing on minjung-centered nationalism, literature since the fifties can be divided broadly into two periods: the formative stage of minjung consciousness in the 1950s and the 1960s; and the period thereafter, during which its practice has emerged in a concrete form. Created in response to situations outside literature, growth in minjung consciousness in each period has been spurred by intense social, economic, and political conflicts. The Korean War of the 1950s, the April 19 student-led revolution of the 1960s, the Yusin "revitalization" reforms of the 1970s, and the Kwangju uprising of the 1980s are the material manifestations of these conflicts.

The absolute demands of the first half of the 1950s were to obliterate the cultural legacies of the colonial era, to establish a national literature, to restore the national language, and to overcome the aftereffects of the Korean

War and the division of Korea.[2] Poems and novels depicting the historical impact of the war and the division were prevalent, and a feeling of victimization due to circumstances beyond one's control dominated this literature. For the minjung, in the sense used today, survival was essential, and so in the literature of this period existential questions dealing with the terrible conditions following the war took precedence over analysis of historical catastrophes. Victimization by circumstances beyond one's control, the consequent breaking up of value systems, and agonizing speeches about loss of lives by the bereaved were the dominant themes. The protagonists in Sŏ Kiwŏn's *Amsa Chido* (Sketch map), Son Ch'angsŏp's *Hyŏl Sŏ* (Writing in blood), and An Sugil's *Chesam Ingan Hyŏng* (Third human type) are portraits of a consciousness in which the maimed values, ethics, and bodies are all manifest.

This sense of victimization is likewise revealed in literature that deals with ideology. The ideology of the 1950s is one element in a broader category of seeking to understand the irrational features of this era of turmoil and suffering. Confrontations in ideology were not existential reflections. More than existential reflections, confrontations in ideology can be summarized—as in the outburst of a farmer in Hwang Sunwŏn's *Kainŭi Huye* (Cain's descendant)—as catastropic and nihilistic experiences of "the whole world completely turning upside down."

The impoverished conditions of the time were far too dreadful to allow writers simply to absorb the shocking historical events and discover therein the impetus to push forward, and one gets the impression that this impoverishment united even nationalistic fervor in the years following liberation. Since thereby the logic of national security became absolute in politics and culture, the official division of Korea after the 1950–1953 war had precluded the possibility of ideological objectivity taking root in literature. Nevertheless, the division thus established did create two different types of nationalism. One is an official, formal nationalism based on anticommunist ideology; the other, an antiestablishment nationalism that arose under dictatorship and the process of industrialization. The gap between the two steadily became wider and firmer.

From Ambivalence to the Pursuit of National Identity

The April 19 student uprising of 1960, an attempt to transcend the postwar mentality, took the difficult step from the sense of victimization to the overcoming of self, and as such provided a stepping-stone to the realization of one's national identity. However, the literature of the 1960s shares the successes and failures of the student uprising. The literature of this era was written by a generation of writers educated in *han'gŭl*, the vernacular phonemic script. It can be summarized, like all other areas of this time, as "an oscillation between temptation and fear in response to foreign powers."[3] In view of the coup d'état of 16 May 1961, the student uprising, taken as a historical event, was a dismal failure. But this failure itself nevertheless prompted reflection on the ambivalent nature of the citizens' consciousness, an ambivalence that emerged in the process of modernization begun in 1960 and arose out of an awareness of civil identity based on imported Western liberal concepts and the material comforts of a Western-oriented consumer society. In literature, the failure led to the debate between "pure" and activist literature.

Ambivalence is characteristic of the 1960s in many ways. Ch'oe Inhun's novel *Kwangjang* (Public square), which overshadowed the 1960s, deals with division. The protagonist of the novel, Yi Myŏngjun, establishes the "private chamber" (South Korea) and the "public square" (North Korea) as confrontational entities, which suggests the epistemological structure of the time. The paradigm of the first is the pure art and modernism argument, and of the latter, participation and realism. However, the seemingly confrontational entities have a common element in that both pursue what is "mine, ours," even if the former does so from an individual's perspective and the latter from a collective standpoint. As a consequence, the confrontation becomes logically ambivalent. Nevertheless, the basis for minjung nationalism, even when the term had not yet been coined, was more actively sought after in the latter paradigm. Increasingly, the original ambivalence became transformed into confrontational and mutually exclusive positions, particularly in the 1980s.

The pursuit of national identity gave birth to social consciousness, and this in turn fertilized the minjung debates of the 1970s. Authors of the older generation "established the place for epics which deal with Korea's survival methods," by studying the intellectual history of a nation, as in An Sugil's *Puk Kando* (North Chientao), which was completed in 1967; these efforts were continued in Pak Kyŏngni's *T'oji* (The Earth), which commenced publication at the end of 1960s. The new generation educated in han'gŭl began to see in their contemporary conditions, particularly in the class alienated by the process of modernization and industrialization, elements that belied the existence of a single, unitary nation.

Individual writers seek a setting for issues that pertain to their world of experience. Many works of the 1960s deal with a member of the urban petite bourgeoisie who gradually becomes callous due to empty values and mammonism (Yi Hoch'ŏl's *Sŏurŭn Manwŏnida* [Seoul is jammed full, 1967]). They also deal with farming and fishing villages that became victims of industrialization and invisible power (Kim Chonghan's *Moraet'op Iyagi* [Story of a sandbank, 1966] and Pang Yongung's *Pun'ye Ki* [Account of Punye, 1967]); divided consciousness stemming from the national division (Yi Hoch'ŏl's *P'anmunjŏm* [Panmunjom, 1961]); and victims of foreign—American—violence (Nam Chonghyŏn's *Punji* [Chamber pot, 1965]). All these settings of a variety of realities are not so much isolated issues as the germination of those issues which would arise thereafter out of comprehensive analyses forged amid the overwhelmingly absurd mechanism of the present reality.

Now, as in the case of the novel by Nam Chonghyŏn, *Chamber Pot*, most of the protagonists in these 1960s works are anonymous victims who can only be referred to as "somebody." They criticize and form accusations rather than resolving problems. Emotional responses to injustice and violence are more prevalent than analyses of existing problems through reconstruction of reality. Furthermore, narratives regarding the circumstances of victimization comprise a larger proportion of the literature than do objective characterizations of the victimizers themselves.

Issues relating to the formation of national identity are acutely reflected even in questions of literary language and genre. Variety and verisimilitude are attained through use of regional dialects, the rhetoric of the lower class, and satires (as in Kim Suyong), while traditional genres such as *p'ansori* (solo narrative drama) and *madangguk* (open-air theater) are revived in new ways. In poetry, the suddenly inflated reality causes the question of national identity to expand to genres such as *sasŏl sijo* (narrative *sijo*), a *sijo* of commoners, collective poetry (Yi Songbu's *Chŏllado* [Chŏlla province]), lengthy poems, and epics (Sin Tongyŏp's *Kŭmgang* [Kŭm river, 1967]).

In particular, *Kŭm River* greatly influenced the national literature of the next generation by attempting to capture historical struggles in an epic form through the transformation of a farmer, Hanŭi, who represents the "everlasting sky," symbolic archetype of the culture of the Korean people. This is a truly rare work of the 1960s, which deals with the origins of the power and sentiments of the minjung while conveying a comprehensive sense of society and history. However, in the 1980s the familiar questions regarding typification of minjung characters and hero-types must be approached from a different angle, something to which we shall return shortly.

National Literature as Minjung Leadership

Discussion of minjung national literature became concrete in the 1970s, being subdivided according to differences in logical process and standpoint. It dealt with commitment in theoretical and critical discourses rather than with the actual literary works. The various stages of transformation this discussion underwent in sum encompassed the debates concerning committed literature and social reality that had appeared from the 1920s to the 1950s— for example, populism, proletarian literature, and socialist realism. However, Korea's minjung national literature was not yet inextricably tied to the official line of a political party, as is the case with socialist realism, Marxism, and communist literature.[4] Here it differs also from European proletarian literature, where, in the case of France's Ecole de littérature proletarienne, authorship is limited strictly to those of proletarian-class background (although this limitation is being insisted upon in recent debates on minjung nationalist literature), and in which originality is emphasized in opposition to doctrinal Marxist literature.[5] Furthermore, Korea's minjung literature exhibits clear distance from a populism that rejects all political engagement, chooses the "people" alone as its theme, and devotes all its energies to presenting their reality.[6]

However, these superficial comparisons are rendered meaningless by the division of the Korean nation, which, together with the official prohibition on leftist ideologies, has limited all literature in South Korea, wherein lies the fundamental difference between Korea's minjung literature and the people-oriented or proletarian literature of the West that was formed in relation to stages of industrialization. Hence, it is its nationalistic character that distinguishes Korea's minjung literature from the various comparable movements in the West. This distinction also helps to explain why the Korean movement resists limiting minjung to simply "the people" or the proletariat. Hence, the connection with nationalism is not only the principal differentiating characteristic but also the absolute condition of Korean minjung literature.

According to Paek Nakch'ŏng (Paik Nak-chung):

> There has to be some concrete national reality that demands firm adherence to the concept of national literature. That is to say, there have to be people who are the subjects of national literature, while at the same time the need must exist to distinguish under "nationalist literature" especially that literature which, amidst the whole gamut of literary activities possible to a particular people, is demanded by the human development and survival as subjects of that people. In other words, this literature is the product of a crisis mentality concerning the survival of the people and their well-being in the face of serious threats, the realization that a proper attitude toward national crises is precisely the factor that determines the positive development of Korean literature itself.

The concept of nationalist literature understood in this way assumes, then, a thoroughly historical character.[7] People as the agents, a crisis mentality concerning the survival of the many, and a people's sense of history as summarized above are the fundamental issues and indices of the concrete appearance of minjung national literature in the 1970s.

Compared to previous decades, the basic feature of minjung nationalism of the 1970s is that it was a "literary response to reality by becoming closely tied to reality." Stated differently, the various contradictions in Korean society of the 1970s changed literature from a descriptive to an active endeavor. This change took place in solidarity with the movements for democratization that were occurring throughout the various levels of society.

Discussion therefore centered on the social functions and objectives of literature. Unlike in the 1980s, literature emerged as the leading arena for social participation. Paek Nakch'ŏng writes about "the particular active nature of creative works that carry forward the mission given to the minjung through their awakened action . . . in order to accomplish the civil revolution, which is the task now facing our society."[8] Kim Chiha, for his part, in "P'ungjanya Chasarinya" (Satire or suicide?) points out the duality of the minjung—the negative characteristics of stupidity, philistinism, and cowardice versus the positive one of progressive power based on wisdom and daring—but elaborates on the path a poet (or literature) must take, as well as the function of literature: "One must submerge oneself in the minjung, affirm the self living and breathing with them, and accept oneself as minjung. A poet must educate the people through minjung satire, awaken them, and show them the direction of their vital spirit by focusing on satire and violence, which expresses the explosion of the people's dissatisfaction."[9]

This view that artistic creators must penetrate the minjung in order to carry out the role of awakening minjung consciousness in literature is also the essence of Sin Kyŏngnim's thought as expressed in "Literature of the Minjung, Literature for the Minjung" in his *Munhakkwa Minjung* (Literature and the minjung). The logic of critical realism versus "pure literature" surfaces as the task at hand in munjung-centered literature for the future of the now suppressed minjung.

Whereas national identity was the pursuit of the 1960s, consciousness as the creator of a new history and nationalism through literary practice were emphasized in the 1970s. There was a move to formalize, in accordance with literary realism, the essence of the minjung as that which fully experienced the contemporary pervasive historical contradictions. An attempt was also made to understand, comprehensively and cooperatively, in the spirit of Third World literary theory, Korea's political and economic national realities within the global capital structure. In this way there emerged in literature the analytic endeavor to group the people's place within the organic interconnections between individual and society, nation and the world.

The satirical attacks contained in Kim Chiha's *Ojŏk* (Five bandits) and *Piŏ* (False rumor) of the 1970s, show a complete change in the awareness of victimization that had dominated the literature of previous eras. These works criticized the injustices of dictatorship by using the traditional p'ansori-style narrative. They also exhibit many of the characteristics of 1970s literature: scrutiny of the victimizer's identity over description of the tragedies arising from various situations; change of focus from the situation of the individual to that of the group; emergence of the notion of organic causality active in contradictions; and the fighting spirit that is aroused in the consciousness of the individual when related to a group.

Critical realism, which was discussed in the early 1970s, required understanding reality from many different angles. Distinctions between the subgenres of peasant literature, proletarian literature, and lower-middle-class literature also emerged. Romans-fleuves, such as Pak Kyŏngni's *T'oji* (Earth) and Hwang Sŏg'yŏng's *Chang Kilsan,* are dedicated to the pursuit of nationalistic traits which maintain continuity across the various temporal divisions that appear on the surface of modern history.

Many works denounced the complex problems that were interrelated with and entangled in the contradictions of the society of the time. Kim Chŏnghan's *Hoenamu Kkol Saramdŭl* (People of the hoe tree valley, 1973), Ch'ŏn Sŭngse's *Nag'wŏldo* (Nakwol Island, 1972), Yi Mun'gu's *Changhan Mong* (A long, sad dream, 1972) and *Haebyŏk* (Sea cliff, 1974) were based on actual firsthand experiences of farming and fishing villages, and revealed a more critical stance. These works decry the dangerously impoverished conditions arising from an industrialized economy based on capitalism. As Emile Durkheim pointed out, the appearance of anomie that came from the modernization process is especially marked in the various central perspectives of the urban lower-middle class, the proletariat, victims of anticommunist ideology, and people in farming and fishing villages. Used broadly, the concept of minjung in the 1970s became more concrete as a class ideology.

However, the minjung depicted in these works are not struggling heroes. They are in the stage of awakening to consciousness of contemporary society. They have not yet found tangible ways to resolve the situational conflicts at either the individual or the collective level. By portraying the tragic lives of the protagonists, such as Cho Yongman in *Sea Cliff* and Kwidŏgi in *Nakwol Island,* authors consciously attempted to portray the complex and inexorable mechanism of victimization and violence that dominates extreme conditions. This process of becoming conscious—although it is far removed from the ideal state in literature demanded by the minjung-nationalist discourse of the time—accomplishes the important function of conveying thoroughly realistic life.

A notable aspect of this period is proletarian literature as the core of minjung literature. Representative works of this period are Hwang Sŏg'yŏng's *Kaekchi* (Far from home, 1971), Yun Chŏnggyu's *Changnyŏlhan Hwayŏm* (Heroic flame, 1972), Yun Hŭnggil's serialized short story *Ahŏp K'yŏlleŭi Kuduro Namŭn Sanae* (Man who was left as nine pairs of shoes), and Cho Sehŭi's serial work *Nanjangiga Ssoaollin Chagŭn Kong* (Small ball launched by a dwarf). The common characteristic of these works is the portrayal of the solidarity of workers in unions or industrial organizations—the realization of the need for the minjung to unite. The conflict arises during the process of organizing unions or gaining basic rights through labor disputes.

Hwang's *Far from Home* is a tension-filled work that uses realistic descriptions of scenes to suggest subtly how labor disputes begin and why they fail. The primary obstacle to unifying the minjung is shown to be the gap between the emotional response of the proletarian class toward inhumane conditions and a rational organization of minjung power. The proletariat's consciousness has not been awakened, and they lack the necessary conviction to participate. In Yun's *Heroic Flame,* the conflict is between proletarians and owners of a business enterprise.

The serialized works in Cho Sehŭi's *Small Ball Launched by a Dwarf* present a gradual intensification of the conflict between the coalescing power of the minjung and the forces that array themselves against it. The early sections show irreconcilable differences in values between the poor and the rich, and the rulers and the ruled. Later, in the sections titled "Kwedo hoejŏn" (Spinning track) and "Kigye tosi" (Mechanical city), the working class's consciousness, represented by Chisŏp, the eldest son of the midget's family, becomes extremely intensified, while in "Nae kŭmullo onŭn kasigogi" (Thorn-fish coming to my net) the victimizer is murdered.

Similar extreme actions can also be seen in Hwang Sŏg'yŏng's *Yagŭn* (Nightshift). The protagonist commits suicide by electrocuting himself when a labor strike is rendered impossible by collusion between the labor union and the management. The fighting spirit based on a willingness to sacrifice even one's life, evident in the death sentence meted out to Chisŏp and the suicide by electrocution in *Nightshift*, plainly indicates the difficulties confronting proletarian literature hereafter.

The New Phase: Rupture or Dialectic Synthesis

In the 1980s, minjung literature seems to have departed from the literary debates hitherto. Although radical changes in the debate on the concept of minjung in literature had already occurred at the end of the 1970s without rejecting the strong flow of nationalism, these changes were even more acutely necessitated by the shock of the May 1980 Kwangju uprising. The foundation for the nationalist literature of the 1980s has been changed and broadened by the younger generation under the label of "minjung national literature." Most of the people in this generation did not personally experience the Korean War of 1950–1953 and grew up in the midst of the relative material wealth that attended rapid industrialization. Therefore, this generation was able to distance itself emotionally from the issue of ideology and fear of impoverishment.

Two major debates, perhaps oversimplified, will be discussed here in order to avoid too hasty a formulation of the present movements. One is the debate on the creators (who writes?); the other, on overcoming the division or on the reunification of Korea. Regardless of their aims, the participants in these debates attempt to overcome insufficiencies in the previous national minjung literature, and to escape from the ideological complexities surrounding these insufficiencies.

As previously suggested, the question of writers of literature firmly rooted "in" the minjung now demands a stronger forward propulsion through a synthesis of the dialectics between literature and practice. The process of popularizing minjung literature again begs the question of authenticity in the representation of reality in literature; this question, in turn, points to the debate on the minjung authenticity of the writers. The problem of a nation, then, is transformed into one concerning social class. Minjung is the main body of the nation, and its class structure is defined by some accordingly: "The proletarian class is the basic foundation but includes the working class, consisting of peasants, small-scale merchants and industrialists, the urban poor, and certain intellectuals."[10] The argument concerning the class authenticity of creative writers is that "professional" writers cannot successfully recreate a minjung reality in literature because of their limitation of belonging to the class of "cultured intellectuals."

This argument creates two chasms. A distance is created between the literature of those professional writers who write for the general minjung and the literature written by the minjung class. Similarly, the main literary genres are dismantled and different genres appear. At first, texts that deal with the realistic aspects or movements of the minjung appear. These new genres may be memoirs, as in Yu Tongu's *Ŏnŭ Tolmaengiŭi Oech'im* (Cry of a stone), written in the late 1970s. They may also be reportages, diaries, and leaflets. Accordingly, genres such as epic poetry, drama in poetry, and open-air drama blend together. The perspective on realism also undergoes reevaluation, and agitprop literature, which gives pride of place to "progressive" movements and situations, becomes dominant. Song Min'yŏp observes that

> the phrase "realism of the third world" is not a subordinate concept within the larger field of Realism. Rather, it is a concept which materializes only when subordinated to the liberation of the minjung of the third world, which is achieved by overcoming the third world reality. In this sense, as literature in the service of liberation movements rather than subject to realist criteria, it is endowed with diverse and unusually comprehensive qualities.[11]

The ascendancy of the realness of literature and its declaratory function are related to the genre of poets who dominated the literary scene in the first half of the 1980s. Poetry spreads quickly: its rhyme scheme and particular rhythmic patterns allow it to be more accessible than prose genres, as it can be readily memorized and thus absorbed into the episodes of various movements. At the same time, the question of the degree of awareness of the minjung as the subjects of history, an issue already recognized in the minjung literature of the 1970s, gained legitimacy through the introduction of the class concept.

These changes created many minjung writers. They also gradually broadened the scope of their influence. By uniting mutually with movements outside literature, minjung literature gained a unique place in the official literary sphere. Furthermore, this literature came to exercise a subtle power termed *dictature des lettres* over the established literary sphere. These changes rely on the validity of movements that are convincing in their efforts to popularize certain aspects of present-day Korea. They are also based on popular responses to the texts of proletarian writers, such as Sŏk Chŏngnam's *Kongjangŭi Pulpit* (Factory lights, 1984), Chang Namsu's *Ppae-*

atkkin Ilt'ŏ (Usurped workplace, 1984), reportages such as Chŏn T'aeil's memoir published posthumously, and Pak Nohae's poetry collection, *Nodongŭi Saebyŏk* (Labor's dawn).

Aside from realness or contemporaneousness, the salient characteristic of this literature is its literary typification.[12] Typification is designed to augment the propaganda power of minjung literature but at the same time hints at its limitations. The problem with typification can be seen particularly in novels, memoirs, and epic poetry. Most of these works adhere to the following typification process in selecting protagonists, plot, and narration of dramatic developments: (1) a sentimental laborer (an individualized minjung); (2) a worker whose consciousness has been raised (collective minjung); (3) their transformation into leaders (subjects: *chuch'e*) of labor movements; and finally, (4) the materialization of the labor movements. Each step of this typification must both report reality accurately and suggest how close the subjects are to the ideal goal of the movement. More than any other, the realism in minjung literature exhibits the irony of being limited by formal criteria of typification.[13] Here one might apply Régine Robin's observation that "in idealized texts which typically portray positive heroes dedicated to changing reality in line with [a theory of] scientific historical movements, one can see an attempt to combine future-oriented romanticism and realism."[14] Therefore, typification is the textualization of a teleological view of history whereby ideological messages, which are presupposed and already constructed, are repeated with great frequency. Thus, like most ideological literature, it is powerfully and effectively disseminated to individuals and organizations through the structural device of redundancy of message[15] and is accepted by them as if it were reality.

The power of typification, which is consciously monologic and centripetal, is indispensable to the success of the movements, but its excessive rigidity entails the danger of becoming a monologue within a closed structure: insofar as typification spreads by consciously relying on the legibility of a few selected codes, it is difficult to avoid the very values and ideological crudity which these codes criticize. These problems in minjung literature must be recognized and overcome to prolong the life of the movement.

Another development in the minjung literature of the 1980s was the debate concerning the overcoming of the nation's division, or reunification. These two issues had been suggested continuously in 1960s minjung literature. They present a comprehensive and analytical understanding of democratization and consciousness-raising of the minjung subjects and a strategic development in the national-minjung movement of the 1970s. These movements are carried out in many dimensions outside literature, and at present a simple diagnosis cannot be made. Readers should refer to Chapter 10, written by Paek Nakch'ŏng, an important leader of this literary movement.[16] For my own part, I shall conclude here by pointing out a few elements that appear in the various stages of national-minjung literature.

First, the challenge of surmounting the division of the nation and the reunification debate stand out as the greatest and most essential developments in the nation-oriented literary movement with minjung tendencies. These minjung tendencies are an unbroken thread in South Korean literature from the 1945 liberation until the present. As such, a deepened, more comprehensive understanding of historical reality, which has been a major pursuit throughout this period, occurred by moving from the stage of recognizing division as the cause of all problems to that of exploring possibilities for healing the division.

Unlike in previous generations, however, it was only in the literary works of the 1980s that the question of division was approached solidly from the minjung's point of view, and a new kind of epic structure can be found in the shift from the declining structure based on individualist or collectivist collapse to a progressive one buoyed up by the burgeoning consciousness of the task of overcoming the division. Although it has limitations, in its engagement with both sides of ideological questions and with the long-accumulating conflicts between the exploited and the exploiting classes, this literature of the 1980s is flooded with multidimensional and dramatic testimonies about division and its aftereffects, and poses fundamental questions for literature in the future.

Since the liberation, numerous positions and movements have ebbed and flowed in Korean literature. However, uniquely among these, the debate over the national-minjung question has preserved considerable continuity even as it has undergone a transformation of its original avant-garde intent in the midst of the rapid changes affecting South Koreans. Nevertheless, in order to move beyond simplistic platforms or transitory struggles and become an enduring literary practice, minjung literature will need to engage in more dynamic and dialectical—even self-critical—reflection. Further, to enable it to become a concrete and leading literary movement, rather than simply the subject of debates by Kim Chiha and others who follow, a more scientific and systematic sociocritical analysis of literature's intrinsic qualities must be the aim. Such an objective must be given highest priority at the present stage, in which South Korean literary discourse is dominated by debates over minjung-national literature.

10

The Reunification Movement and Literature

Paik Nak-chung

Translated by Kenneth M. Wells

[Paik Nak-chung was prevented from attending the minjung conference by a travel ban imposed on him by the South Korean government in reaction to his involvement in plans by the National Writers' Union (Minjok Munhwa Chakka Hoeui) to hold a North–South writers' conference in March 1989. This chapter was originally published under the title "T'ongil Undonggwa Munhak" in *Ch'angjakkwa Pip'yŏng* in the spring of 1989. It was occasioned by the author's reflections on a symposium on "Reunification and Literature" held in Seoul in December 1988 under the auspices of the National Writers' Union. Finding his and others' discussions at the symposium somewhat abstract, he resolved to pursue the question of the relationship between literature and Korea's reunification through direct examination of relevant works from the standpoint of the minjung. In order to emphasize this more concrete approach, Paik Nak-chung added "movement" to the title, and it is with his discussion of this choice of title that the translation begins.—EDITOR'S NOTE]

ALTHOUGH ONE may have reservations about an overly cavalier use of the word "movement," I have decided to use it because it seemed important to raise once again the obvious fact that, at least where reunification is concerned, this can only be achieved through a sustained *movement* of the people of North and South Korea. That is to say, as with "democratization" or "attaining autonomy," so too "reunification" is a historical process involving all manner of vicissitudes, not some once-and-for-all event that can be simplistically conceived in terms of whether it will or will not take place. What the content of unification will be, or even whether it can be achieved directly or through some interim form, cannot be settled in advance; and where it has yet to be realized, it is necessary to distinguish between processes where the system of division is being weakened and those where it is being strengthened. And the whole thing depends on Koreans actively taking charge of the situation themselves. There are some who worry that, unlike the democratization and autonomy movements, emphasizing reunification might lead to a defeatist feeling that until it is attained nothing at all can be done; but this anxiety derives from a failure to grasp the reality of the reunification question as a task that requires a concrete movement.

Adding "movement" to reunification also naturally involves a call for a scientific understanding of the task in question. Some have concluded that the idea of giving central importance to a unification movement, a movement to overcome national division, is itself unscientific, on the grounds that "division," "unification," and so on are concepts with no recognized basis in social-science theory. And it is true enough that, even setting aside those which have from the outset been ruses to mislead the people, the greater part of the unification arguments to date have as often as not been lacking in scientific integrity or class content. It is precisely to make good that deficiency that I have been emphasizing the need to understand, and have myself endeavored to understand, the system of division in terms of a "contradiction." Yet, while this may be blamed partly on my own deficiencies, it seems that even where controversial points have been advanced lucidly enough, logical debate on their pros and cons has been very rare. For instance, one would have expected some awareness that understanding the system of division in terms of a contradiction infers a scientific grasp of the "contradiction between the division system and the populace of north and south," rather than a "contradiction between the northern and southern systems." Yet despite repeated explanations to this effect, a surprisingly large number of debaters continue to take comfort in reiteration of the claim that the very notion of a division contradiction is unscientific and petit bourgeois. One suspects that social-science and "movement" theories in Korea have yet to catch up with the concrete realities of the era and society of division in which Koreans live.

Be that as it may, in line with my own objectives, I chose to add "movement" to "reunification," while deciding on the other hand to leave "literature" as it was: neither "national literature" nor "literature movement." At this point it seemed meaningful for once simply to say "literature," and leave it at that. It is necessary to question the basis and limitations of science ceaselessly, if only to ensure that science renders its proper service to "movements." This is a task science cannot accomplish on its own; and without the constant illumination provided by creative literature, a science in the service of human emancipation—a science united to a philosophy of praxis rather than mere instrumental knowledge—is impossible. But rather than advancing a detailed theoretical argument, which in any case I have attempted elsewhere, I will confine myself here to drawing attention once again to the need for constant reflection on the nature of literature not only for its own sake but also in order to safeguard the health of science and political movements, and will now shift my focus to discussion, unavoidably selective, of the actual works of literature themselves.

It seems advisable to preface this discussion with a word of explanation concerning my repeated insistence that a discussion of literary performance must include the most exacting judgment of a work's artistic merit. Now though from one corner of Korea's literary world we still hear charges that proponents of "national literature" substitute political and historical judgment for literary judgment, there is a tendency among those on the "national literature" side to deem insistence such as mine on a work's "artistic quality" as proof of a halfhearted commitment to the minjung cause. If the qualitative standard in question really is outmoded and wrong, then it is quite in order to denounce it. But the notion that it is possible to detach the artistic merit of a work from its political and historical meaning and treat it in isolation betrays an extremely naive conception not only of literature but of politics and history as well. At the risk of belaboring the obvious, we need to be reminded that the nature of the artistic quality emphasized in the "national literature" debate is completely different from that of the aesthete. By way of illustration, the latter is like an epicure who fusses only about taste and takes no thought at all for the effects of food on the life and health of the eater. It is clear that this is not a correct understanding of the "quality" of food or of eating. Nevertheless, the taste of food is not irrelevant to mental and physical health, and so it is unreasonable to exclude taste from discussion of a food's quality. To complicate matters further, one cannot reliably decide whether a given food is beneficial to one's health on the basis of its taste. Any authoritative pronouncement on the quality of food, then, requires the ability to grasp eating in its relation to the whole of life in all its aspects; and this is only possible if we overcome the tendency to absolutize either the taste of food or its generalized nutritional value.

This is of course merely an illustration, but concern for a work's quality is obviously indispensable to the health of literature and art; and surely a proper awareness of every aspect of life, from eating to politics and history, inevitably involves such a qualitative judgment. It would be no exaggeration to say that this is precisely the essence of dialectical thinking. For does not dialectical thinking consist in evaluating whatever is under consideration not simply as a manifest fact but in terms of what kind of movement inheres in it and what direction it is taking, and thereby participating or intervening in the movement oneself?

The Progress of Korean Literature
after the June 1987 Uprising

It is my belief that after the June 1987 uprising, which ended the military's direct domination of the nation and ushered in limited democratic reforms,

Korean literature entered a new stage. I first made this claim in an article published in spring 1988 in the revived *Creation and Criticism* journal, under the title "National Literature and the National Movement Today." My criteria for this new stage were, above all else, the *fruits* borne in the literary and national movements. I am not unaware that, broadly considered, the May 1980 Kwangju uprising had already inscribed itself as the big moment of the new era; but I judged that only in the June 1987 uprising did its historical significance begin to emerge on a large, nationwide scale, and that in the literary realm its full effects were felt only after that struggle. Hence I have adhered to the claim I made in autumn 1985 that, although Korean literature had then reached the threshhold of a new stage, it had not yet crossed it ("A New Stage in Minjung Literature," in *Creation and Criticism*, no. 57), and I see no reason even now to relinquish that position so long as "fruits of active engagement" remain the standard—and so long as by change in "stage" we mean some larger-scale transition than a mere change in the "situation."

The question is whether the actual achievements following the uprising have reached a sufficient level to be clearly distinguished from what pertained before. Of course, it must be remembered that while on occasion a change in literary stage may be effected by a single stroke through the appearance of a single work of literature, normally it is accomplished more slowly than are advances in political history. And in the present case, too, it is difficult to find any clear-cut qualitative leap from the achievements which I considered heralded a new stage in 1985 to the works I identified in my 1988 article as early signs that the new stage had by that point been entered. Indeed, the same applies to the more recent important works that I wish to examine here. For instance, the two works that in my view deserve to be considered the most outstanding literary achievements of 1988—Ko Ŭn's *Maninbo* (Ten thousand lives) and Hwang Sŏg'yŏng's *Mugiŭi Kŭnŭl* (In the shadow of war)—comprise but a part of the long accumulated labors of these well-known, established writers and, more particularly, represent the continuation or completion of works begun prior to June 1987.

Hence, although developments since 1988 only strengthen my conviction that a new stage in Korean literature has certainly been entered, this conviction is not founded on a claim to have discovered some sudden creative leap. Rather than a leap, what strikes the eye is the untiring devotion of a number of established writers, to which we may add the rise of some active new figures and significant advances in other areas that lie outside a narrow definition of Korea's "literary world." It is these things together which compel the conclusion that, in terms of the vitality of Korean literature, a definite momentum has been attained which differs clearly from the situation hitherto. I wish now to turn to a more concrete examination of the various factors involved in this.

First of all I would like to discuss the significance of Ko Ŭn and Hwang Sŏg'yŏng, who represent the generation of established writers. It could be somewhat disappointing to critics who demand a more striking or revolutionary degree of change than that denoted by the term "stage," that the major share of literary production should continue to be shouldered by this senior generation right down to the end of the 1980s. Yet the appearance of more than just one or two such writers who have persevered in their activities and continued to develop for several decades is itself a comparatively new phenomenon in Korea's modern literary history, and without this sort of accumulated effort, any really meaningful leap or revolutionary change can hardly be expected.

Of course, the work Ko Ŭn accomplished in the 1980s was made possible by both the activities of other writers during the same period and the foundation laid by his own continuous development during the 1970s. In any case, it is clear that his performance over the last few years is solid lively grounds for speaking of a new stage, not as a concept but as a reality. In terms of his personal history, I would judge that the biggest change in his poetic life occurred in the 1970s and that he entered a new phase in his writing after his release from prison in the early 1980s, with the successive publication of *The Collected Poetical Works of Ko Ŭn* (Minŭmsa, 1983), extensively revised and newly arranged in two volumes, *Star of the Homeland* (1984), *Pastoral Poems* (1986), and *Fly, Poetry, Fly* (1986). Yet even in the midst of this remarkable progress, his publication in 1986 of volumes 1, 2, and 3 of *Ten Thousand Lives* marked another new departure, and it is this, followed by the completion of the epic poem *Mount Paektu*, Part I (1987) after the June 1987 uprising and the successive publication of the collection *The Pupils of Your Eyes* (1988) and volumes 4, 5, and 6 of *Ten Thousand Lives*, that strengthens the conviction that, at least in terms of the history of modern Korean poetry, it is a quite unprecedented performance.

Regarding *Ten Thousand Lives*, I wrote a brief afterword when the first three volumes came out, and Kim Young-moo's most meticulous and pertinent piece of criticism, "Liberated Language and the Artistic Practice of National Life," appeared in *The Sound of My Waves* (Nanam, 1987), an anthology of Ko Ŭn's writings. But, rightly or wrongly, mention of *Ten Thousand Lives* is rather rare in the copious discussions on Korean national literature. It is a general characteristic of Ko Ŭn's writing that, although it does not stand squarely within any fixed scheme of minjung literature, it cannot be properly attacked as non-minjung national literature either. It seems to have been even easier to exclude *Ten Thousand Lives* from the radical debates of the 1980s than his other writings, on the ground that its content has so far been limited mostly to the portrayal of folk in his home village whom he had known in his earlier years. But take away the six-volume *Ten Thousand Lives*, and not only would debate over contemporary Korean literature easily descend into irrelevance and vacuity, but the opportunity would be lost to gain the experience, so urgently needed for the better development of Korean literature, of discovering its present significance as great litera-ture, even where the work's themes do not directly deal with the class and national issues of the 1980s. It is for this reason that I have decided first of all to make a number of points concerning the second set of volumes of *Ten Thousand Lives*, while not attemping anything like a thorough critique.

One way of indicating the contribution made by *Ten Thousand Lives* to opening a new stage in Korean national literature is to mention that the numerous poems that have already appeared (around a thousand verses if combined with those appearing throughout 1988 in *Wŏlgan Kyŏnghyang* [Kyŏnghyang monthly]), while for the most part retaining their poetic flavor, read like an absorbing novel. I do not mention this as some vague eulogy: it is something which will have to be rigorously tested against a standard I pro-posed in 1985, that "a full-fledged work of sustained literature" was what had to be achieved in order to propel Korean literature into a new stage (*A New Stage in National Literature*, 29ff.). I should like, however, to post-pone this more rigorous examination till after *Ten Thousand Lives*—and also *Mount Paektu*, which in the author's scheme of things bears an inseparable relation to the former—has advanced to a further point of development. Here I will satisfy myself by expanding a little on my personal impression, on first reading *Ten Thousand Lives*, that it came closer than anything else I had read to the flavor of Hong Myŏnghŭi's novel *Im Kkŏkjŏng*.

I suspect many readers would agree that, more than in other recent poetry, the naturalness and abundance of vernacular words one meets in *Ten Thousand Lives*, and the emotions of the people and the joys and sorrows of the minjung they evoke, come close to the world of Hong Myŏnghŭi. Of course, as a long novel, *Im Kkŏkjŏng* has a structure and continuity of plot that is absent in *Ten Thousand Lives* and possesses, besides, those unique strengths and aesthetic virtues of Hong which Ko Ŭn lacks. But to say that each of the poems in *Ten Thousand Lives* possesses individual vitality as a self-contained short piece, while together they support the sustained inter-est that one associates with *Im Kkŏkjŏng*, is to recognize strengths which the latter lacks. In the first place, in its poetic ambience and compressed beauty it excels *Im Kkŏkjŏng*'s rather tedious passages, and this, rather than being a matter of difference of genre, indicates that the poet's historical and autho-rial consciousness in the 1980s has attained a different dimension than those of the authors of the 1930s. In fact, in terms of realist accuracy, and intensity also, one does not encounter in *Ten Thousand Lives* the absurd actions one finds now and again in "P'ijangp'yŏn" (vol. 2 of *Im Kkŏkjŏng*), or the far-fetched connections between historical persons and events made in "Yang-banp'yŏn" (vol. 1), or the happy-go-lucky popular novel kind of atmosphere of the passages on Kkŏkjŏng's life in Seoul in "Hwajŏkp'yŏn." This is not unrelated to the fact that Ko Ŭn in *Ten Thousand Lives* is writing to his contemporaries or to his decision in *Mount Paektu* to deal with anti-Japanese struggles in the not so distant past, whereas Hong remained within the confines of *Suhoji*-type bandit novels° (though one must of course take into account the constraints of his time).

This is why consciousness of the reunification issue manages repeatedly to surface in *Ten Thousand Lives,* even though the work is as yet confined to portrayals of childhood or boyhood acquaintances of his home village. The author's historical consciousness is more clearly revealed in his evaluation of the historical figures who now and then find their way into the work, in poems such as "Chŏng Yakjŏn," "Kim Ch'unch'u and Kim Yusin," "Hong Taeyong," "King Kwanggaet'o," "Tosŏn," and so on, but the works that portray the lives of the common rural folk with such precision and yet such solicitude themselves bear witness to an unusual faith in the nation and the minjung. This—to take a short poem as an example so that the whole may be quoted—is arranged as a terse credo in "Ich'adon":

> The blood of vengeance is blue
> The blood of martyrdom is white
>
> But neither matches the red blood
> Of these homely bodies of ours

and attains dazzling radiance in "Changsun of Mije Village":

> Like a frosted chestnut
> Her white face
> White joy bubbling over
> Pegging a full load of washing
> Up on a long clothesline
> Her joy hoists the pole and overflows
> Till the joy breaks free in singing
> Rich and melodious—
> "Far fly the seabirds to shores of southern lands."

Yet, on the other hand, it is always accompanied by a dispassionate awareness of the pitiful national reality, as in "Hai! Hai! Woman!" and the wretched life of the minjung, as in "A Certain Mother"—and of the lesson of "Hong Chongu": "History also provides living-space for those who turn their backs on history" (vol. 6).

The "interest" of *Ten Thousand Lives* lies in this kind of faith and this kind of awareness, and its fusion of generous sympathy with dispassionate distance is the characteristic sentiment of the working and struggling minjung themselves, something which activists would do well to embody in their lives also. Although *Ten Thousand Lives* has not yet dealt with people

---

°That is, *Shui-hu chuan* (The water margin), a vernacular Ming Chinese classic, translated by Pearl Buck as *All Men Are Brothers.*—TRANSLATOR'S NOTE

actively engaged in the current movement to overthrow the national division of Korea, it is no accident that among the diverse writings Ko Ŭn has concurrently produced we find, as a natural extension of his *Ten Thousand Lives,* such significant contributions as "Let Liberation Live through These Deaths," a cycle of poems dedicated to martyrs of the national democracy movement of the 1970s and 1980s, from Chŏn T'aeil to Pak Naejŏn.

To recapitulate, these works of Ko Ŭn share both in the advancement of the whole national democratic reunification movement and in the hard-won achievements of poets from Pak Tujin, Kim Kyudong, and others of the older generation, to numerous contemporary and younger poets, including Sin Kyŏngnim, Min Yŏng, Cho T'aeil, Kim Chiha, and Kim Namju. The activities of these poets, too, have been indispensable to the opening of a new stage, but I wish to finish my discussion of poetry here and move on to the field of novels, which more properly belong to the category of long literature.

As one who has read but little, I must refrain from making firm statements about how far the extraordinary quantitative growth of full-length novels in South Korea includes also an elevation in quality. But having explained that the concept of a new stage in Korea's national literature is not derived from a consideration solely of creative writings in the south, I think I may be excused from offering a comprehensive evaluation of the numerous recent novels. If among those which I have read there was none that even approached, let alone actually measured up to, being a full-length novel that gave an adequate and comprehensive picture of our times, then whatever other factors may apply, that in itself would be sufficient to cast doubt on my whole thesis. Fortunately, a reading of Hwang Sŏg'yŏng's *In the Shadow of War,* the fruit of many years' labor, put to rest any doubts that Korea's novelistic literature had definitely advanced a good step beyond the standard of previous literature.

I include in "previous literature" Hwang's historical novel *Chang Kilsan* (1975–1984), which I have mentioned on several occasions as an invaluable contribution. Various aspects of the work itself are, however, open to criticism; but, more pertinently, it departs from the actual contemporary issues which, as is evident from *Kaekji* (Alien land, 1971) or *Hanssi Yŏndaegi* (Chronicles of Mr. Han, 1972), ought to be the main concern of this writer, and leaves a general sense of loss that he had regressed to a world modeled on *Im Kkŏkjŏng.* In this respect, *In the Shadow of War,* which deals with the Vietnam War, is an especially pleasing signal of his return to the present. Of course, the Vietnam War he experienced directly and portrayed in his novel was already over two decades in the past. However, quite apart from the obvious fact that participation in that war remains a vivid part of Korea's contemporary history, it is clear that the war itself is not irrelevant to Korean society today, where anti-American and anti-imperialist issues have risen to prominence as matters of considerable urgency. In other words, the choice of Vietnam as the setting is significant not only in broadening the subject matter of Korean novels but in its function also of shedding new light on Korea's situation in the 1980s; and this stems from Hwang's treatment of this material as a writer actively engaged in the present national democratic movement.

As a novel depicting an unfamiliar land and society, *In the Shadow of War* is surprising for its realistic immediacy. I cannot vouch for the accuracy of every detail, but as a novel to be read by Koreans rather than Vietnamese or Vietnam specialists, a lifelike evocation of the country's overall atmosphere and the general feeling of the war there would be more important than precision on matters of detail. If one may hazard a guess at how Vietnamese readers might respond, there is a distinct possibility they would feel that certain aspects, such as the family life of the Pham Guyen family, do not capture the flavor of a specifically Vietnamese ethos too well, while on the other hand they might acknowledge that it would be difficult even for one of their own writers to depict so vividly the black market of Danang in which Koreans also were involved.

In any case, whereas one would expect difficulties in achieving a strictly factual representation when a foreign setting is chosen, by the same token there is in such cases a correspondingly lower level of expectation in this regard on the part of the readers. But the real problem in these circumstances is whether it does not perhaps occasion impairment of what is more fundamental than descriptive facticity, namely, a novel's "artistic truth." If this weakness may be said to exist in *In the Shadow of War*, it is found in the hero, Corporal (later Sergeant) An Yŏnggyu, whose brilliant skills and exploits are dazzling to the point of romantic heroism. For example, granted that, knowing some English to begin with, he is by nature a very clever person quick to learn practically anything, there is yet not the slightest indication as the novel progresses that he experiences language difficulties in any abstruse debate or in the execution of any complex plan. (Hwang deliberately translates English dialogues in a somewhat stilted style in order to make the scenes more real to readers.) The help given Yŏnggyu by the native assistant Thoy in his brilliant exploits as a member of the Criminal Investigation Corps is considerable. But on reading this part one suspects that, had this been a novel in which the characterization of Thoy had taken place in a Korean setting, the author would have maintained a much more rigorous sense of reality. A person of such talent as Thoy, if he did not join the liberation front, would likely as not succeed in some moneymaking venture in a big way; but having served the whole time as a faithful messenger of the Korean army personnel, it is only at the eleventh hour that he seizes on some weakness in the liberation-front army and plots a quick fortune. And the end of all this is first his and then the liberation-front guerrilla Phan Min's death in battle. Hwang's breathless treatment of this denouement may

seem sufficient to put to rest doubts over the delineation of Thoy's character; but on second thought there is some difficulty in accepting that Thoy is
the type of person who, even for the sake of making a scoop, would meddle
in the affairs of the liberation front—and so clumsily at that.

Beneath the various questions surrounding the main characters lies curi-
osity over what sort of life Yŏnggyu led before coming to Vietnam. The
author seems to skirt this question intentionally, and leaving this entirely to
the reader's imagination is certainly one expedient to avoid interrupting the
flow with awkward reminiscences and so making the novel overly wordy. But
it is a different matter if this absence of Yŏnggyu's background is a corollary
of a lack of awareness of Korean realities. In my view, although the vivid portrayal of one cross-section of the Vietnam War and of Yŏnggyu's enlightenment there does prompt one to think afresh not only of the Korea of the
1960s but of the 1980s as well, it fails to give sufficient guidance toward how
to think of Korea in concrete terms. For in relying largely on the vantage
point of the Vietnamese minjung, the novel merely hints at the general
validity of its anti-imperialist or anti-American consciousness as something
also applicable to Korea and is silent on the specific nature of that applicability. Of course, if one assumes that the gist of national liberation in the
Vietnamese case is more or less what the Korean situation demands, it could
be maintained that the lesson of Vietnam for Korea hits home all the harder
by omitting direct reference to it in the book. But insofar as the cause of
national liberation in Vietnam was so unambiguous and the distinction
between patriot and traitor so clear-cut, there must have been particular historical factors at work that differ from those in contemporary Korea. In contrast to Korea, where a system of division has been established by the
intervention of outside powers and, as a part of that system, state organizations with a limited yet definite autonomy have arisen, the Vietnam War was
a continuation of the war of liberation from the old colonialism even after
the main actor changed from France to the United States—a desperate
attempt on the part of the foreign powers to *create* a divided system like
Korea's. If this distinction is allowed, then it follows that while *In the
Shadow of War* has raised the issue of anti-imperialist and anti-American
thought which is so central to today's movement to overcome the division, it
has failed to attain the degree of concrete historical consciousness the movement requires.

This question of the consciousness of reality demanded by the present
stage of the national democratic movement bears an inseparable relationship to the "interest" or "persuasive power" and similar questions pertaining
to artistic quality, and here the demand for factual accuracy takes on formidable importance. Verisimilitude is not the whole of realism, nor is it in
every instance an indispensable component, but in novels that do not
employ fantasy from the outset, close attention to facts is one gauge of an

author's integrity, and an important factor that may prevent an author's endeavor to present the whole shape of reality from falling into formularization or sloganism. The fact that not one of the many recent South Korean novels that deal more directly than *In the Shadow of War* with the present national democratic movement can be considered superior to Hwang Sŏg'yŏng's Vietnam War novel, seems to derive first and foremost from a deficiency in such rudimentary realist discipline. This impression is reinforced when one observes how the several novels using the *ppaljjisan* (partisans) as their subject matter pale before Yi T'ae's memoirs, *Nambugun* (The southern brigade). Whereas no one can deny how inspiring the latter is as a full-blooded, firsthand account of actual experiences, regardless of the ideological position of the author, the absence of this inspiration cannot be compensated for even by a "progressive" message, whether we are talking of a record of facts or a product of the imagination. But it needs to be reiterated that the lack of such inspiration based on the truth—where the tendency of the work rather than that of the individual author is at issue—is itself a lack of true progressiveness and a departure from commitment to the minjung side. Bearing this point in mind, I intend to wind up my discussion of the literary world in South Korea since the June 1987 uprising with a few brief comments on the activities of some recent writers.

Among novelists who have recently attracted notice, Chŏng Tosang, whose "Sibobang Iyagi" (Room 15) stole the limelight in 1987, is an unusually prolific writer. However, his products are of uneven quality. For instance, it is glaringly obvious that his medium-length work, "Yŏgi, Singminŭi Ttangesŏ" (Here, in this colonial land, [*Nokdu Kkot* I, Nokdu, 1988]), was written in haste without regard for even the most elementary discipline of realism, for the sake of giving expression to anti-United States, antifascist consciousness. (In this work, Korean troops sent out as KATUSAs [Koreans attached to the U.S. Army] observe firsthand the corruption of the U.S. superior officers and the two Korean sergeants who curry their favor, Chŏn Taehwan and No T'aeuk,* by whom they are then treated brutally.)

Compared to this, "Saebyŏk Kich'a" (Dawn train [*Silch'ŏn Munhak* 10, Summer 1988]), which deals with a labor struggle in an American-owned clothing factory called Grand Prix Fashion, is a little more credible. The notion of a fundamental link between the problem of attaining self-reliance vis-à-vis foreign powers and the struggle for the laborers' right to a livelihood is valid, and in choosing a rather wavering labor-union member named Sundŏk as the main character and tracing the process whereby she cannot help but turn into a much stronger fighter, Chŏng composes many vivid,

---

*The names Chŏn Taehwan and No T'aeuk are transparent allusions to the former president Chun Doo-Hwan (Chŏn Tuhwan) and the current president of the Republic of Korea, Roh Tae-woo (No T'aeu), both of whom are military products, former army generals.—TRANSLATOR'S NOTE

convincing passages. Nevertheless, the work as a whole fails to free itself from trite stereotypes. One finds this in the usual run of hackneyed incidents—from the father ruined by plummeting livestock values to the battering and gang-rape of a female factory worker. In particular, one suspects that the unwitting revelation of their links with the company by the gangsters, who babble on about "ten million wŏn" before they run off, is not so much a slip on their part as a false step by an author in a hurry to bring the novel to some kind of close. Moreover, the long, verbose passage in which a student-cum-laborer called Miran explains the significance of the Grand Prix Fashion strike to her fellow workers, is a far cry from the realism demanded of true minjung literature: "As one round in the long war against America, we must stage a fight in this company. To be sure, higher wages and the victory of the democratic labor union are our immediate objectives, but ultimately, the object is to oust all American imperialists, beginning with Grand Prix Fashion, and so we must direct all our powers to that end as effectively as we can." It is not that student laborers who talk like this do not exist, but the stance of the author toward this kind of talk ought—if it is to correspond with the view of the awakened workers—to exhibit a certain skepticism and irony, and give some indication that he is urging readers to reflect critically on the substance of a speech that seems to regard the labor movement simply as a means or vehicle of anti-Americanism.

Hence, although in Chŏng Tosang one detects a general awareness that both national self-reliance and labor movements are pressing issues and that a healthy combination of the two is the principal task of the whole minjung movement, his works, which deal directly with these matters, have not as yet made any noteworthy contribution toward a solution. A more substantial contribution has been made in a roundabout way by a novella in which neither laborers nor the United States of America make an appearance: "Ch'in'gunŭn Mŏlli Kassŏdo" (Though my friend's gone far away), in Ch'ae Kwangsŏk and Kim Myŏngin, eds., *Pamgirŭi Saramdŭl* (People of the night road [Seoul: P'ulpit, 1988]). This story deals with the harrowing experiences of one Kim Wŏnt'ae, who, while engaged in the student movement, is forcibly drafted and posted to the front before becoming the object of the so-called greening (reeducation) program. It draws an unusually graphic and lifelike picture not only of the merciless torture perpetrated by the National Security Forces but also of the inhuman nature of military life as a whole that makes the existence of such a National Security Force possible. Indeed, even compared to Yu Simin's "Tal" (Moon, [*Creation and Criticism*, Summer 1988]), its description is far more vivid and the events themselves more shocking and arresting in their impact. Furthermore, whereas the perspective of "Moon" appears to go no further than criticism of military culture according to the standards of civilian rule, "Though My Friend's Gone Far Away" takes one into territory that belongs more clearly to the culture of fascist oppression and the insane ideology of division.

Still, the ending of the piece is a little disappointing. Standing, on his return from a home leave, at the crossroads of betraying his comrades or submitting to continued dreadful torture, Wǒnt'ae is leaning toward the latter; but the author, himself perhaps unnerved at the prospect of what is to ensue, dodges the issue by introducing an absurd land-mine accident. There is no explanation why Wǒnt'ae was permitted to engage in work when he was still subject to isolation and surveillance; and his death, an almost pure accident, neither a "suicide suspiciously like a murder" nor an "accident suspiciously like a suicide" (of which we had so many examples in the days of General Chun Doo-Hwan's rule), wholly departs from the novel's theme. Evidently, the author would do well to take some time out for more adequate training in the art of writing.

One can sense also in Kim Hansu's short novel *Sǒngjang* (Growth [*Creation and Criticism* 62, Fall 1988]), that there are many instances where a faithful representation of even partial reality is more fruitful than a sense of theme that leaves the sense of reality behind. Although in many repects the immature debut of a novice, this work holds a special place among the recently mushrooming labor novels for its minutely drawn inside view of the life of a poor laborer's family. In most of the labor novels to date, perhaps because they have been written by university graduates, one usually finds that the actual lives of the laborers who comprise the large majority of those engaged in the radical work-site confrontations with which the novelists deal, are either omitted or treated only in extreme generalities. For instance, although it does not exactly fit the "labor novel" category, the most regrettable feature of Hong Hǔidam's "Kippal" (Flag [*Creation and Criticism* 59, Spring 1988]), the first piece to tackle successfully the Kwangju uprising from a clear class and anti-imperialist perspective, is that the concrete everyday lives of all the laborers who appear, beginning with the main female protagonist, Sunbun, are all but invisible.

In this respect, the first two chapters of Kim Hansu's *Growth* are a breath of fresh air. Here, the main character, Ch'angjin, begins to realize that, having grown up under a father who, even though he was basically a good person, was unable to escape from lifelong poverty, drink, and the family disharmony this created, he himself was to some extent treading the selfsame path. Yet for a novel to end here would surely render it susceptible to the criticism that it had not budged an inch from naturalism, and so the author is quite justified in attempting in the third chapter to render the process whereby the protagonist becomes enlightened and turns away from the kind of life his father led. But in rushing rather too quickly through the confrontation in the factory with the villainous company president, the demolition of the neighborhood shantytown, and other such incidents, the writer seems to be putting his own conclusions before the hitherto composed delineation of the protagonist's life. (As an obvious example, the settlement or "mutual agreement" between the president and Ch'angjin after the latter split the former's head open—not through some chance blow of the fist but with a club during a murderous fit of rage at the end of a labor-management dispute—by using money left over from Ch'angjin's mother's sale of their tenancy rights and procurement of a boarding room, is hardly credible in the real world of Korea.) This further confirms that some degree of naturalist monotony was inevitably there even in the more successful first two chapters. But in spite of these shortcomings, the scene at the end, where Ch'angjin, perched atop a removal truck in the falling snow, strengthens his resolve and accepts even the unhappy memory of his father with a smile, is not so awkward. Indeed, it is quite moving. It is moving because the prolonged "period of oppression" suffered by his family has been so faithfully reproduced, and because the snowflakes in this final scene are not flakes appreciated by leisured people but are flakes unambiguously situated in the experience of the laborer Ch'angjin.

> It was fine powdered snow. As fine as the rice flour people ground for rice-cakes on festival days, when he used to cry from hunger and eat earth off the ground. Snow is fine and clean to everyone. It is equally fine and clean to poor and rich alike. All things in the world ought to be like the snow. That one cannot achieve alone. It is possible only when the I of every downtrodden I, when our we, becomes one.

Apropos of *this* snow, Ch'angjin says: "There is nothing dead in the world. Some things just appear to be dead. Look, look at father's tears in that snow, enfolding the whole world in a smile"; and with this deep emotion he himself is also able to smile "strong and bright."

Finally, Kim Hyangsuk's collection of stories, *Surebak'wi Sogesŏ* (In the wagon wheel [Ch'angjakkwa pip'yŏngsa, 1988]), cannot be omitted from a discussion of Korea's recent literature. The two long and five short stories in this anthology were all released in 1988, and their elaborate structure, meticulously polished language, and deeply penetrating descriptions could, in terms of the priority given to "activism" in today's South Korean novels, be considered to be behind the times. But if the eyes of the minjung who are awakened as a class demand above all a high degree of artistry, then it ought to be possible to evaluate Kim Hyangsuk's "artistic" prowess according to the criteria of "activist" accomplishments as well. That the actual sweep of the author's eye encompasses a definite activist rather than mechanistic or psychologistic horizon may be gleaned from the fact that all five short stories treat either casualties of the democratization movement or those who are at one and the same time victim and victimizer, in addition to the lives of those around them.

To acknowledge that Kim Hyangsuk's short stories depict mainly the life of the middle class or that the acute problems of the times barely surface in her ambitious longer piece, "In the Wagon Wheel," need not lead to the conclusion that her critical consciousness is limited to a bourgeois or petit bourgeois dimension. Although her writings as a whole may not have attained in full measure the qualities of minjung literature, they hardly remain rigorously within the confines of middle-class literature even when they address only middle-class life through the eyes of a middle-class narrator. It may be that genuine rigor refuses any inept compromise, but then again, neither does it countenance any self-indulgence in the form of mere grumbling or abstract negation. In fact, the son who laid down his life in "Purŭi T'ŏnŏl" (Tunnel of fire) and the daughter in "Karaannŭn Sŏm" (The sinking island) who is violated by the "dirty hand" and then plunges into factory life, are not liberalist activists, as one might expect of the middle class. More importantly, the author's unostentatious yet scathing judgment on Unsuk's daughter, who is regarded by others as a model middle-class maiden ("Tunnel of Fire"), and the mother's "sudden thought" that she actually rather envied her troublesome daughter Kiok ("The Sinking Island"), are not irrelevant to the perspective of the minjung movement.

Moreover, a notable aspect of Kim Hyangsuk's fictional world is that a specifically woman's consciousness permeates her writings in a way that fully integrates it with the issues raised in the overall minjung movement. At work in Kiok's mother's gradual awakening are her disillusionment over the revelation of her husband's adultery, committed in order to obtain a son, and her recognition of her own incorrigible subservience in nevertheless involuntarily sympathizing with her husband's rationalization; while mixed in with the painful awakening of the victimizer's son, Chongha, in "Ŭiinŭi Tol" (The stone of a righteous person), is the belated realization that his paternal grandmother, in standing up unconditionally for him and his father while lashing out verbally without compunction at his younger sister, mother, and maternal grandmother, is actually an oppressor. Indeed, Chongha's role as the dimwit who perceives the true situation only long after his mother and the young Chonghye do, is in large measure due to his being a boy who has been coddled by traditional notions of male superiority.

The Broadened Horizon of National Literature

As I observed earlier, although one can point to remarkable vitality in Korean poetry and fiction from 1988 and to a new energy in drama and filmmaking also, there is plenty of room to question whether the performance up to now in itself justifies talk of entering a new "stage." Not only is there no publicly agreed-upon measure of exactly what degree and kind of output is needed for a new stage, but I myself have not been without some dissatisfaction concerning the works that I consider to be of relatively superior quality. This is precisely one reason why I have advocated undertaking a comprehensive examination of a variety of areas of progress besides Korea's "domestic creative products" in a narrow sense. If we take into account other factors directly affecting national literary creativity, it is very likely we shall be persuaded that the vitality exhibited by recent Korean literature is of a nature which promises genuine continuity and growth.

Surely the most significant reality for the Korean nation as a whole is that, even after the cooptative June 29 declaration and the inauguration of the Sixth Republic, minjung initiatives in the national democratic movement are actually being strengthened, without buckling under to the system of division. Speaking of what may be considered the direct preserve of the cultural sphere, the lifting of the ban on ideological works and on works of art and literature by people who went north after the country was divided or who have worked in the north all along, the partial invigoration and democratization of the mass media, the increase in contacts with the socialist bloc and with progressive Western intellectuals and literary figures, and the freeing, finally, of poets such as Kim Namju along with the mass release of political prisoners at the end of 1988, are all consequent on the general advance of the minjung movement.

In the process, the wall that had hitherto so strictly separated the "establishment" from the "movement" has also largely collapsed. Of course, there is always the danger in such cases of being coopted by the system, and in fact a partial defection of progressive membership in precisely this manner is already observable. But unless the national democratic movement is to remain indefinitely a mere "counterculture," without ever exercising any effectual leadership over the whole of society, such a risk is unavoidable. In point of fact, the erection of the wall between the movement and the establishment groups was necessitated by the overpowering dominance of the latter. Even giving due recognition to the dangers involved, it is therefore only natural that, as their power increases, the movement groups should step up their efforts to infiltrate and gain control of the established institutions.

In this respect, the founding of the *Han'gyŏre Sinmun* (One people newspaper) in May 1988 and, before that, the resumption of publication of so-called oppositional quarterlies like *Ch'angjakkwa Pip'yŏng* and *Silch'ŏn Munhak*, are significant outcomes of the June 1987 uprising. Further, the fact that, among all the oppositional cultural organizations, the Chayu Silch'ŏn Munin Hyŏbŭihoe (Writers for Practice of Freedom) was the very first to reorganize and broaden itself as the Minjok Munhak Chakka Hoeŭi (Korean National Writers' Union) in September 1987 may be taken as evidence of the relative maturity of the literary sphere. This may seem a rather self-serving judgment, but the existence of very broad sympathy for the basis on which the new Writers' Union was formed was confirmed in December of the same year, when artists in other fields participated en masse in the foundation of the Han'guk Minjok Yesurin Ch'ongyŏnhap (abbreviated as Minyech'ong: Federation of Korean National Artists), in response to their sense of the need for a body that could essentially supersede Yech'ŏng, the existing government-sponsored federation, as opposed to simply ignoring or criticizing its member organizations.

But eschewing discussion of organizations and the media, I wish here to make some mention of works which, while not new compositions by domestic authors, have at a stroke extended the horizons of Korean national literature and the reading experience of the public. In the broad sense of the term, there is no reason to deny that the aforementioned *Nambugun* (The southern brigade) is a "new composition by a domestic author"; but however that may be, the great broadening of freedoms not only concerning that phase of modern history but also in scholarship, art, and thought through the publication of a memoir about the long-forbidden topic of the activities of the "partisans," and its auguring a formidable advance in the discernment of readers, is a good example of the far-reaching effects of developments taking place outside "creative literature." Furthermore, the publication of *Nambugun* demonstrates that the pioneering efforts made by publishing activists throughout the 1980s in the face of bans, confiscations, searches, interrogations, incarceration, and so on, are beginning to yield more tangible fruit since the June 1987 uprising.

Literature written in the colonial period by Koreans who remained in or crossed over into the north after the division had already been actively published before the Ministry of Culture and Information lifted its ban on it. The public announcement by authorities in that ministry that not only must the writings of Hong Myŏnghŭi, Yi Kiyŏng, Han Sŏrya, Cho Yŏngch'ul, and Paek Injun remain banned but also works by "released writers" that were written after the August 15 liberation, has also long since evaporated as so much ineffectual verbiage. Quite suddenly, the battle lines in the confrontation advanced to the issue of materials distributed in contemporary North Korea, so that in January 1989 confiscations and interrogations recommenced, but this time in the wake of the publication of *Minjungŭi Pada* (Sea of the minjung [Han Madang, 1988]; original title: *P'ibada* [Sea of blood]), *The Selected Works of Kim Il-Sung*, and *Pukhan Hyŏndaesa* (Modern history of North Korea), among others. But it would be no exaggeration to say that suppression even of original materials from North Korea, which in a sense is the last frontier for the publishing culture of this era, has in point of fact become meaningless.

In the midst of the hubbub occasioned by the above, translations of works by progressive Koreans resident in Japan, such as Kim Sŏkpŏm, Lee Hoesŏng, and Kim Talsu, which had been deemed dangerous at the time of their original publication, together with texts by writers in Yanbian such as Kim Hakch'ŏl and Yi Kŭnjŏn, were published in South Korea without causing any particular ruckus, and this, too, has contributed to a marked broadening of the horizon of Korean national literature. Having read only a few of these, I cannot discuss them at length, but fortunately we can draw on Hwang Sŏg'yŏng's skillful and vigorous treatment of several of them in his "Hangjaeng Ihuŭi Munhak" (Literature after the uprising [*Creation and Criticism*, Fall 1988]). Among these, Hwang has expressed particular appreciation of Kim Hakch'ŏl's *Kyŏkjŏng Sidae* (Age of passion, 3 vols. [Seoul:

P'ulpit, 1988]): "Here indeed is a novel that has kept intact the native literary tradition we ourselves have lost, yet containing a firm core of strength beneath its easy-going air." In his review article, "Minjung Saenghwalsaŭi Pogwŏn'gwa Hyŏngmyŏngjŏk Nakkwanjuŭiŭi Ppuri" (The restoration of minjung history and the roots of revolutionary optimism [*Creation and Criticism,* Fall 1988]), the poet Sin Kyŏngnim has commented, while examining in more detail its virtues as a novel, that "in truth, it was a long time since I had so savored the joy of reading a novel."

In my view also, *Kyŏkjŏng Sidae* merits recognition as a precious addition to Korea's national literary harvest of the 1980s. Since it was published in the Korean Autonomous Prefecture of Yanbian in 1986, and was written in Korean about Koreans, it fully meets even the formal criteria of Korean national literature, but these alone do not capture the really important aspect of the work. It is not merely written in Korean: the type of Korean used is reminiscent of the language and expression unique to Korean that one finds in *Im Kkŏkjŏng,* while its characters are authentic Koreans of the 1920s and 1930s with the authentic faces of Korean compatriots involved in the anti-Japanese resistance in China. As Shin Kyŏngnim correctly observes, this is not an effect solely of having the advantage of living memory of people who actually existed, but lies in the author's skill as a novelist and "the author's great love" on which that skill is founded. Further, what was probably decisive in the sense of authenticity conveyed in *Kyŏkjŏng Sidae,* as is made clear in the author's afterword, was his sense of mission in writing "biographical literature that borrows the form of the novel" in order to fill in "historical lacunae that certain factors created."

But regardless of whether it is biographical literature or fiction, for the purposes of this discussion our evaluation must abide strictly by the standards of a literature demanded by the present phase of the reunification movement. Needless to say, the history of anti-Japanese resistance fighters in China and the sentiments and language of Koreans of the past restored to us in *Kyŏkjŏng Sidae* provide valuable nourishment and also some direct stimulation to our movement and literature. On the other hand, however, it gives little clue to how that resuscitated history and those lives reflect the total reality of the time or how one is to grasp the historical relationship between that era and the present. Indeed, even had he not said so himself in the afterword, the author's intention to record only those things he had himself experienced is clearly revealed in the novel's abrupt ending just as the battle of Mount T'aehang was at its height. (Kim Hakch'ŏl was severely wounded at this point, lost consciousness, became a POW, and was hauled off to Japan, where he underwent amputation of a leg and suffered imprisonment.) I am not arguing that the novel should have been broader in scope, but that it is the basic requirement both of writers of authentic realist novels and of responsible historians that, however limited the particular event being drawn, the writer must in some way imbue it with his/her own sense of the whole canvas of the period.

Measured against this standard, *Kyŏkjŏng Sidae* clearly falls short. After the main protagonist, Sŏ Sŏnjang, leaves Korean territory, one gets the impression that Korea's concrete reality disappears not only from the experiences of Sŏ but also from the author's consciousness; and encaged in the limited perspective of the Chosŏnin Ŭiyongdae (Korean Patriotic Corps), even the anti-Japanese struggle in China proceeds like so many snapshots of Sŏ's life, with almost no connection to the whole picture of the Korean liberation movement or the movement of the Chinese minjung. Of course, these snapshots are all vivid and convincing enough, and the very fact that each follows the other without any special attempt to create a structure to tie them together may be an expression of the "revolutionary romanticism" cherished by the author and his characters alike. But just as revolutionary romanticism is only one among many qualifications of a revolutionary, so is it nothing more than one among a number of desirable virtues of the realist novelist. In terms of *Kyŏkjŏng Sidae*'s sheer "readability," too, the fact that the interest of the first volume steadily diminishes as one moves into the second and third volumes is due to the failure, once he finishes describing his youthful life in Wŏnsan, of the author's optimism to measure up to the sense of ultimate oneness with life of a true realism that sublates the protagonist's romanticism.

Insofar as "works by literary figures who went north" had been read continuously by numerous Koreans before the August 15 liberation and during the period immediately following it, they are not especially unfamiliar works. But with their release for general publication, it is only now, when all can read them freely and make their own evaluations, that the basic conditions have been established for sound critical debate. However, since neither space nor my own state of preparation allows it, my own participation in this debate will have to await another opportunity.

The recent introduction of North Korean works beginning with *KKot P'anŭn Ch'ŏnyŏ* (The flower girl), *P'ibada* (Sea of Blood), and *Han Chawidanwŏnŭi Unmyŏng* (The fate of a self-defense corps fighter), and other such works classified today in North Korea as "Immortal Classics," is an event of quite another order. Through a brief critique of *P'ibada*, I propose now to share some thoughts on the import of this momentous development for Korean national literature.

What needs to be clarified at the outset is that, originally composed and staged as a drama, *P'ibada* was made into a musical, a film, and a novel only much later, and for my discussion I shall be relying solely on the South Korean edition of the novel version, titled *Minjungŭi Pada* (Sea of the minjung). In volume 2 of their *Chosŏn Munhak Kaegwan* (Survey of Korean literature [Indong, 1988]), North Korean scholars Pak Chongwŏn and Yu Man state: "Composed during times of hardship when the main forces of the Chosŏn Inmin Hyŏngmyŏnggun (Korean People's Revolutionary Army), which had operated victoriously in Musong prefecture, were advancing on

Changbaek under the Great Leader around the end of August 1936, the immortal classic *P'ibada* was staged as a play in the village of Man'gang in Musong." Recently, a researcher in the south has introduced the classic as follows: "[In North Korean literature] in the 1970s, a task of considerable significance was performed, as works composed by Kim Il-Sung during the armed resistance to Japan, such as *P'ibada, Han Chawidanwŏnŭi Unmyŏng,* and *KKot P'anŭn Ch'ŏnyŏ,* were reworked as modern novels, films, and musicals. In North Korea's literary history, these works hold an important place as classics of the revolutionary artistic tradition and are positively evaluated as genuine examples of socialist realism in literature and art" (*Sahoewa Sasang* 2 [1989]: 375). Needless to say, quite apart from various practical problems, passing judgment on such works is something that critics who are in the dark concerning North Korean social realities and literary-artistic customs must undertake with extreme caution. But granting the necessity of a very cautious, tentative evaluation, I believe the time has come for public debate consistent with the principles of minjung national literature.

In actuality, it is extremely difficult to place *P'ibada* accurately in the experience of South Korean readers. The content itself, which, while dealing with the armed anti-Japanese struggle by communists, repeatedly emphasizes that revolution is the only alternative, is unfamiliar and even threatening to readers in the south; but the difficulty in placing it "in the right niche" does not derive from that alone. The whole atmosphere or makeup of the novel does not easily fit into the notion of "serious" versus "popular" literature to which South Koreans are accustomed in domestic and foreign works. Measured against the customary standard of artistic refinement, *P'ibada* clearly contains many elements of popular literature. On the other hand, there are virtually no examples of popular literature with which I am acquainted where the level of earnestness associated with serious literature is sustained as much as in *P'ibada.* Apart from the fact that its subject matter or political message could not coexist with notions of the "popular" in the south, its dedication to and practiced skill in choosing and refining pure vernacular Korean alone would have to be judged a not inconsiderable achievement in South Korea's present circumstances.

Of course, the boundary between serious and popular literature is not clear, and the proper meaning of the concepts themselves is distorted by a social system in which artistic refinement is divorced from mass culture. Hence there is no inherent mystery in the fact that *P'ibada* fits neither category. The terms serve as a means of expressing one's first impressions on reading the story, a point of departure for a more careful examination of the accuracy of this impression and of how closely *P'ibada* may have approached the ideal of a genuine blend of artistry and popular culture. Needless to say, we must undertake this enquiry in an attitude of humility, whether for the sake of recovering the nation's common heritage or as a fitting intellectual response to the unfamiliar. At least it is necessary to transcend differences in systems, thought, and ideology and to honor the great national pride that fills the book, as well as to recognize as one cause for that pride its search for and usage of many an indigenous word which in the south has mostly been buried between the covers of dictionaries, notwithstanding the efforts of a few exceptional writers.

What quickly come to mind as examples of a desirable blend of high art and popular culture are Tolstoy's *Anna Karenina* and (though these do not command the same broad consensus as Tolstoy) the masterpieces of Balzac and Dickens. The impression *P'ibada* gives is quite different from these. This seems not simply a difference between "critical realism" and "socialist realism." The peculiar problems arising from the transformation into a novel of what was originally written as a drama and the difficulties attending communal composition of a novel may be more important factors. In this case, a far more apposite contrast can be made with Maxim Gorky's *Mother*, which was written by one person and as a novel to begin with. What catches the eye here is the similarity of plots: the belated awakening to history through her son's plunge into the underground movement of a mother who has spent half her life in nothing but tears, misery, and wretched suffering, and her own subsequent induction as a revolutionary fighter. Now, I have read only the English translation (Gorky, *Mother* [Moscow: Raduga Publishers, 1949]), but I do not think it quite measures up to its renown. Gorky himself reportedly considered this a "novella"; but in fact, while being too long for a novella, it lacks the full development of a full-scale novel, so that it is neither one thing nor the other. As a result, there are a number of more or less meaningless and tiresome passages. For instance, it would be reasonable in a work of this length to depict the factory life of Pavel Vlassov; and the mother's activities, too, except for the opening and final dramatic scenes, tend to fall into monotonous repetition because they are unsupported by a sufficient delineation of related characters and situations.

By contrast, in *P'ibada,* the shock of the woman losing her husband and of the village being completely razed by the Japanese troops' surprise punitive expedition in part 1, or the process in parts 2 and 3 where the mother, against a background of the bitter sorrows suffered in common by the destitute, stateless Korean women of the time, realizes the need to fight alongside her children and finally awakens the neighboring womenfolk and organizes the Women's Association, are full of very vivid and moving episodes. When, in part 4, preparations for the "revolt" encounter difficulties, the mother voluntarily infiltrates a mining village and succeeds in stealing gunpowder by winning over the concubine of the pro-Japanese mine owner; later, following her arrest by Japanese troops, she manages to withstand torture and free herself. In contrast to Gorky's novel, this part is filled with vibrancy and conveys an emotion over and above the interest of following the plot. This is doubtless because, rather than the more or less idealistic

creed concerning the future life of humanity so frequently advocated in
Mother, the concrete need to struggle against actual, visible oppressors on
behalf of national liberation and a more humane life is expressed so poignantly. Further, the strong emphasis placed on the Koreanness of the virtues
appearing in the struggle and on the good-heartedness of the "have-nots,"
also stands in contrast to the failure of Pavel in Gorky's novel ever to become
a particularly admirable human being.

True, one can regard the portrayal not only of Pavel but of several other
characters in *Mother* as fraught with human failings as evidence of Gorky's
realistic truthfulness. (The novel's ending not with a dramatic victory but
with the mother's arrest may also be taken in the same sense.) And it is true
that in the Korean society of *P'ibada,* apart from a few "running dogs" of the
Japanese, there may be poverty and misery but no villains, traitors, internal
conflict, or corruption. This may be attributable to transposing into novel
form a dramatic framework designed for immediate rapport with the audience, but in any case it imbues the work as a whole with a kind of legendary
atmosphere. Indeed, the intention of *P'ibada* from the outset was obviously
not to reconstruct a particular episode in the armed struggle against the Japanese according to the facts à la *Kyŏkjŏng Sidae,* but to create a type of
nation-building myth that symbolizes the victory of the struggle to liberate
the homeland. Setting aside the question of how far it conforms to the historical facts of the battle in Musong prefecture, it is clear that the victory at
the end (part 5) which is achieved in concert by the peasants' and miners'
uprisings, the planned revolt in the fortress, and the commando unit's attack,
is not itself the final victory of the Paektu Mountain unit's anti-Japanese
resistance, and even less the triumph of the national liberation movement.
That the novel ends with the mother, as she watches the receding ranks of
the resistance fighters, gazing "intently along the road to revolution—a wide
road stretching far into the future—through tears glistening with violet
light," likely enough stems from the fact that the victory in the prefecture is
regarded as the pattern for the ultimate triumph of the revolution.

To what extent does the novel *P'ibada* realize the typicality thus aimed
at? A more fundamental issue here is the question of the historical sound-
ness of the aim itself. For instance, one cannot judge this issue without
inquiring into the actual role the unit which led the Musong battle played in
the founding of the DPRK and, beyond this, the proper weight to be given
that tradition in planning the future reunified Korea. But here it seems best
to focus on the question of how convincing the novel's design is in giving the
Musong victory the status of a nation-building legend or myth.

As the narrative moves into part 5, the legendary elements become ever
more prominent. Now we see the mother, having sustained another punitive
raid and witnessed her youngest son's tragic death, rebound superhumanly
to glorious participation in the following day's insurgency. Although community art forms such as drama, opera, or film may be up to it, or even epic and

dramatic poems that draw on the power of poetry to confer a higher dimension of reality upon their legendary elements, it is questionable whether a novel is equal to the task of incorporating such scenes as these into its narrative structure. To start with, they were not constructed with sufficient eye to detail to obviate doubts concerning verisimilitude, nor was any other innovative form created to accommodate it. Thus the treatment of the actions of the Japanese comes across as being far too inept. The instant he hears a garbled report of the clash with the guerrilla Cho Tongch'un, the border control captain makes an impromptu reprisal raid on the whole village of Sangdong but neglects to request reinforcements to finish it off, or even in response to reports of an impending revolt; and apparently the mother, already fingered as a suspect, encountered no difficulty in passing through the fortress gates to participate in a secret meeting on the eve of the rebellion.

It may have been more suitable to deal with such episodes as the comic death of the self-defense corps leader Pyŏn Changguk with something like Kim Chiha's balladic technique based on *p'ansori*. Again, the incongruity would have been obvious had one tried to film such scenes as that concerning Cho Tongch'un's corpse, where, on receiving the "report of Kumamoto's death from Pyŏn Changguk, and that they barely managed to track down the guerrilla who had disappeared into the swamp, but since he was already dead were unable to discover any clues," the border patrol captain yelled out orders to cut down the whole village; and yet Kapsun, returning only after the massacre had begun, hugged her mother and the dead Ŭllam and, at the end of a long period of wailing, "ran off and found the guerrilla Cho Tongch'un already dead where he lay in the swamp." These problematic aspects are especially conspicuous in part 5 but are examples of how, overall, the novel *P'ibada* fails to attain the happy goal of a realist novel in which legendary, romantic elements are harmonized with firm adherence to lifelike details.

Having said this, however, it must be acknowledged that the initial respect with which we began our critique of the novel remains intact, and it is undeniable that, along with other classics of North Korean literature, it has occasioned a considerable enlargement of the horizon of national literature. Confronted by a populism of such a different nature, the low-quality popular novelists of the south cannot but be spurred on to better things, and we are now at the stage where the vice of thinking some important advance in national literature has been made merely by raising the topic of the armed resistance tradition or of revolutionary thought can be put behind us. What at any rate is clear is that, as in the cases of the several other publications that have greatly altered the reading environment of South Koreans recently, here too the opportunity *P'ibada* provides for a new stage in national literature can only be fulfilled through our thoughtful and active response to it.

Perspectives on the Period after the June Uprising

Although it is universally recognized that the June 1987 uprising stands as one of the truly momentous events in Korea's modern history, opinion differs over the hypothesis that it marks the beginning of a new stage in Korea's national literature. It is not my intention to get too bogged down in the controversy over whether to call the progress made since the June uprising a new "phase" or a new "stage," or whether one may accurately date the achievement of new accomplishments from June 1987 or from later in 1988, or even 1989. The important thing is not pedantic concern for preciseness of classification but rather how accurately the actual, concrete products themselves are evaluated and how Koreans should understand their historical significance, the better to attain the optimum course of practice in the future. I propose, therefore, to broaden a little the purview of the debate that so far has stressed literary productions, in order to clarify the original import of the theory of a "new stage" through an examination of the various perspectives on the situation as a whole since the June uprising.

These perspectives may be divided into three broad tendencies. First, there is the "middle-class" perspective, which views June 1987 as *the* decisive turning point. Here one finds a cleavage between the positions advanced by the government side and the official opposition parties. The "new stage" theory of the former I judge to be nothing more than a deceitful play on words, in that even while emphasizing the epochal significance of the June 29 Declaration they are devoting themselves to minimizing all substantive differences between the Fifth and Sixth republics. In particular, by their rejection of the general view that June and its aftermath are the long-term results of the May 1980 Kwangju uprising, they are repeating the sorry performance of the Chun regime which, bypassing May 18 (the day of the Kwangju uprising), blustered about the "new era" being opened instead on 17 May 1980 (that is, the date of Chun's coup d'état). It is debatable whether the conservative opposition differs substantially from the government on this point, but it can at least be observed that the two opposition parties (then led respectively by Kim Young-sam and Kim Dae-jung), which participated in the June uprising, more faithfully represent the view of the majority of the middle class that June 1987 heralded a decisive new stage in the process of democratization.

Insofar as this perspective is not confined to the middle class alone but corresponds also to the gut feeling of considerable numbers of citizens—perhaps a mistaken feeling but still no mere phantasm—it can by no means be ignored by the national literature or unification positions. But the basic problem with this perspective is that, while it possesses an earnest yearning for democracy, it lacks the mass base necessary for its attainment. The democracy these people have in view is remote from the aspirations of the core class of minjung, who comprise the greatest portion of Korean society and who have suffered the most from the dictatorships, and it also falls short in terms of the political will to satisfy the deeply cherished desire for reunification of the majority of the nation. When the aspirations of the minjung and minjok (nation) move beyond the established parameters of what is called "liberal democracy," this perspective almost completely lacks the power to wage a costly struggle for their genuine freedom as distinct from the power to stifle democracy itself on the pretext of "safeguarding the liberal democratic system." Herein lies the reason for the tendency of the larger part of the conservative opposition to show willingness to compromise even in the midst of pressing for an inquiry into the truth of the 1980 Kwangju uprising, and to be taken in by the ruling class' strategy of distorting it as a regional problem.

Hence, despite the fact that the middle-class perspective correctly understands one aspect of the post-June political situation, it cannot but be challenged by more "radical" positions. One of these actively seeks to reflect the desire for national reunification and so makes that the supreme task. In this case, too, there is not necessarily unanimity on the post-June era. There are those who fasten onto 1988 as clearly marking a new stage, in view of the heightened thirst for reunification among all classes that year and especially the nationwide expansion of the movement centered on the (unfulfilled) plans for the south–north student conference on June 10. But others argue that 1988 failed to mark a decisive turning point in the reunification movement as that year also gave considerable cause for celebration among the forces of division, with the success of the Olympic Games without the presence of North Korea and the trend toward recognition by socialist countries of two Koreas on the peninsula. Considering the added momentum gained in 1989 by the government's so-called northern policy, and the fact that visits to the north by leaders of *chaebŏl* (big business) conglomerates and plans for opening up tourism in the north have become the dominant topics among South Koreans, skepticism concerning the advent of a new stage would seem to be the more accurate position if one applies the single standard of "national liberation."

Finally, there is the perspective which attaches importance to class contradictions within South Korean society above all else. According to this position, the middle-class theory of a new stage is a fallacy that reduces "democracy" to "liberal democracy," nothing more than a part of the ideological offensive to strengthen the hegemony of the bourgeoisie, while absolutizing national liberation/reunification is a manifestation of a petit bourgeois tendency that lacks any class conception. But, here again, there are internal differences over how to regard the post-June political situation. Two views are possible: first, that the labor struggle of July and August which followed on the heels of the June 29 declaration did usher in a new stage; and second, that when judged by the standard of "the solidification of the leadership of the working class," no leap forward has occurred, regardless of other developments. Again, so long as one insists on the sole standard of "working-class hegemony," this latter, more skeptical evaluation seems closer to the truth.

Then what is the standpoint concerning the whole political situation after the June 1987 uprising of a national literature theory which asserts that in the course of 1987 and 1988 Korean literature has entered a new stage? While introducing the three different positions above, I pointed out that, on the face of it, the skeptical perspectives were closer to the truth than those supporting the new-stage theory. And if one intends nevertheless to claim the advent of a new stage, it can only imply an attempt to synthesize dialectically the valid elements of each of the existing positions without accepting any of them in toto. In fact, I would go so far as to say that the new development of most moment in the post-June political situation is that, while revealing more clearly their respective premises and problematics in the enlarged historical space opened up by the June victory, these three hitherto coexisting perspectives have themselves raised the need for a new synthesis. Indeed, one can say that they have disclosed the practical possibility of a new synthesis for the first time. With a view to making some contribution to this synthesis, I wish to elaborate a little on the standpoint of the national literature theory.

First, the national literature theory is also a minjung literature theory, which believes that minjung power centered on the working class is the chief motive force of the unification movement. It therefore has no argument with raising the issue of class contradictions in South Korean society and endeavoring to identify, on the basis of a scientific understanding of these contradictions, the social force to take charge of the democratization and unification movements. But Korea's minjung literature is a minjung literature of a physically divided society, and one that aspires to lower the curtain on the division era, and so taking one's cue from theories or practices of working-class leadership developed in societies where no system of division intrudes, is an overly ideological attitude. Although the limitations of the present stage of the Korean labor movement are the direct result of suppression under military dictatorships, at a deeper level they exist because the development of working-class power, which had continued through the period of the Japanese empire's colonial, fascist rule and had risen to a not inconsiderable level after liberation on 15 August 1945, was artificially cut short by the solidification of the system of division by the Korean War of 1950 to 1953. It is thus a fallacy to view matters as if lack of a theoretical grasp of class contradictions were the principal factor inhibiting minjung leadership, without taking into account the special characteristics of a divided country; and to expect, under circumstances of continuing division, a decisive victory—as opposed to merely relative growth—of minjung power, is to be in danger of resurrecting, mutatis mutandis, the liberalist thesis of democracy first, unification second. For instance, where a supposedly scientific understanding of the system's anti-minjung character fails to grasp that it is a system of *division*, it is insufficiently scientific. Hence, in the debate over whether to view the present situation as a new stage, neither side can expect to be convincing so long as such a vague grasp of concrete realities remains the norm.

Second, it is equally difficult to grant that making national liberation and autonomy the absolute standard reflects a scientific grasp of the system. Although raising the problem of division that the other two streams relatively neglect deserves the highest commendation, this position fails to understand adequately that it is a division *system*, covering the whole Korean peninsula. As a result, there is lacking any scientific endeavor to understand North Korean society's achievements or problems in relation to the conditioning effects of the system of division—indeed, there is little to choose between scholars of any persuasion on this point—and even when discussing South Korean society it is common practice to ignore completely the distinction between old and new colonialisms. Indeed, even where discussion of autonomy is premised on the concept of neocolonialism, the charactersistics of a neocolonial society which forms one side of the system of division—that is, its unique combination of unusual development with unusual dependency—are not accurately understood. Consequently, there are far too many unscientific discussions that apply without any modification the yardstick of colonial or dependent nations which suffer no division. For example, focusing only on the dependency which the system of division enforces, and then overlooking the certain degree of autonomy it does allow and the possibility of a relative expansion of that autonomy, is to encourage a kind of autonomy-first, unification-second theory, which considers it possible to obtain full and final autonomy as opposed to a relative growth of it, before overthrowing the system of division. Contrary to this, the kind of understanding of the division which the literary works and critical debates of the national literature camp have fostered highlights its anti-minjung nature, in the light of which South Korea's internal democratization is perceived to be the primary task, while the progress of antiforeign, self-reliance forces are evaluated as one part of the movement to topple the system of division. This is why the national literature camp does not see the lack of a decisive advance in national autonomy after June 1987 as in itself a sufficient ground for relinquishing the claim for a new stage.

I have already noted that the middle-class exaggeration of the visible changes since the June uprising is fraught with difficulties. But the point is that those who favor theories of class or national contradiction need to synthesize and adjust their views so that they center on the movement to overthrow the division within the space newly opened up after June 1987, and that in the process it would be advisable for them to adopt a more positive stance toward the series of limited democratizing measures in South Korean society which have created that space. These changes, often dubbed "liberalist reforms," may partake of the nature of a tactical retreat by the ruling party or a reformist strategem of "power-holders" conceived in a broader sense than those who belong to a particular political party. But the fact that despite the failure to oust the ruling party in the 1987 elections the recent changes are surging ahead under the continued propulsion of the minjung (in many respects more so than in the Philippines, Argentina, and Brazil, where military regimes have already been replaced by civilian governments), is a phenomenon fundamentally and directly related to the special nature of the system of division. That is to say, because it is a divided country the seizure and maintenance of power by antidemocratic forces is in some ways unusually easy, but these forces are nevertheless constantly and permanently in the fragile position of never being able to secure or legitimize themselves as a class hegemony in the true sense of the term.

Insofar as the system of division, unlike normal relations between two states, operates and is perceived as an antinational, anti-minjung system, it is impossible for the government to maintain power in default of pretentions to seek reunification. In other words, it represents the self-contradiction of a "system of division aiming at (or at least claiming to aim at) unification." For this reason, if even a little room for debate on the real nature of the system is permitted, a barely containable "confusion" arises. It is a general phenomenon that liberalist reforms of any substance in developing Third World states possess an explosive power not inferior to the antifeudal revolutionary character of liberalism in early capitalist societies, but this applies even more in a divided society. Of course, in nations where the desire for unification is not great, or among citizens who are greatly wanting in democratic capacity, reform measures can before long operate as a means of once again stripping away the substance of the people's freedoms. Korea is not invulnerable to the same danger; but should the post-June 1987 changes be accurately and scientifically understood as a process of reunification that has no parallel in world history, it is not the degree of desire for unification or the democratic staying power of the general minjung that one will need to worry greatly about. Rather, it is the inertia of a portion of the intellectuals and activists who, on the grounds that the present developments do not fit any existing framework, conclude that only to respond on a tactical level is an expression of the most thoroughgoing revolutionary logic, which must be overcome with all haste.

The creative role of literature is vital both in promoting this kind of self-criticism and tuning among intellectuals and in activating minjung power. Of course, this is not the exclusive preserve of literature, nor is it the role of our literature alone. But unless Korea's reunification movement is a creative movement of the highest order, it will be difficult to succeed in its aim of overcoming this unprecedented system of division, under which nevertheless both north and south, while being exceptionally brutal and rigid, have borne their respective fruits, to the surprise of the rest of the world. The reunification movement must be pursued as a creative art, so to speak, and all reunification activists must become artists—artists of history. Only as one branch of this art can Korean literature bloom to the full; but if the art of the national tongue fails to do its part, it will be vain to expect artists of historical action to turn out for duty.

Principal Authors Cited in Text

Cho T'aeil	b. 1941; imprisoned 1977
Chŏng Tosang	b. 1960; imprisoned early 1980s
Han Sŏrya	1900–?; imprisoned 1930s
Hong Hŭidam	b. 1944
Hong Myŏnghŭi	1888–?; imprisoned 1930s; his multivolume epic work, *Imkkŏkchŏng*, was serialized between 1928 and 1940
Hwang Sŏg'yŏng	b. 1943; imprisoned since 1933
Kim Chiha	b. 1941; imprisoned 1964, 1970, 1974–1980; nominated for Nobel Prize in Literature, 1970s
Kim Hakch'ŏl	b. 1916; imprisoned early 1940s
Kim Hansu	b. 1964
Kim Hyangsuk	b. 1951
Kim Kyudong	b. 1923
Kim Namju	1946–1994; imprisoned 1973, 1979–1988
Kim Sŏkpŏm	b. 1925
Kim Talsu	b. 1919
Ko Ŭn	b. 1933; imprisoned 1977, 1978–1979, 1980–1982; his six-volume poetic work, *Maninbo* (Ten thousand leaves), was published by 1988
Min Yŏng	b. 1934
Pak Tujin	b. 1916
Sin Kyŏngnim	b. 1935; imprisoned 1961, 1980
Yi Hoesŏng	b. 1935
Yi Kiyŏng	1895–1984; imprisoned 1930s
Yi Kŭnjŏn	b. 1929
Yi T'ae	b. 1934; imprisoned early 1950s
Yu Simin	b. 1960; imprisoned 1980s

11

The Nation, the People, and a Small Ball: Literary Nationalism and Literary Populism in Contemporary Korea

Marshall R. Pihl

The Background of Literary Nationalism

National literature (*minjok munhak*) is defined by contemporary Korean criticism as a literature based upon a thorough understanding of the nation as a whole, in terms both of its historical conditions and its current realities. It embraces the whole of national life and imparts meaning and value to the individual lives of those who constitute the nation.

The broad genre referred to as "national literature" dates back to the era of sudden social change that characterized the late nineteenth century. Fueled by the enlightenment movement, "new" literature in the early twentieth century began to look beyond the life of the individual and toward a social context, while developing literary forms that were more suitable to the new consciousness. But, overwhelmed by the political, economic, and cultural tsunami of Japanese aggression, the logical development of literary theory slackened and the expression of a national consciousness was thwarted and distorted. By the late 1930s, the fate of such literary activity was sealed by the Japanese New Order, a cultural policy which decreed that all literature must serve the needs of the state. In terms that could almost be called Stalinist, it was deemed that literature "exists only because of the State and is something which must exist only to practice the Way of the Subject."[1]

In the turbulent years of ideological struggle that followed a liberation embittered by national division, no progress was made in the discussion of a national literature. After the war and recovery, a long and mostly silent hiatus ensued in the area of theoretical development. From the early 1950s to the middle 1960s, when literature was estranged from the barren reality of the times, its focus of concern fell short of a broader conception of life and concentrated on war and individual experience.

When Korea entered a period of rapid industrialization in the 1970s, a reemergence of literary nationalism (*minjok munhangnon*) seemed a natural response to the social and political situation. Kwŏn Yŏngmin [Kwon Young-min] of Seoul National University characterizes that response in the following way:

> In particular, as Koreans entered the decade of the 1970s, the crisis in the social and political situation, confrontation and discord among social classes, and the withering of spiritual culture prompted a realistic awareness of the fact that the autonomous being of the nation and the equilibrium of life for most of its constituents were facing an absolute threat; and, in the field of literature, a realistic basis for literary nationalism was naturally established in response to a need to search for the total meaning of the life of the nation and the recovery of its wholeness in order to counter this threat. Therefore, in the context of the state of the times during the 1970s, literary nationalism took its place as an exceedingly dynamic notion that embraced the whole of literature and society.[2]

Stressing the affirmative nature of the literary nationalism of the 1970s, Kwŏn points to three ways in which it differed from its earlier stages. First, he identifies an attempt to establish a national literature that could stand on its own terms, in contrast to the literature produced during the colonial period, when Japanese aggression tended to serve as a reference point for Korean writers. Second, the literary nationalism of the 1970s differed from that of the past because of its shift in orientation from style and form as the primary concern toward an emphasis on value and content. Third, the new emphasis on value and content meant that literary nationalism gained a historical aspect, which it had to have in order to portray the whole picture of Korean cultural life.

The National Literature of the 1970s

The decade of the 1970s was unique in Korean history. It was a period characterized by rapid economic development, which produced both social and regional discord, as well as a rigid political orthodoxy that invited ideological confrontation. In the social sphere, Korea saw an increase in rural poverty as uprooted workers flocked to the major cities, which were dominated by a burgeoning, materialistic bourgeoisie seeking to reap the benefits of the commercial culture.

At the same time, a national self-awareness began to take shape as part of an effort to reunify the nation and recover a shared sense of national identity. In response, Korean literature began to give form to the new realities facing modern Korea and, thus, to participate in the crucial process by which Korea could redefine itself. This was the essence of literary nationalism, which Kwon Youngmin sums up as "an effort to surmount and reconcile, from a spiritual standpoint, the Korean social contradictions that started to crop up as the country entered a stage of industrialization."[3]

National literature came to embody the zeitgeist of the 1970s, grasping its significance and giving form to the national experience. The form of this literature was so interrelated with the spirit of the period that it became known by the catchphrase, *ch'ilsimnyŏndae munhak*, "literature of the 1970s," identifying it as a distinct unit of literary history—much to the consternation of the antihistorically minded, who conceive of literature as an autonomous and uninterrupted flow.

In the field of literary criticism, it became necessary to conceptualize a basic framework for the emerging literary nationalism. In July 1974, Paek Nakch'ŏng (Paik Nak-chung) of Seoul National University discussed the basics of national literature in his seminal article "New Unfolding of the National Literature Concept."[4] Paek points to the deeply historical nature of Korean national literature, recalling the colonial experience, and he stresses that it must not only reflect the people's consciousness but also take an active lead by challenging the people with new ideas and concerns. He relates literature, reality, and the role of a "national" literature in the following terms.

> There must exist certain concrete national realities that demand tenacious adherence to the concept of a national literature. There must exist a nation to serve as the principle element of a national literature. At the same time, a need must actually exist to distinguish "national literature" from among all the literary activity possible for that nation—that is, particularly needed for that nation's autonomous existence and human development. That is to say, this sense of need results from an awareness that the nation's autonomous existence and the welfare of the majority of its constituents face imminent danger; and it is based upon a judgment that the correct posture for meeting such a national crisis is ultimately also a prime factor governing the healthy growth of the literature of that nation's people.[5]

In the search for an appropriate applied methodology for national literature, critical discussion became focused on the theory of realism in the 1970s and based itself increasingly on the ideas of such Western theorists as Arnold Hauser *(The Social History of Art)*, Lucien Goldmann *(Towards a Sociology of the Novel; The Hidden God)*, and Georg Lukács *(Aesthetics; History and Class Consciousness; The Theory of the Novel; Realism in Our Time)*. The work of Lukács, in particular, appears to have been influential in recent Korean literary criticism.

Georg Lukács, a proponent of the Hegelian-Marxist vision, has been a seminal force in literary criticism since the 1920s. Fundamental to his definition of literary realism is the idea that works of art cannot be separated from their historical and political contexts. To Lukács, realism is a great art that embraces totality, typicality, and history, thereby linking the fictional hero to social and historical reality. In his view, the greatest writers of realism can use this approach to recapture and recreate a harmonious union of human life. In Korea, his concepts of "totality," "typicality," and "concreteness" gained currency in the 1970s.

According to Lukács' conception of "totality" in literature, fictional detail is irrelevant without reference to outer reality; it is the writer's task to give form to life and thereby reveal its totality. He does not intend to depict the totality of society by including every minute detail; rather, he wants to suggest the whole through selected details, so that "the whole is constantly present in the parts."[6] Lukács' concept of the "typical" is summed up by Terry Eagleton in the following way:

> By the "typical" Lukács denotes those latent forces in any society which are from a Marxist viewpoint most historically significant and progressive, which lay bare the society's inner structure and dynamics. The task of the realist writer is to flesh out these "typical" trends and forces in sensuously realized individuals and actions; in doing so he links the individual to the social whole, and informs each concrete particular of social life with the power of the "world-historical"—the significant movements of history itself.[7]

The "world-historical" concept mentioned by Eagleton refers to the idea of "concreteness" which, to Lukács, "involves an awareness of the development, structure and goal of society as a whole."[8] Here Lukács speaks of the historical nature of reality, that is, the social nature of humans and their role in history.

Partly due to the influence of Lukács' theories of realism, Korean fiction of the 1970s tended to emphasize two main themes: the social discord created by the industrialization process and the historical reinterpretation of territorial division. Below we shall look closely at a notable treatment of the social cost of Korean industrialization in Cho Sehŭi's *Small Ball Launched by a Dwarf* (1978).

The Emergence of Populism in the 1980s

"Populism" *(minjungnon)* emerged in the late 1970s and quickly expanded to become a part of the social and cultural mainstream during the 1980s. Indeed, attempts to use the concept of populism in various artistic endeavors could be seen not only in literature, but also in the fine arts, music, and drama. Even in academia, comparable efforts can be found in history, sociology, and economics.

Hence, "populism" in Korea today is more than a literary notion, it is a popular movement whose scope embraces alienated farmers, laborers, intellectuals, and progressive youth. It is an aggressive ideology that is popularly based; its cultural relevance is demonstrated by the fact that it has been welcomed at many levels of Korean society. Its ideology and tactics are problematic to some, but it is bound to gain greater societal acceptance. In response to the popular demand for the democratization of politics and society, its base of support will continue to broaden; and in spite of reservations expressed by some members of the cultural establishment, the people's popular concerns will continue to proliferate in such forms as people's literature, people's drama, people's music, and people's art.

In the field of literature, the predominance of literary nationalism was challenged during the 1970s by the more progressive concept of literary populism (*minjung munhangnon*). Growing numbers of writers, critics, and activists came to conceive of "the people" as the principal element in society, as consumers of literature, and also as a power base. Emerging out of literary nationalism in the 1970s, populism gradually developed into a distinct literary theory with its own theoretical framework.

In the view of Kwŏn Yŏngmin, literary populism showed signs in the 1980s of breaking out of the framework of literary nationalism. Paek Nakch'ŏng, on the other hand, is inclined to treat the two as alter egos in a dialectical relationship.

> Our movement is sometimes called, and calls itself, a people's literature movement. Yet it has also tried to keep its distance from either the ideology of populism or a narrowly proletarian literature. At the risk of indulging in fine phrases, I should say that the twin appellations *minjok munhak* (national literature) and *minjung munhak* (people's literature) point to the genuinely dialectical nature of our conception. "National literature" stresses how, in claiming to be a literature of the people, it yet negates an oversimplified class concept; while the name "people's literature" brings out how this particular national literature refuses an idealistic conception of the nation or national culture.[9]

Kwŏn Yŏngmin distinguishes literary populism from literary nationalism by comparing the role of the people in each of the literary approaches. Literary nationalism of the 1970s put more emphasis on the concept of the people in general than on the search for value in their individual lives. This dilemma is articulated in the following statement: "If literature is to faithfully depict the realities of the life of the people, then it must stress the recovery of the human quality that is demanded by the life of the people."[10] Literary populism, then, arose in response to the need for a literature that would depict real human values and concerns.

The theoretical basis of literary populism attempted to affirm literature's powerful autonomy, ideology, and place in the center of the people's existence. Its major literary goals included strengthening people's autonomy and consciousness. However, since the "people" were seen as the producers and consumers of literature, and since most of the novelists and poets of the 1970s came from the bourgeois intelligentsia, there arose the inevitable question of defining who the "people" are and how, or whether, the intelligentsia could effectively represent them. This issue prompted further theoretical modifications in literary populism, the result being a stronger emphasis on people's ideology and consciousness than on people's autonomy. Because of this view of people's literature both as a *method* to embody people's ideology and consciousness and as a *form,* giving artistic form to the people's consciousness became a primary goal.

Literary Nationalism in Practice: Cho Sehŭi and His *Small Ball Launched by a Dwarf*

The work to be considered here is the most notable product of the "literature of the 1970s." In playful reference to its title, Kim Yunsik (Kim Yoonshik) states that the work "played the role of a big iron ball in Korean society, which moved from the 70s to the 80s, in that it posed the question, what would there be on the other side of the seemingly bright future promised by industrialization?"[11] This work is not only a product of the contemporary scene but responds to the ideological issues of its time as well. As such, it eloquently represents the literature of the 1970s and serves as a good example of Korean literary nationalism in general.

Cho Sehŭi was born in Kap'yŏng, Kyŏnggi Province, in 1942 and was educated at Sŏrabŏl College of the Arts and at Kyŏnghŭi University in Seoul. Cho belongs to a generation that has a unique place in modern Korean history, and he has earned a respected name for himself within that generation. Some speak of them as the *"han'gŭl* generation,"[12] in view of their postliberation education, which distinguishes them from their fathers who were taught in Japanese and their grandfathers who had studied Chinese. Others call them the "liberation generation or "April 19th generation,"[13] after their role in the student-led uprising that toppled the Syngman Rhee government that day in 1960. Those who were then in their teens are now in their late forties, like Cho Sehŭi.

In 1965, the year in which Cho made his literary debut, another member of his generation, Kim Sŭngok (born in 1941), heralded the emergence of a new literary generation with the publication of his award-winning short story, "Seoul: 1964, Winter."[14] Kim and Cho, and others of their generation, share a "point of view that sees fiction not as the presentation of a story but, rather, as the presentation of perception."[15] The academic critic Han Hyŏnggu describes this "April 19th generation" in the course of his study on the place of Kim's writing in Korean literary history.

> Kim Sŭngok is frequently classified as being of the April 19th generation, but one of the elements constituting the distinctive features of this generation is the condition of having experienced [the] June 25 [outbreak of the Korean War] in childhood. Furthermore, this generation's distinctive features also comprise the fact that this was precisely the generation that went through the calamity of internecine struggle in a state of less awakened consciousness, that is, in a state of undeveloped powers of discrimination, and also the fact that they leapt to the fore as leading elements of the student revolution soon after passing through the void of ruin that

immediately followed the war. Such generational characteristics . . . suggest two sorts of complex dispositions . . . which this generation is apt to display toward history and life. That is, they may show a fear of history (given the June 25 and April 19 experiences) or, on the other hand, feel either potency or frustration (as in reaction to [the] May 16 [coup d'état]); with regard to life and living, they may show intense despair (having passed through the void of ruin) or, on the other hand, feel either sardonic or contempt toward life.[16]

As we shall see, this disconcerted worldview profoundly shapes the form of Cho Sehŭi's work. Responding to the economic and social realities of the 1970s, Cho's readers felt a sense of affinity with his way of looking at the world. Cho made his debut as a writer in 1965 with his *Kyŏnghyang Newspaper* award-winning short story, "Burial Boat with No Mast." After exactly ten years' silence, he reemerged on the literary scene with a series of stories that led to his best-selling 1978 collection, *Small Ball Launched by a Dwarf*.[17] In a critical essay on Cho's work, O Seyŏng of Seoul National University reports that over 100,000 copies were sold in the first three years, a rare event for a work of true literary merit.[18]

The book consists of twelve stories published at different times and in different publications between 1975 and 1978:

"The Möbius Loop" [Moebiusŭŭi tti], *Sedae* (February 1976), *Munhakkwa Chisŏng* (Summer 1976)[19]

"Knife's Edge" [K'allal], *Munhak Sasang* (December 1975)

"Space Trip" [Uju yŏhaeng], *Ppuri Kip'ŭn Namu* (September 1976), *Munhakkwa Chisŏng* (Spring 1977)[20]

"Small Ball Launched by a Dwarf" [Nanjangiga ssoa ollin chagŭn kong], *Munhakkwa Chisŏng* (Winter 1976)[21]

"On the Footbridge" [Yukkyo wiesŏ], *Sedae* (February 1977)[22]

"Orbital Rotation" [Kwedo hoejŏn], *Han'guk Munhak* (June 1977)

"City of Machines" [Kigye toshi], *Taehak Sinmun* (20 June 1977)[23]

"Cost of Living of an Ŭn'gang Laborer's Family" [Ŭn'gang nodong kajokŭi saenggyebi], *Munhak Sasang* (October 1977)

"Gods Err Too" [Chalmosŭn sinegedo itta], *Mun'ye Chungang* (Winter 1977)

"Klein's Bottle" [Kullainssiŭi pyŏng], *Munhakkwa Chisŏng* (Spring 1978)

"The Spinyfish Coming toward My Net" [Nae kŭmullo onŭn kashigogi], *Ch'angjakkwa Pip'yŏng* (Summer 1978)[24]

"Epilogue" [Ep'illogŭ], *Munhak Sasang* (March 1978)

Although the cover of *Small Ball Launched by a Dwarf* identifies the work as a "collection of Cho Sehŭi's short stories," critics commonly refer to it as a *yŏnjak sosŏl*, hastening to add that Cho has redefined the meaning of the term. Although this expression had previously been used to designate a collaborative work in which several writers contribute to the making of the whole, Cho Sehŭi's collection can be described as a series of "loosely connected but realistically interrelated stories."[25] A fixed set of characters appear periodically throughout the stories, revealing themselves in bits and snatches as Cho constructs their lives out of discontinuous fragments that are scattered throughout his work. These characters can be seen as groups whose lives parallel, intersect, and collide with each other, summoning up a vision of life in the rapidly industrializing Korea of the 1970s. 0 Seyŏng captures the work in the following words.

> The novel illuminates, through the life of a dwarf and his family, the wretched realities of those who have lost the basis of life in the process of the growth of the Korean industrialized society, their dreams, and the despair experienced in trying to realize their dreams. Their reality is the reality of the uprooted, of those whose economic foundation of life has been lost in what Thomas Hobbes described as a "war of everyone against everyone"; their dream is of a life in which a human being lives like a human being; and their despair is the death of the heroes . . . suffered in their struggle . . . with the enormous forces that oppress them.[26]

The world of the dwarf's family is populated by people who represent a cross-section of contemporary Korean society: entrepreneurs, intellectuals, bourgeoisie, and uprooted workers living on the margins of society. Their values range from humanistic to materialistic, their consciousness from awakened to unawakened, and their morality from human caring to animal egoism.

The primary focus of the stories is upon the dwarf and his four other family members. The dwarf, who is three feet, ten inches tall, takes any work he can find—selling bonds, sharpening knives, washing windows in high-rise buildings, installing pumps, and repairing plumbing. His wife contributes to their income by folding paper in the bindery of a printing plant and peeling bark from logs in the scrap yard of a lumber mill. His first son, who quit school in the ninth grade to work in the engineering department of a printing plant, works as an automobile factory laborer and a helper in a textile plant. In addition, there is the second son, in his middle teens, who already hauls castings and runs a sewing machine, and the youngest child, a daughter.

In the course of their struggle to overcome adversity, the family loses their house the father had built to urban renewal, the first son is tried and executed for the murder of a plant manager, and the father commits suicide. They live cheek-by-jowl with other dispossessed of the city. Juxtaposed with the depiction of their life is the air-conditioned life of the entrepreneurs, their lawyers, and hangers-on who are the driving force of the industrialization, a process that has stirred up a cyclone of urban migration as a result of which uncounted numbers have been uprooted from the close-knit society they had once known.

Cho Sehŭi writes in a lean and clipped style that puts us more in mind of the succinct and unadorned language of Hemingway and the iconoclasm of Vonnegut than the conventionally undulant prose of Korean writers in the generation immediately preceding his. Even the language of Kim Sŭngok, his contemporary, seems relatively conventional in comparison to Cho's. Whereas Kim differs from his predecessors in his brash and sardonic tone, it is a change in language and form that sets Cho apart from the rest. Let us compare the openings of Kim's "Seoul: 1964, Winter" and Cho's "City of Machines" to get a feel for some of the differences.

From "Seoul: 1964, Winter":

> Anyone who had spent the winter of 1964 in Seoul would probably remember those wine stands that appeared on the streets once it got dark—selling hotchpotch, roasted sparrows, and three kinds of wine; made so that to step inside you have to lift a curtain being whipped by a bitter wind that sweeps the frozen streets; where the long flame of a carbide lamp inside flutters with the gusts; and where a middle-aged man in a dyed army jacket pours wine and roasts snacks for you—well, it was in one of those wine stands that the three of us happened to meet that night. By the three of us, I mean myself, a graduate student named An who wore thick glasses, and a man of about thirty-five or thirty-six of whom I could figure few particulars except that he was, in short, obviously poor, and whose particulars, actually, I hadn't even the least desire to know.
>
> The chitchat started off between me and the graduate student, and when the small talk and self-introductions were over, I knew he was a twenty-five-year-old flower of Korean youth, a graduate student with a major that I (who had not so much as gone sight-seeing to a college) had never ever dreamed of, and the oldest son of a rich family; and he probably knew that I was a twenty-five-year-old country boy, that I had volunteered for the Military Academy when I got out of high school only to fail and then enter the army, where I caught the clap once, and that I was now working in the military affairs section of a ward office.
>
> We had introduced ourselves but then there was nothing for us to talk about. For a while we just drank our wine quietly, and then, when I picked up a charred roasted sparrow, something occurred to me to say, and so, after thanking the roasted sparrow, I began to talk.

From "City of Machines":

> July and August that year were unusually humid. Reports of the worst heat in thirty years often covered the newspapers. It seemed like the whole country would dry up and burn to a crisp. But Yunho, for one, had no cause for concern. The air conditioner his father had them install didn't make a sound and pumped out cold air. If one day he had heard that the city looming hugely in his mind suddenly didn't exist, he simply would have studied for the exam in this pleasant setting. The city of Ŭngang remained as a dark picture inside Yunho's mind. The dead dwarf's son and daughter were working there. For Yunho, Ŭngang was no more than just

part of the surface of a small planet. As the means of a life eked out in one part of the dark surface, the dead dwarf's son and daughter sweated in a workshop with machines. They got the work easily. It wasn't that they had superior skills. Even the machines there couldn't do work without the help of people. The dwarf's son and daughter had already undergone many trials. Since they led lives of the lowest standard within a group that was similar to them, their appearances didn't catch one's eye.

When we compare these two openings in regard to such things as vocabulary, tone, point of view, sentence structure, and sentence length, we find similarities that reflect the life of the two writers' generation yet, at the same time, differences that suggest a new departure on the part of Cho Sehŭi.

Their youthful, modern vocabulary of high-frequency words is notable for its distinct quality of explicitness and its concomitantly rare use of vocabulary describing sensory perceptions. This stylistic approach became an essential element in creative writing after the colonial period.[27] The two writers are also comparable in that they share a contemporary worldview distinct from that of their preceding generation. This worldview is expressed through the thoughts and actions of their characters. Kim's slangy and sardonic characters, who brashly reject the reality of life around them, suggest a generation that has tumbled from the heady sense of victory gained in the student revolution into a distrustful frustration engendered by the world of the Park Chung-hee coup d'état.[28] Ten years later, that same generation was to be shaken out of its despair and stirred to action by the brutal realities of industrialization, rediscovering a once-forgotten potency. In this way, Cho uses his characters to reveal a set of social contradictions that is utterly new to the Korean experience.

However, the opening passages also show marked differences between Kim and Cho in their use of the Korean language. Whereas Kim tends to use long and complex sentence structures, Cho's prose is terse and unadorned. In the original Korean of the excerpts quoted above, Kim's five sentences average 111 syllables each and Cho's sixteen sentences average twenty-three syllables apiece; all five of Kim's sentences are compound or compound-complex, incorporating lengthy attributive and conjunctive structures, whereas more than half of Cho's are only simple, subject-object-predicate sentences.

In addition to the obvious differences cited above, there are others that set Cho apart from his predecessors, and even from those within his own generation. His work stands out for its pervasive use of symbols, such as the Möbius loop,[29] the Klein bottle,[30] space, astronauts, the moon, net, fish, fireflies, and so forth. As Kim Yunsik of Seoul National University interprets them, the Möbius loop and Klein bottle symbolically contradict the assumption that there are discrete boundaries in society and, at the same time, assert a seamless totality embracing levels of society—rich and poor, urban and rural, mainstream and marginal.[31] Whereas space, astronauts, and the moon are symbolically linked to the realization of an ideal world, nets and fish connote entrepreneurs and laborers, and fireflies suggest the rootless and alienated in the darkness of their lives.[32] Even the title of the work is symbolic: the "small ball" is an orb of hope launched by the smallest of human beings out of the darkness of his despair (the Korean verb for "launch," *ssoaollida,* is also used to designate the launching of a spacecraft). Related to such symbolism is Cho's verbatim repetition of certain phrases and sentences, within one story or in different stories, as leitmotivs associated with certain places, characters, or situations.

Although Kim Sǔngok and Cho Sehǔi are both explicit writers, Cho's style is more concrete and specific. He chooses his words, particles, and inflections with care, accurately saying no more or less than is needed. Therefore, he does not spell out in detail that which the context already suggests, and the reader must make do with incomplete information at both general and particular levels. Dealing with several sets of characters who lead parallel and sometimes intersecting lives, he creates the cinematic effect of a split screen or jump-cut by juxtaposing bits and pieces of their contrasting experiences. Cho uses this technique without warning in contexts where the reader may be unprepared for it, infusing his overall work with a fragmented and discontinuous quality.

The form of Cho Sehǔi's fiction, therefore, is particularly well suited to the content of his work. This work mirrors the complexity of modern Korean society, a society in which human experience is fragmented and its members suffer from a wrenching alienation that "severs man from the natural rhythms and shapes of creation."[33] Amid this bleak setting, however, Cho's protagonists search, like the dwarf's son Yǒngsu, for meaning and wholeness, for "a world spiritually bonded together by love, a world in which love defines the value of life."[34] As such, *Small Ball Launched by a Dwarf* exemplifies the central thrust of Korean literary nationalism of the 1970s, which sought to recapture the harmonious quality of human life that was being so direly threatened.

In conclusion, it seems that the appearance of Kim Sǔngok and a new generation of writers on the Korean literary scene in the mid-1960s set the stage for change but did not mark such a significant departure from the orthodox order as did the publication of Cho Sehǔi's collection in 1978. The difference between Cho's work and what preceded it is every bit as striking as that between Korean prose of the enlightenment period (1900–1910) and that of the early colonial period (1920s). Cho's work certainly deserves to be characterized as "revolutionary," and we can understand why O Seyǒng would assert that "Cho's . . . response to the call of his imagination moves him beyond classical realism and places his work in the dimension of a neorealism."[35] Indeed, Cho's language and form has had such an epoch-making impact on contemporary Korean writing that Kim Yunsik speaks of drawing a line between literature of the "pre-dwarf" period and that which has followed: "If there is anything tantamount to a revolution in literature, the change triggered by Cho's stories may well be called so."[36]

Notes

Chapter 1

1. Yi Kibaek's (Lee Ki-baik) *Kuksa sillon* (A new theory of Korean history), first published in 1967, was a path-breaking attempt to apply a unified theory to Korean history since early times. Twice revised since, the work has been translated into English by Edward Wagner as *A New History of Korea* (Cambridge, Mass.: Harvard University Press, 1984).

2. See Pak Hyŏnch'ae, *Han'guk kyŏngjeron* (Theory of Korean economy) (Seoul: Kkach'i, 1987), and *Minjok kyŏngjewa minjung undong* (National economy and the minjung movement) (Seoul: Ch'angjakkwa pip'yŏngsa, 1988).

3. Kang Man'gil, professor of history at Koryŏ University, has recently stated that "The 'June 10th democracy movement' [of 1987] was a movement led by the 'minjung,' which consisted of a large spectrum of social classes including student youth, white-collar workers, factory laborers, small urban merchants, the urban self-employed, a section of the farmers, and so on." 6.10 minjuhwa undongŭl toesaeginda," *Han'gyore sinmun* (One people newspaper), 10 June 1993.

4. See the discussion of Yulgok's views in Young-Chan Ro, *The Korean Neo-Confucianism of Yi Yulgok* (Albany: State University of New York, 1989), 32–35.

5. See *Han'gugŭi minsok, chonggyo sasang* (Korean folk and religious thought), vol. 4 of *Han'guk sasang chŏnjip* (Compendium of Korean thought), 6 vols. (Seoul: Samsŏng Publishers, 1981), 4:564–578.

6. Ibid., 569.

7. Chung Chai-sik, "Chŏng Tojŏn: 'Architect' of Yi Dynasty Government and Ideology," in Theodore W. de Bary and JaHyon Kim Haboush, eds., *The Rise of Neo-Confucianism in Korea* (New York: Columbia University Press, 1985), 68–70.

8. Chŏng Yag'yong, *Nongmin Simsŏ* (Seoul: Hyŏn'amsa, 1972). The original work was published in 1818.

9. *The Korea Herald*, 18 October 1989, 1.

10. See Ken Wells, "Between the Devil and the Deep: Nonpolitical Nationalism and 'Passive Collaboration' in Korea during the 1920s," in *Papers on Far Eastern History* 37 (March 1988): 132ff.

11. The same is said by minjung literary figures. In an essay first published in 1984, "Minjungŭi norae, minjokŭi norae" (Song of the minjung, song of the nation), Kim Chiha looks forward to a diffusion of minjung values throughout the whole nation. Kim Chiha, *Pap* (Rice) (Seoul: Pundo, 1984).

12. Richard Johnson, ed., *Making Histories* (London: Hutchinson, 1982), 8, 10.

13. See Herbert Butterfield, *The Whig Interpretation of History* (New York: W. W. Norton, 1965); R. G. Collingwood, *Essays in the Philosophy of History* (Austin: University of Texas, 1965); and E. H. Carr, *What Is History?* (New York: Vintage Books, 1961).

14. See, for example, Nam Chidae, "Yŏksahagŭi Nam-Puk kyoryurŭl wihayŏ" (Toward a south–north exchange on history), in *Yŏksawa hyŏnsil* (History and reality) 2: (1989): 7–17.

15. The whole seventeen-page "Current Comment" *(siron)* section of *Yŏksawa hyŏnsil* 3 (1990): 4–20, is devoted to an explanation of how the study of history is inextricably linked to political action in the present for the future, along the lines of "scientific historical materialism."

16. Despite my wording, I am not referring to Warren Susman's *Culture as History* so much as to Critcher and Johnson, eds., *Working Class Culture* (1979), and Lynn Hunt, ed., *The New Cultural History* (1989), and so on.

17. E.g., Lin Yü-sheng, *The Crisis of Chinese Consciousness: Radical Anti-traditionalism in the May Fourth Era* (Madison: University of Wisconsin Press, 1979).

18. See Ken Wells, "Civic Morality in the Nationalist Thought of Yun Ch'i-ho, 1881–1911," in *Papers on Far Eastern History* 28 (September 1983).

19. *The Independent*, vol. 1, no. 60, 22 August 1896.

20. Editorial, *Tongnip sinmun*, vol. 3, no. 191, 16 November 1898.

21. Editorial, ibid., vol. 1, no. 48, 25 July 1896.

22. Editorial, ibid., no. 39, 4 July 1896.

23. Editorial, ibid., no. 69, 12 September 1896.

24. Editorial, ibid., vol. 2, no. 1, 5 January 1897.

25. *Yu Kiljun chŏnjip* (Collected works of Yu Kiljun), 5 vols. (Seoul: Ilchogak, 1971), 2:264.

26. Editorial, *Tongnip sinmun*, vol. 1, no. 48, 25 July 1896.

27. *Yun Ch'iho ilgi* (Yun Ch'iho diary), 6 November 1898.

28. Kim Ku, *Paekpŏm ilchi* (Seoul: Paekpŏm Kim Ku sŏnsaeng kinyŏm saŏp hyŏphoe, 1947), 187.

29. Editorial, *Tongnip sinmun*, vol. 2, no. 7, 19 July 1897.

30. There is ample evidence of this development. The following are explicit sources: editorial, *Sinhan minbo*, 5 September 1913, and 19 February and 29 April 1914 letters to the editor; Kim Yongsŏp, speech at Tokyo YMCA, 5 September 1917 (*Gendaishi shiryō*, 2:5); Yim Louise (Im Sŏngsin), *My Forty-Year Fight for Korea* (Seoul: Chungang University Press, 1964), 55–56.

31. Sin Ch'aeho is an important theorist of the minjung, but since Kang Man'gil discusses him in Chapter 2 of this volume, I do not devote space to him here.

32. This and the following quotations are taken from a copy of the *Manifesto* that I have in my possession.

33. *Yŏksa pip'yŏng* (Historical criticism) 1 (September 1987): back cover.

34. E.g., besides the two organizations' journals, there are: *Han'guksa kangŭi* (Lectures in Korean history) (Seoul: Han'ul Academy, 1989); *Puk'anŭi Han'guksa insik* (North Korea's conception of Korean history, 2 vols. (Seoul: Han'gilsa, 1990); and *Han'guk minjungsa* (Korean minjung history), 2 vols. (Seoul: P'ulpit, 1986).

35. Kang Man'gil, a professor of history at Koryŏ University, has written a vast amount on Korean history and is a contributor to this volume. His major works in this area include *Pundan sidaeŭi yŏksa ŭisik* (Historical consciousness in the era of division) (Seoul: Ch'angjakkwa pip'yŏngsa, 1978), and, with Song Kŏnho, *Han'guk minjokjuŭi ron* (A theory of Korean nationalism) (Seoul: Ch'angjakkwa pip'yŏngsa, 1982), besides numerous articles in scholarly journals.

36. Cf. Bruce Cumings, "The Abortive Arbertura: South Korea in the Light of Latin American Experience," in *New Left Review* 173 (January–February 1989).

37. Pak Ch'ansung, "Tonghak nongmin chŏnjaengŭi sahoe kyŏngjejŏk chihyang," in Pak Hyŏnch'ae and Chŏng Ch'angnyŏl, eds., *Han'guk minjokjuŭi ron III* (Seoul: Ch'angjakkwa pip'yŏngsa, 1985), 19.

38. Ibid., 55.

39. Ibid., 64–69.

40. Ibid., 70–73.

41. Cf. Choi Chungmoo's Chapter 6 below.

42. E.g., Pak Ch'ansung, (n. 37 above); also Cho Hŭiyŏn, "80 nyŏndae sahoe pyŏnhyŏngnonŭi chŏn'gae kwajŏng," and Chŏng Min, "Minjok haebang minjung minjujuŭi pyŏnhyŏgŭi iron," in *Sahoewa sasang* (Society and thought) (November 1988), 78–94, 95–111.

43. Available in 4 volumes, published in Seoul by P'urŭn sup, 1988.

44. Kang Man'gil, "Nam-Puk'an yŏksa insigŭi kat'ŭn chŏmgwa tarŭn chŏm," in *Changjakkwa pip'yŏng* (Creation and criticism) 63 (Spring 1989): 277–300.

45. Han Wansang was professor of sociology at Seoul National University before his appointment as deputy prime minister. He has written several books, including *Minjunggwa sahoe* (Minjung and society) (Seoul: Chongno sŏjŏk, 1980), and *Chisigin'gwa hyŏnsil insik* (Intellectuals and awareness of the present) (Seoul: Ch'ŏngnyŏnsa, 1986).

46. The recent divergent views of scholars and activists on the significance of the June 1987 events provide a glimpse of the nature of this crisis. See, for example, the range of interpretations offered by Kang Man'gil ("6.19 minjuhwa undongŭl toesaeginda") and Ch'oe Changjip ("Minjuhwa poru simin sahoe ijen han'gye"), both in *Han'gyore sinmun* (One people newspaper), 10 June 1993, and by O Tongnyŏl ("6 wŏl hangjaengŭn onŭl uriege muŏsin'ga?") and Pak Hyŏnch'ae ("Minjudangŭi hyŏnsilgwa kaehyŏgŭi chŏnmang"), both in *Kil* (Way), June 1993. Finally, the whole question of the nature and direction of the minjung movement is taken up again in *Ch'angjakkwa pip'yŏng* 81 (Autumn 1993).

47. On the issue of "internationalization," see Pak Hyŏngjun, "Kukchehwawa chŏn chigujuŭiŭi nolli" (The logic of internationalization and pan-global-

ism), in *Ch'angjakkwa pip'yŏng* 85 (Autumn 1994): 302–319; and the special issue on "Kukchehwa, minjok munhwa, minjujuŭi" (Internationalization, nation, and democracy), in ibid. 84 (Summer 1994).

Chapter 2

1. For example, see Chŏng Ch'angyŏl, "Han'guksa(hak)esŏŭi minjung insik" (Perceptions of the minjung in [the study] of Korean history), in *Yi Yŏnghŭi Sŏnsaeng Hwagap Kinyŏm Munjip* (Seoul: Ture ch'ulp'ansa, 1989).

2. *Kaejŏng Sin Ch'aeho Chŏnjip* (Collected works of Sin Ch'aeho), rev. ed. (Seoul), 2:78.

3. Regarding the change in Sin Ch'aeho's historical perception from heroism to nationalism and again to minjungism, see Kang Man'gil, "Sin Ch'aehŭi yŏn-gung, kungmin'gwa minjung sasang" (Sin Ch'aeho's hero, citizen, and minjung thought), in *Sin Ch'aehoŭi Sasanggwa Minjok Tongnip Undong* (Seoul: Hyŏng-sŏl ch'ulp'ansa, 1989).

4. *Kaejŏng Sin Ch'aeho*, 40–41.

5. Ibid., 42.

6. Ibid., 42.

7. Ibid.

8. See Kang Man'gil, "Sin Ch'aeho."

9. *Kaejŏng Sin Ch'aeho*, 47.

10. "Han'guk nodong ch'onghap yŏnmaeng," in *Han'guk Nodong Chohap Undongsa* (History of the Korean labor cooperative movement) (Seoul: 1979), 170.

11. *Jishō Jōsei Jisatsu Hokoshū* (Collection of reports on ideological trends) (Tokyo: Tōyō bunkasha, 1976), 5:60–61. See also Kim Chŏngmyŏng, ed., *Chōsen Dokuritsu Undō* (The Korean independence movement) (Tokyo: Hara shobo, 1967), 2:540–541.

12. An Pyŏngjik, *Samil Undong* (The March First Movement) (Seoul: Han'guk ilbosa, 1975), 26.

13. Yi Man'yŏl, "Minjung ŭisik sagwanhwaŭi siron" (Essay on constructing a historical view based on minjung consciousness), in *In'gan'gwa Segye'e taehan Ch'ŏrakchŏk Ihae* (Seoul: Samjungdang, 1981), 196.

14. Pak Hyŏnch'ae, "Minjunggwa yŏksa" (The minjung and history), in *Han'guk Chabonjuŭiwa Minjok Undong* (Seoul: Han'gilsa, 1978).

15. Chŏng, "Han'guksa(hak)esŏ," 96.

16. See Kang Man'gil, "1980 nyŏndaeŭi minjung, minjok undongŭi wisang" (The phases of the minjung movement and national movement in the 1980s), in Yi Yŏnghŭi, 134–145.

Chapter 3

1. Han Sangjin, "Minjung sahoehagŭi iron'gwa chaengjjŏm" (Social science theories and issues regarding the masses), in *Sahoe kwahakkwa chŏngch'aek yŏn'gu* (Social Science and Policy Studies) (Institute of Social Science, Seoul National University, 1986), 8, no. 1: 107.

2. Pak Hyŏnch'ae, "Minjungŭi kyegŭpchŏk sŏnggyŏk kyumyŏng" (Examina-

tion of the characteristics of masses in terms of social class), in Kim Chin'gyun et al., *Han'guk sahoeŭi kyegŭp yŏn'gu* (Study of social classes in Korea) (Seoul: Hanul, 1985), 49.

3. Ibid.

4. "Peasants and Artisans in Capitalist Society," in David McLellan, ed., *Karl Marx, Selected Writings* (Oxford: Oxford University Press, 1977), 398.

5. "Bourgeois and Proletarians," in ibid., *Karl Marx, Selected Writings*, 227.

6. Pak Hyŏnch'ae, "Minjungŭi kyegŭpchŏk sŏnggyŏk," 50.

7. Ibid., 51.

8. Ibid.

9. Ibid., 52.

10. Ibid., 53.

11. Hagan Koo, "From Farm to Factory: Proletarianization in Korea," in *American Sociological Review* 55 (October 1990): 669.

12. For detailed empirical studies of industrialization, especially the structure of the labor force and the composition of classes in Korea, see Sŏ Kwanmo, *Hyŏndae Han'guk sahoeŭi kyegŭp kusŏng* (Class composition in contemporary Korean society) (Seoul: Hanul, 1984); and, for a "revised theory" of this topic: Sŏ Kwanmo, "Han'guk sahoe kyegŭp kusŏngŭi yŏn'gu" (A study of class composition in Korea), Ph.D. diss., Seoul National University, 1987; Kim Hyung-ki, *Monopoly Capital and Wage Labor in Korea* (in Korean), ed. Kaegeun Lee and Yun Youngjong (Seoul: Kkach'i, 1988).

13. Charles Tilly, *As Sociology Meets History* (New York: Academic Press, 1981), 179; quoted in Hagan Koo, "From Farm to Factory."

14. According to the analysis of a survey provided by Professor Sŏ Kwanmo of Ch'ungbuk University, the size of the proletariat increased from 36.4% in 1963 to 51.4% in 1983. This survey breaks down Korean class structure into three categories: (1) capitalist classes; (2) petite bourgeoisie; and (3) the proletariat. The proletariat consists of: wage and salary workers, 13.5%; production workers, 26.1%; service and sales workers, 7.7%; and unemployed, 4.1%. For more detailed information, see Sŏ Kwanmo, *Class Composition and Class Division in Contemporary Korean Society*, 46.

15. See, Charles Tilly, *As Sociology Meets History;* Peter Kriedte, Hans Medick, and Jurgen Schlumbohm, *Industrialization before Industrialization: Rural Industry in the Genesis of Capitalism* (New York: Cambridge University Press), 1981.

16. Immanuel Wallerstein, *Historical Capitalism* (London: Verso, 1983), 27.

17. For more detailed information, see Hagan Koo, "From Farm to Factory," 673.

18. C. Johnson, *Political Institutions and Economic Performance: The Government–Business Relationship in Japan, South Korea, and Taiwan;* quoted in F. C. Deyo, ed., *The Political Economy of the New Asian Industrialism* (Ithaca, N.Y.: Cornell University Press, 1987), 6; also in James Cotton, "Understanding the State in South Korea: Bureaucratic-Authoritarian or State Autonomy Theory?" in *Comparative Political Studies* 24, no. 4 (January 1992): 527.

19. Hagan Koo, "From Farm to Factory," 673–674.

20. Ibid., 675.

21. Ibid., 677.

22. Ibid.

23. The prejudice against the labor movement and the state tendency to identify labor-movement activists as "radicals" or "communists," according to many scholars, including Bruce Cumings, are the legacy of the United States Military Government in Korea (USAMGIK, 1946–1948) under General Hodge. Furthermore, Syngman Rhee skillfully maneuvered the anticommunist standpoint of the American government and its representatives in Korea, using it to eliminate his political foes. In his essay "Human Rights in South Korea 1945–1953," Gregory Henderson writes: "Blanket instructions to arrest all leftist leaders and agitators were known to have been issued in the 1946–1947 period. . . . By mid-1947, there were almost 22,000 people in jail, 50–100 percent more than the Japanese had jailed in South Korea. Syngman Rhee . . . needed the police as protection against leftist foes and as support for his regime" (in William Shaw, ed., *Human Rights in Korea: Historical and Policy Perspectives* [Cambridge, Mass.: Harvard University Press, 1991], 137). "The original labor-union movements were increasingly repressed; a right-wing one was established and force-fed by the government. In 1949, Rhee ordered all unions [to be] combined into the Korean Federation of Trade Unions. Except in 1960–1961, a truly free labor-union movement has never thereafter been permitted" (ibid., 145). See Gregory Henderson, "Human Rights in South Korea 1945–1953," 137–145; also see Bruce Cumings, *The Origins of The Korean War: Liberation and the Emergence of Separate Regimes 1945–1947* (Princeton, N.J.: Princeton University Press, 1989), 1:135–151, and George E. Ogle, *South Korea: Dissent within the Economic Miracle* (London and Atlantic Highlands, N.J.: Zed Books, 1990), 47–93.

24. Hagan Koo, "From Farm to Factory," 679.

25. Han Wansang, *Minjung sahoehak* (Sociology of the masses) (Seoul: Chongno Sŏjŏk, 1981), 64.

26. Ibid., 57.

27. Yu Chech'ŏn, "So: Minjung kaenyŏmŭi naep'owa wemyŏn," (Introduction: Content and appearance of the concept of the masses), in Yu Chech'ŏn, ed., *Minjung* (The masses) (Seoul: Munhakkwa chisongsa, 1984), 23.

28. H. H. Gerth and G. Wright Mills, trans., "The Power Position of Bureaucracy," in idem, *From Max Weber: Essays in Sociology* (London: Routledge & Kegan Paul, 1967), 232.

29. H. H. Gerth and G. Wright Mills, trans., "Status Privileges," in *From Max Weber: Essays in Sociology,* 191.

30. Han Wansang, *Minjung sahoehak,* 18.

31. H. H. Gerth and G. Wright Mills, trans., "Status Honor," in *From Max Weber: Essays in Sociology,* 186–187.

32. Han Wansang, *Minjung sahoehak,* 64.

33. David Beetham, trans., "Gesammelte Politische Schriften," in David Beetham, *Max Weber and the Theory of Modern Politics* (London: George Allen & Unwin), 80.

34. Kim Hyung-a van Leest, "Political Satire in Yangju Pyolsandae Mask Drama," *Korea Journal* 31, no. 1 (1991): 92.

35. H. H. Gerth and G. Wright Mills, trans., "The Prestige and Power of the 'Great Powers,' " in *From Max Weber*, 161.

36. Georg Lukács, *History and Class Consciousness: Studies in Marxist Dialectics*, trans. Rodney Livingstone (London: Merlin Press, 1971), 149–222.

37. Han Wansang, *Minjung sahoehak*, 27.

38. Ibid., 28.

39. Ibid.

40. Ibid.

41. Ibid.

42. Ibid., 34.

43. Ibid.

44. Ibid.

45. Ibid., 31.

46. Ibid., 33.

47. James Cotton, "Understanding the State in South Korea: Bureaucratic-Authoritarian or State Autonomy Theory?" in *Comparative Political Studies* 24, no. 4 (January 1992): 527.

48. Han Wansang, *Minjung sahoehak*, 195.

49. Ibid.

50. Ch'oi Woosang and Han Hwagap, *Kim Dae Jung Conscience in Action* (Seoul: Chungdo Publishing Co., 1988), 14.

51. Kim Daejung, *Prison Writings*, trans. Ch'oi Songil and David R. McCann (Berkeley: University of California Press, 1987), cover page.

52. Ibid., 232.

53. Kim Dae Jung, *Mass-Participatory Economy: A Democratic Alternative for Korea* (University Press of America, 1985), x.

54. Ibid., 2.

55. Ibid., 22.

56. For more detailed information, see Kim Hyung-a van Leest, "The Impact of Concepts of Minjung on Thought and Culture in Korea during the Period of Authoritarian Politics (1948–1987)," (M.A. thesis, Australian National University, 1992), 171–186.

57. President Kim's reshuffling of personnel in government and his presidential office since his inauguration has been viewed as the "most dramatic change to overtake South Korea in half a century" (*Far Eastern Economic Review*, 24 June 1993, 18). More than five thousand top-level civil servants (mainly the heads of governmental institutions, including banks and investment institutions, and so on), have been shifted. Of these over three hundred were known to have been personally selected for removal by the president himself (*Sindonga*, May 1993, 181).

58. Kim Hwaju, "Chŏndaehyŏp: T'aep'ungŭi nunin'ga? (Chondaehyŏp: The Eye of the Typhoon?)," *Wŏlgan Chosŏn*, October 1987, 319–322. Also quoted in Ilpyong J. Kim and Young Whan Kihl, eds., *Political Change in South Korea* (New York: Paragon House, 1988), 179.

59. Kim and Kihl, eds., *Political Change in South Korea*, 179.

60. Han Sangjin, "Minjung sahoehagŭi minjungnon pip'an," (Criticism of the social science theories of minjung based on the masses), *Sindonga*, April 1987, 513.

61. Han Wansang, *Minjung sahoehak*, 34.

62. Ibid., 159.

63. "Han'guk kyŏngje, irok'enŭn mossanda (Korean economy: Fears for the future), *Sindonga*, November 1991, 284.

64. Wŏn Chongch'an, Yi Haech'an, Kwŏn Yŏnggil, Yi Chaeun, Kim Sŭngho, Yi Yŏnghŭi, and Pak Chunyŏng, "T'ŭkchip, 90 nyŏndae chungbanŭi simin undonggwa minjung undong" (Special edition: The community movement and minjung movement in the mid-1990s), *Ch'angjakkwa pip'yŏng* 21, no. 3 (Autumn 1993): 6–89.

Chapter 4

1. The sketch of the general cultural orientation in traditional Korea on the eve of Korea's entrance into the family of nations was drawn from part 1 of my manuscript "A Korean Confucian Encounter with the Modern World," which is pending publication.

2. J. Nehru, *Toward Freedom: The Autobiography of Jawaharlal Nehru* (New York: John Day, 1941), 74, quoted in Rupert Emerson, "Nationalism and Political Development," in *Political Development and Social Change*, ed. Jason L. Finkle and Richard W. Gable (New York: John Wiley & Sons, 1966), 159.

3. Karl W. Deutsch, *Nationalism and Social Communication* (Cambridge, Mass.: Technology Press, Massachusetts Institute of Technology, 1953), 152–153.

4. For the fusion of religion and social order, see Robert N. Bellah, "Religious Aspects of Modernization in Turkey and Japan," *American Journal of Sociology* 64 (July 1958): 1–5; Reinhard Bendix, *Kings or People* (Berkeley: University of California Press, 1978), chap. 2.

5. *Hwasŏ sŏnsaeng munjip* (Collected literary works of Yi Hangno) (1899), k. 11 *(Aŏn)*: 9a; k. 12 *(Aŏn)*: 1b, 17a.

6. See my paper "In Defense of the Traditional Order," *Philosophy East and West* 30, no. 3 (July 1980): 355–373.

7. Ch'oe Ikhyŏn, *Myŏn'am chip* (Collected works), 24 vols. (1933), k. 3 *(So)*: 33a–41b (22 January 1876). See also Hatada Takashi, "Kindai ni okeru Chōsenjin no Nihon kan" (The Korean view of Japan in modern times), *Shisō* (Thought) 520 (October 1967): 59–73.

8. *Myŏn'am chip*, k. 1 *(Purok)*: 1:24a–28a; see also k. 3 *(So)*: 3a–16b (1866 *uiso*), 22a–23a (25 October 1868), 38ab (22 January 1876); k. 4 *(So)*: 5a (26 June 1895), 15b (18 September 1898), 34b–35b (9 October 1898), 43a (19 November 1898); k. 4 *(Purok)*: 6a.

9. Tabohashi Kiyoshi, *Kindai Nissen kankei no kenkyū* (A study of modern Korean–Japanese relations) (Keijō: Chōsen sōtokufu chūsūin, 1940), 1:752–766; *Kojong Sillok* (The veritable record of King Kojong), in *Kojong Sunjong sillok* (Seoul: T'amgudang, 1970), 2:3ab, 5a–7a, 14b–16a, 16ab.

10. Kim Yunsik, *Sok Ŭmch'ŏng sa* (Seoul: Kuksa p'yŏnch'an wiwŏnhoe, 1960), 1:156–157.

11. For Ch'oe Ikhyŏn's response to the decree, see *Myŏn'am chip*, k. 4 *(So)*: 5a (26 May 1895).

12. Ibid., k. 2 *(Purok)*: 30a–32b, 32b–33b. For the background, see Yi

Sŏn'gŭn, *Han'guk sa, kŭnse p'yŏn* (A history of Korea: modern era) (Seoul: Ŭryu munhwa sa, 1963), 716–724.

13. *Myŏn'am chip*, k. 5 *(So)*: 8b (23 September 1904).

14. Susanne K. Langer, *Philosophy in a New Key: A Study in the Symbolism of Reason, Rite, and Art* (New York: New American Library of the World Literature, 1948), 241–242, 244.

15. *Myŏn'am chip*, k. 2 *(Purok)*: 33b–34a, 35a–37b; k. 4 *(So)*: 29b–32b; Yi Sŏn'gŭn, *Han'guk sa*, 723–745; Yu Insŏk, *Soŭi sinp'yŏn* (Seoul: Kuksa p'yŏnch'an wiwŏnhoe, 1975).

16. *Myŏn'am chip*, k. 4 *(Purok)*: 3a–5b.

17. Ibid., 5b–6a.

18. Ralph Linton defines a nativistic movement as "any conscious, organized attempt on the part of a society's members to revive or perpetuate selected aspects of its culture." Ralph Linton, "Nativistic Movement," *American Anthropologist* 45 (1943): 230.

19. For a comprehensive English-language survey of the Tonghak, see Benjamin B. Weems, *Reform, Rebellion and the Heavenly Way* (Tucson: University of Arizona Press, 1966). For the study of the Tonghak as a case of the search for personal and cultural identity, see Chai-sik Chung, "Religion and Cultural Identity: the Case of 'Eastern Learning,'" *International Yearbook for the Sociology of Religion* (Koln und Opladen: Westdeutsch Verlag, 1969), 5:118–132.

20. See Roland H. Bainton, *Here I Stand: A Life of Martin Luther* (New York: Abingdon-Cokesbury Press, 1950), 268–280; J. M. Porter, ed., *Luther: Selected Political Writings* (Philadelphia: Fortress Press, 1974), 85–88.

21. *Myŏn'am chip*, k. 4 *(Purok)*: 10a.

22. *Hwangsŏng sinmun*, 29 July 1904; see also Hwang Hyŏn, *Maech'ŏn yarok* (Collected works of Hwang Hyŏn) (Seoul: Kuksa p'yŏnch'an wiwŏnhoe, 1955), 1: 124–125.

23. *Myŏn'am chip*, k. 4 *(So)*: 25a–26b (9 October 1898).

24. Ibid., 27a; see also *Kojong Sillok*, 3:78a–80b.

25. *Myŏn'am chip*, see also *Kojong Sillok*, 3:79a.

26. Unless otherwise noted, all translations are the work of the author. *Myŏn'am chip*.

27. Hwang, *Maech'ŏn yarok*, 124–125, 228–229. See the memorials by Yun Ch'iho and others advocating popular rights and political participation in *Kojong sillok*, 3:46a–47a, 47b–48a; and see more about the disputations in 3:58b–59b, 60a–61a, 61b–62a, 71b–72a, 77ab passim.

28. *Myŏn'am chip*, k. 4 *(So)*: 26a. For the various traditional forms of protest, see Yi Kŭngik, *Kug'yŏk yŏllyŏsil kisul* (Narrative history in translation) (Seoul: Minjok munhwa ch'ujinhoe, 1966–1968), 8:51; 10:47, 540.

29. *Tongnip sinmun*, 4 June 1896.

30. For correlative cosmology in traditional China, see John B. Henderson, *The Development and Decline of Chinese Cosmology* (New York: Columbia University Press, 1984).

31. Yu Insŏk, *Ŭiam sŏnsaeng munjip* (Collected literary works) (Seoul: Kyŏngin munhwasa, 1973), 2:513a.

32. Ibid., 513b.

33. The term *chagang* was used as early as the beginning of the 1880s synon-

ymously with *kaehwa* (enlightenment) and *pugang* (wealth and power). For the use of these terms, see *Kojong Sillok,* 1:619ab; 2:12ab, 60ab. For general background, see Kyō Zaiken (Kang Chaeŏn), "Richō makki no jitsuryoku baiyō—jikyō undō" (The cultivation of real ability toward the end of Chosŏn Korea—self-strengthening movement), *Shisō* 585 (March 1973): 40–67; *Han'guk tongnip undong sa* (A history of the Korean independence movement) (Seoul: Kuksa p'yŏnch'an wiwŏnhoe, 1965), 1:83–87, 333–357, 391–405; *Taehan chaganghoe wŏlbo* (Seoul: Asea Munhwasa, 1976), no. 1, 9–10.

34. Chai-sik Chung, "On the Quest for Confucian Reformation," *Journal of Social Sciences and Humanities* 49 (June 1979): 4–10. See also Pak Ŭnsik, "Without the Rise of Education Survival Is Impossible," *Sŏu hakhoe wŏlbo* 1 (December 1906): 8. For Pak's view of education and knowledge, see his *Hakkyu sillon* (A new discourse on the rules of learning) (Seoul: Pangmun sa, 1904). For the hackneyed culture of the past, see his article "On Reforming Old Customs," *Sŏu hakhoe wŏlbo* 2 (January 1907): 8.

35. See the two articles Chu wrote about why it was necessary for Koreans to learn their own national language ("Chaguk munŏn," "Kugŏ wa kungmun") in *Chu Sigyŏng chŏnjip* (The collected writings of Chu Sigyŏng), ed. Yi Kimun (Seoul: Asea munhwa sa, 1976), 1:21–24, 25–33.

36. Pak Ŭnsik, *Han'guk t'ongsa* (Seoul: 1910); Sin Ch'aeho, "Toksa sillon," in Tanjae Sin Ch'aeho sŏnsaeng kinyŏm saŏphoe, ed., *Tanjae Sin Ch'aeho chŏnjip* (The collected works of Sin Ch'aeho) (Seoul: Hyŏngsŏl ch'ulp'ansa, 1977), 1:467–513. For the dominant mentality of the intellectual world, which was subservient to China, see "Nonsŏl," *Taehan maeil sinbo,* 4 August 1909; see also *Pak Ŭnsik chŏnsŏ* (Collected works of Pak Ŭnsik) (Seoul: Tan'guk taehakkyo ch'ulp'anbu, 1975), 3:201.

37. *Hwangsŏng sinmun,* 3 May 1906. See also an editorial on "Patriotism" in three parts, in *Mansebo,* 26, 27, 28 July 1909.

38. "Nonsŏl," *Hwangsŏng sinmun,* 5 May 1906. See also the editorials in *Hwangsŏng sinmun,* 8 March 1910, 14 January 1909, 20 March 1908.

39. "Nonsŏl," in ibid., 12 September 1905.

40. "Nonsŏl," ibid., 10 April 1905; "Nonsŏl," *Sŏbuk hakhoe wŏlbo* 13 (June 1909): 1–3; "Nonsŏl," *Sŏu hakhoe wŏlbo* 3 (February 1907): 5–8.

41. See 6 April 1902 in vol. 5 and 11 March 1894 in vol. 3 of *Yun Ch'iho ilgi* (Yun Ch'iho's diary) (Seoul: Kuksa p'yŏnch'an wiwŏnhoe, 1973–1986).

42. Ibid., 27 May 1904, in vol. 6.

43. Ibid., 30 March 1889, in vol. 1.

44. "Nonsŏl," *Tongnip sinmun,* 12 September 1899; Philip Jaisohn, "What Korea Needs Most," *The Korea Repository* 3 (March 1896): 109.

45. *Sŏbuk hakhoe wŏlbo* 10 (March 1909): 13–15.

46. Especially see "Kusŭp kaeryang non" (On reforming old customs), *Sŏu hakhoe wŏlbo* 2 (January 1907): 6–10.

47. See Chai-sik Chung, "On the Quest for Confucian Reformation," *Journal of Social Sciences and Humanities* 49 (June 1979): 1–38.

48. Pak, "Yugyo kusin non," 12–15.

49. *Tanjae Shin Ch'ae-ho,* 4:105–107, 108–110.

50. *Sŏbuk hakhoe wŏlbo,* 12 (May 1909): 28–30.

51. Song Pyŏngsŏn, *Yŏnjae sŏnsaeng munjip* (Collected literary works of Song Pyŏngsŏn), 24 vols, k. 8 (*So*): 8b, 9a.

52. Emile Durkheim, *Suicide* (New York: Free Press, 1951), 210–216.

53. Ibid., 228, 283.

54. Hyŏn Sangyun, *Chosŏn Yuhak sa* (A history of Korean Confucianism) (Seoul: Minjung sŏgwan, 1949), 456–459. See Song's memorial in *Kojong Sillok,* 3:411ab, 416ab, and also Song Pyŏngch'an's memorial, 3:423ab.

55. See *Han'guk tongnip undongsa* (A history of the Korean independence movement) (Seoul: Kuksa p'yŏnch'an wiwŏnhoe, 1965), 1:114, 116–118; and also the memorial by Min Yŏnghwan and others in *Kojong Sillok,* 3:406b, and the entry on his death in 3:408b. For the numerous memorials protesting against Japan's control of Korea, see the entries of November and December 1905 and January and February 1906 in *Kojong Sillok,* 3:394b–417b, 418a–424a passim.

56. Kwak Chongsŏk, *Myŏn'u chip* (Collected literary writings of Kwak Chongsŏk) (Seoul: Asea munhwa sa, 1984), *yŏnbo,* 4:676–683, 686–688.

57. Ibid., *Kwŏnsu* 1 (February 1904), 12–13; (8 September 1904), 21–23 (17 October 1904), 14–15.

58. Ibid., *Kwŏnsu* 1 (1 October 1905), 23.

59. Ibid., *Yŏnbo* 4 (29 August 1910), 739.

60. See Chŏn U's critical reviews of the theories of the relationship between *i* and *ki* held by Yi Hangno, Ki Chŏngjin, and Yi Chinsang from the perspective of Yi Yulgok and Song Siyŏl, in *Kanjae sŏnsaeng munjip chŏnp'yŏn* (Collected literary works of Chŏn U, pt. 1) (my private collection, n.d., 17 *kwŏn*), k. 13: 59a–65a, 65a–77b, 92a–93a, 93ab, 93b–94a. See also Yi Pyŏngdo, *Han'guk Yuhak sa* (A history of Korean Confucianism) (Seoul: Asea munhwa sa, 1987), 473–494.

61. See Kwak's critique of Yu Chunggyo, who challenged his mentor Yi Hangno's view in Kwak Chongsŏk, *Myŏn'u chip,* k. 16 (*Chapchŏ*), 3:599Ua–610Lb, especially 609Ua–La.

62. *Myŏn'am chip,* k. 16 (*Chapchŏ*): 47b–48b.

63. See k. 161, *Myŏn'u sŏnsaeng munjip,* 4: 364Lab.

64. Ibid., 4:364Lab, 365Ua–Lb, 365Lb–366Ua, 368Ub–La, 369Uab, 371Ub, 373La–374Ua. See also the same point made by Kim Ch'angsuk in the inscription he wrote on the monument erected at the tomb of Kwak Chongsŏk, in *Simsan yugo* (Posthumous writings of Kim Ch'angsuk), no. 18, Han'guk saryo ch'ongsŏ (Seoul: Kuksa p'yŏnch'an wiwŏnhoe, 1973), 232–233; cf. 251–252.

65. See *Simsan yugo,* 252; also 200–201.

66. *Myŏn'am sŏnsaeng munjip, Kwŏnsu,* 1.

67. For a general discussion of these events, see Cho Chihun, "Han'guk minjok undong sa" (A history of the Korean nationalist movement), in *Minjok kukka sa* (A history of people and nation), ed. Han'guk munhwasa taegye (Seoul: Kodae minjok munhwa yŏn'guso ch'ulp'anbu, 1964), 1: 639–669; Kuksa p'yŏnch'an wiwŏnhoe, ed., *Han'guk tongnip undong sa* 2 (1966).

68. Even Kim Ch'angsuk, one of the more open-minded Confucian leaders, unwittingly uses the term *tongbi* (the rebels of Tonghak), following the common usage among the members of Yurim. See *Simsan yugo,* 240, 297.

69. *Simsan yugo,* 313.

70. Kim Ku, one of the outstanding leaders of the Korean independence movement, gives telling evidence about how crucial it was for the independence of Korea to educate the ignorant masses, who cared for nothing but their own immediate needs and concerns, thus awakening in them a patriotic, national

consciousness. See his *Paekbŏm ilchi* (Autobiography of Kim Ku) (Seoul: Kyomunsa, 1982), 94, 192, 291–292.

71. *Simsan yugo,* 130.

72. Kim Yunsik, *Sok ŭmch'ŏng sa,* 2:500.

73. See the inscription on the tombstone of Haesa Kim Chŏngho written by Kim Ch'angsuk in *Simsan yugo,* 277. See also Hŏ Sŏndo, "Samil undonggwa Yugyo kye" (The March First movement and the Confucian circle) in *Samil undong osipchunyŏn kinyŏm nonjip* (Papers in commemoration of the fiftieth anniversary of the March First movement) (Seoul: Tonga ilbo sa, 1969), 284–285.

74. Ibid. See Kim Ch'angsuk's inscription on the mausoleum in memory of his mentor, Kwak Chongsŏk, in *Simsan yugo,* 231–232; see also his letter to Cho Kukhyŏn, 130–133, and his recollections of his seventy-three years of life, 309–316.

75. *Myŏn'u sŏnsaeng munjip,* k. 3 *(Yŏnbo),* 4:758–759.

76. Ibid., 760–761.

77. Ibid., 761–762.

78. Ibid., 764–765, 768–769.

79. Kim's *Simsan yugo* is a valuable source for the study of his life and thought. His personal recollections of seventy-three years of his life (k. 5) shed much light on the relatively unexplored problem of the role played by Confucianism in the struggle for national independence.

80. *Simsan yugo,* 102, 116, 117, 151–153, 214, 356–357.

81. See Boyd C. Shafer, *Nationalism: Myth and Reality* (New York: Harcourt Brace, 1955), 5.

82. On the usage of the term "cultural nationalism," see Sallo Wittmayer Baron, *Modern Nationalism and Religion* (New York: Meridan Books, 1960), 4–5.

83. Martin Buber, *Kampf um Israel, Reden und Schriften (1921–1932)* (Berlin, 1933), 232, cited in Baron, *Modern Nationalism,* 3.

84. See Sin Ch'aeho's verdict on Korean Confucianism in *Tanjae Sin Ch'aeho chŏnjip,* 4:108–109.

85. See Michael Edson Robinson, *Cultural Nationalism in Colonial Korea, 1920–1925* (Seattle and London: University of Washington Press, 1988).

86. See Cho, "Han'guk minjok undong sa," 669–836; Chong-sik Lee, *Politics of Korean Nationalism* (Berkeley: University of California Press, 1965), chaps. 4 and 5.

87. Joseph R. Levenson, " 'History' and 'Value': The Tensions of Intellectual Choice in Modern China," in Arthur F. Wright, ed., *Studies in Chinese Thought* (Chicago: University of Chicago Press, 1953), 150.

Chapter 5

1. For minjung Buddhism, see Park Sung-bae, "Theoretical Background of Minjung Buddhism in Korea," a paper given at the Conference on Religion and Contemporary Society in Korea, University of California at Berkeley, 11 November 1988.

2. In this paper, I use "minjung Christianity" as an umbrella term, so that I can include but not be limited to what is known as "minjung theology."

3. The encyclical *Gaudium et Spes*, quoted in Deane William Ferm, *Third World Liberation Theologies* (Maryknoll, N.Y.: Orbis Books, 1986), 7.

4. See Deane William Ferm, "Gustavo Gutierrez," in *Profiles in Liberation: Portraits of Third World Theologians* (Mystic, Conn.: Twenty-third Publications, 1988), 154–158, and "Liberation Theology—Its Message Examined: An interview with Gustavo Gutierrez," *Harvard Divinity Bulletin* 19, no.1 (Spring 1989): 6–7.

5. For a discussion of the current social and political orientation of the National Christian Council, see Yun Ilung, "Kidokkyo kyohoe hyŏbŭihoe (NCC) ŭi silch'e," *Wŏl'gan Chosŏn* (August 1988), 196–207.

6. Documents circulated by missionaries in Seoul and declarations by the Catholic Priests for the Realization of Justice and the Support Committee of the Families of the Arrested, in the author's possession. For the People's Revolutionary Party case, see U.S. Congress, *House Journal*, 93d Cong., 2d sess., "Human Rights in South Korea; Implications for U.S. Policy: Hearings before the Subcommittees on Asian and Pacific Affairs and on International Organizations and Movements of the Committee on Foreign Affairs," 30 July, 5 August, and 20 December 1974.

7. See Sugwon Kang, "The Politics and Poetry of Kim Chi-ha," *Bulletin of Concerned Asian Scholars* 9 (April–June 1977): 3–7.

8. The circumstances of the Ogle deportation are explained in "Human Rights in South Korea; Implications for U.S. Policy," 136–137 and 266–269. At about the same time, American Maryknoller Father James Sinnott, who had been organizing fishermen and factory workers on islands in the Yellow Sea, was also forced to leave Korea.

9. "Theological Declaration of Korean Christians, 1973," in Peggy Billings, *Fire Beneath the Frost* (New York: Friendship Press, 1984), 80–81.

10. Donald N. Clark, *Christianity in Modern Korea* (Lanham, Md.: University Press of America / The Asia Society, 1986), 34.

11. Copies of the manifesto in the writer's possession. For the event, see "Crackdown in the Cathedral," *Newsweek* (Asia edition), 22 March 1976, 6–7.

12. For a chilling account of one such experience, see David Kwang-sun Suh [David Suh], *Theology, Ideology, and Culture* (Hong Kong: World Student Christian Federation, 1983), 9–13.

13. Suh Kwang-sun David [David Suh], "A Biographical Sketch of an Asian Theological Consultation," in *Minjung Theology: People as the Subjects of History,* ed. Commission on Theological Concerns of the Christian Conference of Asia (Maryknoll, N.Y.: Orbis Books, 1981), 16–17.

14. The Asia Watch, *Human Rights in Korea* (Washington, D.C.: The Asia Watch Committee, 1988), 309–312. Pak Hyŏnggyu was the pastor arrested at the Easter sunrise service in 1973. Later, in between his many arrests, he served as director of the Human Rights Committee of the National Christian Council.

15. Billings, *Fire Beneath the Frost*, 74.

16. I will leave it to others in this book to attempt a definition of *han;* but my own sources for it include: Suh Nam-dong, "Towards a Theology of *Han*," in *Minjung Theology: People as the Subjects*, 55–69; and Kim Chiha's discussion of his work "Chang Il-dam," in his "Declaration of Conscience" (1975), which appears in many places, including *Bulletin of Concerned Asian Scholars* 9, no. 2

(April–June 1977): 8–15. An interesting, recent variation on the theme of han and liberation from it is expressed by Hwang Tong-gyu in "Passage to the Bronx," a poem about the han of getting mugged in Manhattan in broad daylight. *Korea Journal* 29, no. 8 (August 1989): 48–50.

17. Suh, *Theology, Ideology, and Culture*, 50–51.

18. Cyris H. S. Moon, *Korean Minjung Theology: An Old Testament Perspective* (Maryknoll, N.Y.: Orbis Books, 1985), passim.

19. Suh, "A Biographical Sketch," 22.

20. Han was a pastor in Sinŭiju who came south with his congregation and built up the Yŏngnak Church congregation in Seoul. See Clark, *Christianity in Modern Korea*, 23–24.

21. Moon, *Korean Minjung Theology*, 75.

22. As both of my grandfathers were presidents of this seminary in the 1930s, I feel a certain filial reticence about mentioning this.

23. Suh, "A Biographical Sketch," 21.

24. The well-known objections of the Western missionaries to Shinto shrine worship by Christians in the later stages of Japanese rule notwithstanding, the general attitude of even the most anti-Japanese missionaries was that Koreans should acquiesce in the here and now and wait for judgment in the hereafter.

25. Sometimes, however, minjung theologians except present-day missionaries from this criticism (for example, see Moon, *Korean Minjung Theology*, 74), although it must be added that Moon himself was a missionary of the Presbyterian Church U.S.A. for more than ten years.

26. Kim Kwangok, conversation with author, 6 May 1989.

27. Hyun Young-hak, "A Theological Look at the Mask Dance in Korea," in *Minjung Theology: People as the Subjects*, 53–54.

28. For which see George Ogle, *Liberty to the Captives* (Atlanta: John Knox Press, 1977).

29. For an example of one UIM worker's activities, see "Cho, Wha Soon: A Modern Apostle," in Billings, *Fire Beneath the Frost*, 58–65. A collection of first-person accounts of attempts by Korean UIM missioners to organize workers is in George Ogle, "On Becoming the Body of Christ" (mimeograph, 1971), 32–68.

30. T.K. [pseud.], *Letters from South Korea* (New York: International Documentation, 1976), passim.

31. Shirin McArthur, letter from Presbyterian Volunteer-in-Mission in Seoul, 20 April 1987.

32. Tony Dawson, "Ferment at the Yeast Factory: Urban Industrial Mission in Yong Dong Po, Korea" (typescript, 1985). Dawson served several years as a UIM worker on assignment from the Uniting Church of Australia.

33. Ibid.

34. William R. Garrett, "Liberation Theology and Dependency Theory," in *The Politics of Latin American Liberation Theology*, ed. Richard L. Rubenstein and John K. Roth (Washington, D.C.: The Washington Institute for Values in Public Policy, 1988), 181.

35. Leonardo and Clodovis Boff, *Introducing Liberation Theology* (Maryknoll, N.Y.: Orbis Books, 1986), 28.

36. The literature criticizing liberation theology in this vein is extensive, with much of it emanating from conservative Catholic scholars in North America. Good examples are Michael Novak, ed., *Liberation Theology and the Liberal Society* (Washington, D.C.: The American Enterprise Institute for Public Policy Research, 1987); Ronald Nash, ed., *Liberation Theology* (Milford, Mich.: Mott Media, 1984); and James V. Schall, S.J., ed., *Liberation Theology in Latin America* (San Francisco: Ignatius Press, 1982).

37. See, for example, Kim Chiha's frequent references to the people and events that shaped liberation theology in his "Declaration of Conscience," cited above (n. 16).

38. Some minjung theologians, weary of treating Marxist social analysis like a dead cat, confront it head-on. An Pyŏng-mu, for example, contends that it was Karl Marx who helped open the eyes of the oppressed to the enormous injustice of a capitalist society. See "Ahn Byung-mu," in Ferm, *Profiles in Liberation,* 79.

39. Tong Hwan (Stephen) Moon, "Korean Minjung Theology: An Introduction," in *Korean-American Relations at Crossroads,* ed. Wonmo Dong (Princeton, N.J.: The Association of Korean Christian Scholars in North America, 1982), 13.

40. Ham Sok Hon, *Queen of Suffering: A Spiritual History of Korea* (Philadelphia: Friends World Committee for Consultation, 1985), 182.

41. See, for example, Cardinal Kim's "The Future Cannot Be Built on Lies and Cover-up" (26 July 1986), "Democracy Is the Road to Reconciliation with God" (9 March 1987), "Politicians Must Be Afraid of the People" (15 March 1987), and his Easter message (19 April 1987), all available from the Korea Coalition, 110 Maryland Avenue, N.E., Washington, D.C. 20002.

42. See Kim Ok-hy, "Women in the History of Catholicism in Korea," *Korea Journal* 24, no. 8 (August 1984): 28–40.

43. Sister Rose Guercio, interview with author at the Maryknoll Mission, Seoul, 21 July 1988.

44. The Pastoral Congress Committee for the Bicentennial of the Catholic Church of Korea, "An Introduction to the 'Schemata' of the Pastoral Congress of Korea" (print, 1985), 37–38. A more assertive statement is the "Conference of Korean Bishops' Social Pastoral" (5 July 1985), which defines the church as the "protector of human rights and human dignity." (Documents from the Catholic Conference of Korea, Seoul).

45. Avery Dulles, *The Reshaping of Catholicism: Current Challenges in the Theology of the Church* (San Francisco: Harper and Row, 1988), 148.

46. My notes on a sermon by Paul Cho Yonggi, Yoido Full Gospel Church, Seoul, 24 July 1988.

47. Moon, *Korean Minjung Theology,* 73.

48. Suh Nam-dong, "Cultural Theology, Political Theology and Minjung Ideology: A Review of Choan Seng Song's *Third-Eye Theology* (1979), *The Compassionate God* (1982), and *Tell Us Our Names: Parables for Folk Theology* (1983)," in *Theological Thought: the Quarterly of the Korea Theological Studies Institute* 42 (Fall 1983); translation distributed by the North American Coalition on Human Rights in Korea (no page numbers on manuscript).

49. Suh Nam-dong [Sŏ Namdong], "Historical References for a Theology of Minjung," in *Minjung Theology: People as the Subjects,* 177.

Chapter 6

1. Franz Fanon, "The Pitfalls of National Consciousness," in *The Wretched of the Earth*, ed. Franz Fanon (New York: Grove Weidenfield, 1963).

2. Kang Man'gil, "Han'guk minjokchuǔiǔi ihae: Song Kǒnho minjokchuǔironǔl chungsimǔro" (Understanding Korean nationalism: Song Kǒnho's theories of nationalism), in *Han'gukǔi minjokchuǔi undonggwa minjung* (The Korean nationalist movement and the minjung) (Seoul, 1987).

3. See, for instance, Michael Robinson, *Cultural Nationalism in Colonial Korea, 1920–1925* (Seattle: University of Washington Press, 1988).

4. Much of this argument on the notion of culture industry is supported by the Frankfurt School thinkers. The intellectual relationship between the anti-capitalistic minjung culture movement and the theories of culture industry championed by such scholars as Adorno and Horkheimer will be discussed elsewhere.

5. Paek Nakch'ǒng (Paik Nak-chung), "4.19ǔi yǒksajǒk ǔiǔiwa han'gyesǒng" (The historical significance of 4.19 and its limitations), in *Sawǒl Hyǒngmyǒng-non* (Discussions on the April revolution), ed. Kang Man'gil et al. (Seoul: Han'gilsa, 1983).

6. Ibid. and Yi Chaeo, *Haebanghu Han'guk Haksaeng Undongsa* (The history of the students' movement during the postliberation period) (Seoul: Hyǒng-sǒngsa, 1987), 185.

7. Yi Chaeo, 206–217.

8. Note that instead of the term "nation" *(minjok),* or "people" *(minjung),* as was often used in the 1980s, the students of the 1960s employed the term "native land" *(hyangt'o).* This may be an indication of the evolution of the notion of nationality into *ethnicity* as South Korean life is increasingly syphoned into the transnational capitalistic system.

9. Yi Chaeo, *Haebanghu Han'guk,* 228.

10. M. M. Bakhtin, *Rabelais and His World* (Bloomington: Indiana University Press, 1984), 109.

11. Cho Tongil, *Han'guk Kamyǒn'gukǔi Mihak* (Aesthetics of Korean maskdance drama) (Seoul: Hanguk Ilbosa, 1975).

12. For detailed discussion, see my *Frost in May: Decolonization and Culture in Korea,* forthcoming.

13. Kim Chiha, "P'ungjanya chasarinya?" (Parody or suicide?); reprinted in his *Minjokǔi norae minjungǔi norae* (Song of the nation, song of the people) (Seoul: Tonggwang Ch'ulp'ansa), 1984.

14. Abdul R. JanMohammad, "The Economy of Manichean Allegory: The Function of Racial Difference in Colonialist Literature," in *"Race," Writing, and Difference,* ed. Henry Louis Gates, Jr. (Chicago: University of Chicago Press, 1985).

15. Michel Foucault, "Nietzsche, Genealogy, History," in his *Language, Counter-memory, Practice* (Ithaca, N.Y.: Cornell University Press, 1977).

16. Sin Tongyǒp, *Anthology of Sin Tongyǒp* (Seoul: Ch'angjakkwa Pip-'yǒngsa, 1975).

17. As the corruption of the government system and officials proceeded

more intensely toward the end of Chosŏn dynasty (1392–1910), a large number of tenant farmers, unable to meet the heavy taxation, usurpation, extortion and corvée, abandoned their homes and became vagrants. They subsisted as illegal mine workers, itinerant entertainers, or simple beggars. Many of them even engaged in banditry. However, their level of social knowledge was limited, and therefore they were unable to initiate powerful resistance against the feudal system. See Pyŏn Chusung, "19segi yuminŭi silt'aewa kŭ sŏnggyŏk" (The nature and characteristics of nineteenth-century vagrants), master's thesis, Koryŏ University, 1990.

18. Both Chŭngsan'gyo and Tonghak are millenarian new religions that emerged in the late nineteenth century. Tonghak, established by Ch'oe Cheu, was a syncretic religion calling for social reform and human equality. Chŭngsan'gyo was established by Kang Chŭngsan, incorporating many Tonghak ideas but relying heavily on Maitreya tradition. Therefore Tonghak's drive for social and political reform was substantially dissipated in Chŭngsan'gyo.

19. Ever since the notion of ture became situated in the minjung discourse, studies on ture in this light have proliferated as the debates on collective community *(kongdongch'e)* continue.

20. Kim Yŏlgyu, *Han'guk minsokkwa munhak yŏn'gu* (Korean folklore and literature) (Seoul: Ilchogak, 1971), 274.

21. Ch'ae Hŭiwan, "Kamyŏn'gukŭi minjungjŏk miŭisik" (Popular aesthetics of mask-dance drama), master's thesis, Seoul National University, 1977.

22. Ch'ae Hŭiwan and Im Chint'aek, "Madanggugeso madang kusŭro" (From madang theater to ritual), in *Han'guk munhagŭi hyŏndan'gye* (The current state of Korean literature), ed. Paek Nakch'ŏng et al. (Seoul: Ch'angjakkwa Pip'yŏngsa, 1982).

23. Paek Kiwan, "Minjokkwa kut" (Nation and shamanic ritual), in *Minjokkwa kut* (Nation and shamanic ritual), ed. Minjok Kuthoe (Seoul: Minjok Kuthoe, 1987), 12–13.

24. Ibid., 12.

25. Robert Young, "Disorienting Orientalism," in *White Mythologies, Writing History and the West* (London and New York: Routledge, 1990). More recently, Patrick Williams and Laura Chrisman echo the same concern in their introduction to *Colonial Discourse and Post-colonial Theory* (New York: Columbia University Press, 1994).

Chapter 7

1. The national security law is widely understood as the umbrella which has allowed indiscriminate tyranny of the state in the name of national security and anticommunism. For a longer treatment of this movement, see Abelmann, forthcoming.

2. The university school year begins in the spring. Koryŏ University had a particular tie to Koch'ang because of its founder, Kim Sŏngsu.

3. Chuch'e is also the cornerstone concept of Kim Il Sung's North Korean chuch'e sasang, or subject ideology, which refers to the state's autonomous political, social, cultural, and economic existence. During my fieldwork in rural

Korea, I noticed a more daily use of the word to refer to matters of personality, such that "a person with subject-consciousness" meant someone with formed opinions who exerts control in her life.

4. All names of farmers, students, and other activists are pseudonyms; corporate representatives, however, are referred to by their actual names. The place-names that appear here are the actual names.

5. The CFU representative documented his involvement in a twenty-odd-page narrative for circulation among a small number of movement participants. The document describes the representative's frustrations in dealing with Yun and the Relinquish Committee.

6. With the early stirrings of dissent, Samyang lowered the rents.

7. Most people in a similar income bracket to his either had no phone or used the phone only for incoming phone calls and local calls and in all other cases traveled to the market town by bus to make long-distance phone calls at a pay phone at the bus station. Private phones in the region were always locked, and a real source of worry. In a sense, phones were beyond their means and thus frightening. In the case of one couple I knew, the husband would not even give his wife the key to the phone, causing constant arguments. Cho was fond of repeating that it had been because of CFU and the movement that he—a welfare recipient (stressing his poverty)—had installed a phone, thus bragging about the extent of his commitment.

8. The landlords also owned and managed salt fields contiguous to the rice fields; the salt-field ownership was not contested in this protest.

Bibliography for Chapter 7

87nyŏn nongch'ŏn hwaltong charyojip (1987 Agricultural Action Resource Collection). Seoul: Koryŏ taehakkyo nongch'on hwaltong chunbi wiwŏnhoe (Preparation Committee of the Koryŏ University Nonghwal), 1987. Cited as Agricultural Action Resource Collection.

Abelmann, Nancy. *Memory and Mobilization: The Practice and Politics of History in a South Korean Tenant Farmers Movement.* Berkeley: University of California Press. Forthcoming.

Choi Chungmoo. "Shamanism and the Making of the Revolutionary Ideology in Contemporary Korea." Social Sciences Research Council Conference. Thailand, May 4–8, 1989.

Cumings, Bruce. *The Origins of the Korean War: Liberation and the Emergence of Separate Regimes.* Princeton, N.J.: Princeton University Press, 1981.

Dong Wonmo. "University Students in South Korean Politics: Patterns of Radicalization in the 1980s." *Journal of International Affairs* 40, no. 2 (Winter/Spring 1987): 233–255.

Mun'gwadae nonghwal 2 ch'a tapsa pogosŏ (The Second Agricultural Action Investigation Report of the College of Arts). Koryŏ University: n.p., June 1987. Cited as The Second Agricultural Action Investigation.

"Taehaksaeng nongch'on hwaltong" (University students agricultural action). *80nyŏndae minjungŭi ssaumgwa tu'jaeng yŏksa* (The history of the fights and struggle of the people in the 1980s), 406–427. (Seoul: Pip'yŏngsa, 1986. Cited as University Students Agricultural Action.

Chapter 8

1. Han'guk minjungsa yŏn'guhoe, *Han'guk Minjungsa II* (Seoul: Pulpit, 1986), 267.

2. It is interesting to remember that this category of spirits might very well include Kŭn Simbang's husband; thus the initiation dream also narrates a powerful and very personal story.

3. Kim Minju and Kim Ponghyŏn, *Chejudo Inmindŭrŭi 4.3 Mujang T'ujaengsa charyojip* (Materials on the history of the April 3 uprising of the Cheju people) (Osaka: Munchosa, 1963).

4. This is described in the short stories of Hyŏn Kiyong; see *Suni Samch'on* (Aunt Suni) (Seoul: Ch'angjakkwa pip'yŏng sa, 1979).

5. See Bruce Cumings and John Halliday, *Korea: The Unknown War* (New York: Pantheon Books, 1988).

6. See Hyŏn Kiron, *Chejudo Changsu Sŏlhwa* (Legends of generals of Cheju Island) (Seoul: Munhakkwa chisŏng, 1981).

7. Ibid.

8. See Yi Sunok, *Yi Chaesu Silgi* (A biography of Yi Chaesu) (Osaka: Chung-do Munhwatang, 1932).

9. Compare this to Bruce Mannheim, "A Semiotic of Andean Dreams," in *Dreaming: Anthropological and Psychological Interpretations*, ed. Barbara Tedlock (Cambridge: Cambridge University Press, 1987).

10. Compare again Bruce Mannheim, "Discursive and Presentational Form in Language: Subliminal Patterning in a Quechua Folksong," unpublished manuscript, 1989.

11. See Walter Benjamin, "N[Theoretics of knowledge: Theory of progress]," in *Philosophical Forum* 15 (1983–1984): 1–2.

12. Ibid. Compare with Susan Buck-Morss, "Benjamin's Passangenwek: Redeeming Mass Culture for the Revolution," *New German Critique* 29 (1983): 2211–2240.

13. Walter Benjamin, *Reflections* (New York: Harcourt Brace, 1978), 159.

14. Cf. S. R. F. Price, "The Future of Dreams: From Freud to Artemidorus," *Past and Present* 113 (1986): 3–37. He is concerned with Greek dreams.

Chapter 9

1. Kwŏn Hyŏngmin, comp., *Haebang Sasimnyŏnŭi Munhak* (Literature of the forty years since the liberation) (Seoul: Minŭmsa, 1985), 4:13.

2. Kim T'aejun et al., *Han'guk Hyŏndae Munhaksa* (Modern history of Korean literature) (Seoul: Hyŏndae munhaksa, 1989), 205.

3. Chŏng Kwari, "Chagi chŏngnip ŭi noryŏkkwa kŭ chŏnmang" (Efforts to establish selfhood and its prospect), *Yŏksa, Hyŏnsil kŭrigo Munhak* (History, reality, and literature), ed. Kim Pyŏnggol and Ch'ae Kwangsŏk (Seoul: Chiyangsa, 1985), 142.

4. Régine Robin, *Le Réalisme socialiste: Une esthétique impossible* (Paris: Payot, 1986), 67.

5. Arthur Greenspan, "Le Nouvel Age de Populaille et la littérature prolétarienne," *Revue des Sciences Humaines*, no. 190 (1982–1983), 70.

6. Réné Garguilo, "Du réalisme socialiste au réalisme sans rivages," *Roman, Réalités, Réalisme* (Paris: P.U.F., 1989), 152.

7. Paek Nakch'ŏng, "Minjok munhak kaenyŏmŭi chŏngnibŭl wihae" (On establishing the concept of national literature), *Haebang Sasimnyŏnŭi Munhak,* 4:178–179.

8. Ibid., 184.

9. Kim Chiha, *P'ungjanya Chasarinya* (Satire or suicide?).

10. Pak Hyŏnch'ae, "Munhakkwa kyŏngje" (Literature and economics), *Yŏksa, Hyŏnsil kŭrigo Munhak* (History, present, and literature) (Seoul: Chiyangsa, 1985), 65.

11. Chae In'yong and Song Min'yŏp, "Minjung munhagŭi nolli" (The logic of minjung literature), *Minjok, Minjung, kŭrigo Munhak* (People, minjung, and literature) (Seoul: Chiyangsa, 1985), 132.

12. Paek Chin'gi, "Nodong munhak, kŭ silch'ŏnjŏk kanŭngsŏngŭl hyanghayŏ" (Proletarian literature, toward the possibility of its practical application), *Minjung, Nodong kŭrigo Munhak* (Seoul: Chiyangsa, 1985), 229.

13. Philippe Hamon, "Un discours contrainte," *Poétiques,* no. 16 (1973).

14. Robin, *Le Réalisme socialiste,* 69.

15. Susan Suleiman, *Le Roman à thèse, ou, l'autorité fictive* (Paris: P.U.F., 1983), 229.

16. Paek Nakch'ŏng, a professor of English literature at Seoul National University and a contributor to this volume, has already written extensively on the relations between literature and national issues, as, for example, in *Minjok Munhagŭi Sae Tan'gye* (Seoul: Ch'angjakkwa pip'yŏngsa, 1990).

Chapter 11

1. Kim Tonghwan, in the 19 November 1940 *Maeil sinbo,* quoted in Kim Yoon-shik (Kim Yunshik), *Han'guk kŭndae munye pip'yŏngsa* (A study of recent Korean literary arts criticism) (Seoul: Ilchisa, 1976), 408.

2. Kwŏn Yŏngmin [Kwon Youngmin], "Minjok munhangnonŭi nolliwa silch'ŏn" (The logic and practice of national literature), in *Han'guk minjok munhangnon yŏn'gu* (Studies in Korean literary nationalism) (Seoul: Minŭmsa, 1988), 521.

3. Ibid., 524.

4. Paek Nakch'ŏng [Paik Nak-chung], "Minjok munhak kaenyŏmŭi sin ch'ŏn'gae" [New unfolding of the national literature concept], in *Wŏlgan chungang* (July 1974), 81–91; reprinted as "Minjok munhak kaenyŏmŭi chŏngnibŭl wihae" (Toward the theoretical establishment of the national literature concept) in a collection of Paek's critical essays, *Minjok munhakkwa segyemunhak* (National literature and world literature) (Seoul: Ch'angjakkwa pip'yŏngsa, 1978), 123–138.

5. Ibid., 82.

6. Georg Lukács, *Realism in Our Time* (New York: Harper Torchbooks, 1971), 99.

7. Terry Eagleton, *Marxism and Literary Criticism* (Berkeley: University of California Press, 1976), 28.

8. Lukács, 96.

9. Paek Nakch'ŏng, "What the Other Korean Writers Think: A Message to the Foreign Participants of the 1988 Seoul PEN Congress," 5.

10. Kwŏn, "Minjok Munhangnon," 533.

11. Kim Yunsik [Kim Yoon-shik], "The Korean Novel in an Age of Industrialization," *Korea Journal* 29, no. 6 (1989): 23–28.

12. Among others, Kwŏn Yŏngmin, "Pundan shidaeŭi munhagŭrosŏŭi han'-gugŭi tangdae munhak" (Contemporary Korean literature as the literature of a period of division), in *Han'guk munhak* (1985).

13. Kwŏn, "Minjok Munhangnon," 526;Han Hyŏnggu, "Kim Sŭngok munhagŭi munhaksajŏk sŏnggyŏk" (The nature of Kim Sŭngok's literature in terms of literary history), in Yi Chuhyŏng et al., *Han'guk hyŏndae chakka yŏn'gu* (Studies on contemporary Korean authors) (Seoul: Minŭmsa, 1989), 221.

14. "Sŏul, 1964 kyŏul," first published in *Sasanggye* (June 1965), won the 1966 Tongin Literary Prize.

15. Han Hyŏnggu, 221.

16. Ibid., 222.

17. (Seoul: Munhakkwa chisŏngsa, 1978), 341.

18. O Seyŏng, "Cho Sehŭi ron: sarangŭi ippŏpgwa sabŏp [On Cho Sehŭi: Legislation and adjudication of love], in *Han'guk hyŏndae chakka yŏn'gu* (Studies of contemporary Korean authors) (Seoul: Minŭmsa, 1989), 359.

19. Translated as "Möbius Loop" by Hyon Joongshik and Han Hakjoon in *Modern Korean Short Stories* (New York: Larchwood Publications, 1981).

20. Translation by Timothy Jay Warnberg, University of Hawai'i, in progress.

21. Translated as "A Dwarf Launches a Little Ball" by Chun Kyung-ja, in *Korea Journal* (January 1987).

22. Translated as "On the Overhead Bridge" by Adrian Buzo, in *Korea Journal* (October 1980).

23. Translated as "City of Machines" by Marshall R. Pihl, in *Korea Journal* (March 1990).

24. Translated as "The Bony-Fish That Came into My Net" by Sol Sun-bong, in *Korea Journal* (November 1978).

25. Kwŏn, "Minjok Munhangnon," 529.

26. O, "Cho Sehŭi ron," 362.

27. I have in mind vocabulary related to sensory perception, which expresses qualities of sound, shape, motion, color, texture, smell, and taste. This kind of vocabulary usage is not so prevalent in Chosŏn period literature as it was in the fiction and poetry of the colonial period and in the work of postliberation writers.

28. This is an age of distrust, said Prime Minister Kim Chongp'il, in an accusatory frame of mind when speaking to Seoul National University students in the early 1960s.

29. Called Möbius strip or loop, after August F. Möbius (d. 1868), who invented a figure that is a one-sided surface formed by holding one end of a rectangle fixed, rotating the opposite end through 180 degrees, and then applying it to the first end.

30. A device, invented by Felix Klein (d. 1925), which has a surface closed in such a way that it is possible to pass from a point on one side to the corresponding point on the opposite side without passing through the surface, and that is

formed by passing the narrow end of a tapered tube through the side of the tube and flaring this end out to join the other end.

31. Kim, "The Korean Novel," 27.
32. For a full treatment of these symbols, see O, "Cho Sehŭi ron," 374–379.
33. Lukács, *Realism in Our Time,* 12.
34. O, "Cho Sehŭi ron," 367.
35. Ibid., 36.
36. Kim, "The Korean Novel," 26.

INDEX

Christianity. *See* Catholic Farmers' Union; Catholic Priests' Association for Justice, Catholicism; Christian Farmers' Union; Confucianism; Han'guk Theological Seminary; Kim Suhwan; Presbyterianism; Protestantism; shamanism; theology; and Urban Industrial Mission

chuch'e ideology, 52, 237–238

Chu Hsi, 64–65, 75, 78

Chun Doo-Hwan. *See* Chŏn Tuhwan

Chŭngsan'gyo, 114, 116, 237

class, 2, 4, 8, 14, 31, 174, 184, 191, 225; analysis of, 11, 13, 39–46, 176; as distinct from status groups, 48, 52; contradictions between, 203–205, 218; middle class (bourgeoisie), 8, 29, 32, 34–38, 55, 56, 101, 103, 106, 112, 117, 170, 192–193, 210; proletarian, 32, 34–38, 41–46, 56–58, 170, 174, 176; struggle between, 18, 24, 43, 46, 56, 58, 98, 100, 103, 115, 137, 174, 178

Cold War, 3, 106, 139, 144

colonialism, in Asia, 34, 35, 37, 188; decolonization, 8, 105, 112; Japanese, 1, 3, 12, 15, 20, 26, 28, 31–37, 45, 61, 65, 68, 76, 80–85, 93, 107, 109, 111, 119, 199–200, 204, 209, 210. *See also* imperialism; neocolonialism

communists, 35, 46, 48, 85, 89, 127, 144, 156–157, 161, 171, 198

Confucianism, 5, 6, 17, 20, 52, 61–86, 136; attitude to economics, 46; and Christianity, 62–64, 66, 75–76, 78–79; and common people, 62, 70–72, 75–76, 81, 110; and Tonghak, 69–70; view of history, 15–16, 74–80, 83.

Cultural Assets Conservation Act (1962), 11, 115

Culturalists, Korean (1890s–1930s), 5, 17–18, 20–24, 27–28, 34, 107

"Declaration of the Korean Revolution" (1923), 32–34

decolonization. *See under* colonialism

Democratic Justice Party, 54

Democratic Party (of South Korea), 53

DPRK. *See* North Korea

drama, 95–96, 108, 110, 213. *See also* madangguk; Malttugi Association

Durkheim, Emile, 67, 77, 174

fascism, 85, 106–107, 189, 190, 204

Gorky, Maxim, *Mother,* 199–200

Ham Sŏkhŏn, 89, 98

Han Chawidanwŏnŭi Unmyŏng (Fate of a self-defense corps fighter), 197–198

Han Sŏrya, 195, 207

Han Wansang, 4, 29, 39, 47–52, 54–59, 223

Han'guk Theological Seminary, 89, 95

han'gŭl movement, 74, 76

Han'gyŏre Sinmun (One people newspaper), 194, 221, 223

Hanmindang, 134–135

Historical Issues Research Center (Yŏksa munje yŏn'guso), 18, 25

Hong Hŭidam, 191, 207

Hong Myŏnghŭi, 195, 207; *Im Kkŏkjŏng,* 184–185, 186, 196

Hwang Sŏg'yŏng, 183, 195, 207; *Chang Kilsan,* 173, 186; *Kaekchi* (Far from home), 174, 186; *Mugiŭi Kŭnŭl* (In the Shadow of War), 182, 186–189

Hwangsŏng Sinmun (Hwangsong newspaper), 69, 73

Hwang Sunwŏn, *Kanaŭi Huye* (Cain's descendant), 169

imperialism, 2, 12, 59, 75, 98, 106, 113, 116, 122, 191; Japanese, 12, 23–24, 34, 61–62, 65–68, 72, 76, 78–80, 82, 102, 204; and Leninism, 18, 23; western, 62–66, 69, 78–79, 102, 106, 118, 186, 188, 190

Im Sugyŏng, 99

Independence Club (Tongnip Hyŏphoe), 21, 27, 70, 73, 75, 80

Japanese colonialism. *See under* colonialism

Contributors

Nancy Abelmann, an assistant professor of anthropology at the University of Illinois in Urbana-Champaign, has carried out extensive research on Korean farmers' movements.

Choi Chungmoo is an assistant professor at the University of California at Irvine, where she teaches mainly Korean cultural anthropology in the Department of East Asian Languages and Literatures.

Choi Hyun-moo teaches French literature at Sŏgang University in Seoul, where she is an associate professor. In 1992 she was awarded the Tongin Prize in Literature for her creative writings.

Chung Chai-sik, an authority on Korean Confucian social thought and formerly a professor of sociology at Yonsei University in Seoul, is now Walter G. Meulder Professor of Social Ethics at Boston University School of Theology.

Donald N. Clark specializes in modern Korean history, including religious history, and is a professor at Trinity University in San Antonio, where he teaches Korean and East Asian history.

Kang Man'gil is a professor of Korean history at Koryŏ University in Seoul. Besides being an active participant in movements related to the minjung, he is among the first and most respected scholars to undertake research on Korean history from a minjung perspective.

Kim Hyung-A is a doctoral student at the Australian National University in Canberra. She has studied many aspects of Korean culture, including drama and nationalist culture, and is currently studying the cultural roots and implementation of self-reliance ideology in North and South Korea.

Kim Seong Nae has focused on Cheju Island shamanism and teaches Korean anthropology at Kangwŏn National University in Ch'unch'ŏn.

Paik Nak-chung is a professor of English literature at Seoul National University. Since founding the quarterly journal *Ch'angjakkwa Pip'yŏng,* which he continues to edit, in 1966, he has stood at the forefront of minjung literary theory and criticism.

Marshall R. Pihl was, until his death in 1995, a specialist in modern Korean literature and professor in the Department of East Asian Languages and Literatures at the University of Hawai'i.

Kenneth M. Wells studies nationalism in modern Korea and was an associate professor in the Department of East Asian Languages and Cultures at Indiana University in Bloomington before moving in January 1994 to the Australian National University in Canberra, where he now teaches Korean history.